FULFILLED

Fulfilled

THE PASSION & PROVISION STRATEGY
FOR BUILDING A BUSINESS WITH
PROFIT, PURPOSE & LEGACY

Kathryn & Michael K. Redman

LIONCREST
PUBLISHING

FULFILLED
The Passion & Provision Strategy for Building a
Business with Profit, Purpose & Legacy

ISBN 978-1-5445-0797-2 *Hardcover*
      978-1-5445-0796-5 *Paperback*
      978-1-5445-0795-8 *Ebook*
      978-1-5445-0798-9 *Audiobook*

To Grandpa and Grandma Mullen, for modeling what a fulfilled life can look like. To Michael's mom, for showing us what sacrificial love can accomplish. And to our daughter, Jenna, for believing in us. Thanks for not only loving us as parents, but calling us friends.

Contents

Introduction

"It is impossible to have a great life unless it is a meaningful life...And I believe it is very difficult to have a meaningful life, without meaningful work."[1]

JIM COLLINS, AUTHOR OF *GOOD TO GREAT*

We didn't realize how bad it could get until the money started pouring in.

Sure, there had been challenges in our first few years of running "Half a Bubble Out," our marketing and business consulting startup, but they'd been relatively typical. Mostly, they centered around not having enough cash. There had been months where we didn't know if we could make our mortgage payment. We experienced the embarrassment of telling our staff we needed a few more days before we could make payroll. Friends from our church anonymously dropped off groceries on our front doorstep. It was bad.

But it was about to get worse.

---

1   Jim Collins - Good to Great. "Jim's Seven Questions: Learning From Young Leaders Full Talk." YouTube. YouTube, January 12, 2018. https://www.youtube.com/watch?v=LHs_2tSw-M4.

Thanks to a wildly successful marketing campaign over (of all things) a toenail fungus treatment, our business blew up. Suddenly, we were the go-to marketing agency for podiatrists across the country. We learned more about toenail fungus than we could ever hope to forget. We also grew 400 percent in a matter of months.

Almost overnight, we were an entrepreneurial success story, flush with cash, business, and clients. But there was one major problem: our small operation was not prepared to meet the new staggering demands. We didn't have enough staff, nor did we have adequate systems in place to keep up with our new capacity. We began to hire as fast as we could—which was a major mistake.

Out of desperation, we made two hires that were not a good fit. Our Myers-Briggs temperaments were all out of whack, and they didn't mesh with our management style. These employees became unmotivated, packing up their bags at 4:50 p.m. and at the door, waiting to leave, at 4:55 p.m. Clearly, they weren't excited about the work they were doing, and we had no idea how to motivate them. In addition to our inadequate systems, we were now realizing that, apparently, we couldn't hack it as leaders either.

We also secretly resented some of our clients. Assuming that all business was good and needed, we hadn't been choosy about who we worked with. Unfortunately, the toenail fungus biz had led us to some colorful characters who did not care, for instance, that we were at Costco on a Saturday with our daughter. For some of our clients, that seemed like the perfect time to chew us out over the phone while our ten-year-old waited patiently in the car—and what's worse, we let him! We began compromising our values because we felt we *had* to respond to our clients at any time of day or night. Work life spilled over into our personal lives and we started working insanely long hours.

What was happening?! "Success" was pouring into our bank accounts but we were ready to throw the whole thing away. Both of us said to each other at different points, "I *hate* going to work." If this was success, it was miserable!

Then, it all changed. Right in the middle of the Great Recession, the niche we were in collapsed.

Many of our clients determined they no longer had room in their budgets for a marketing agency. It didn't feel good to watch our client list shrink—yet we also experienced profound relief. Suddenly, we had a chance to regroup.

We started having conversations that helped us identify our Core Values: we needed to enjoy the people we worked with, and we needed to prioritize our family's health over the bottom line of our business. We urgently sought out new training to tighten up our systems and improve our management. We learned that we needed to be faster to either fire or coach people who weren't a good fit.

In two years, our business had grown by 200 percent. Granted, we managed that by growing 400 percent and then shrinking by 50 percent. It's a lousy trajectory to achieve doubled growth, but we were thankful to get there either way. In the process, we'd been forced to get smart and think about what really matters.

What did we have at the end of those crazy years? A strong foundation, a good reputation, and quite a few battle scars.

We redoubled our efforts to serve our clients well and make sure everything we did honored our values. Our business developed a reputation for consistency and quality work. Although we'd always made a point to give back to the community, we redoubled our commitment to invest in our neighbors and further earn their respect. We were newly equipped with lessons we'd learned about hiring, sales, management, defining our processes, and building relationships with clients. We had codified our values. Best of all, we still had a solid marriage and a solid relationship with our daughter.

Both of us are teachers at the core, so along the way, we mused to each other, "Wouldn't it be great if we could pass on some of the lessons we learned? You know, so that we could help other people avoid the extremes we reached?"

THE PROBLEM

The two of us know what it's like to pour your blood, sweat, and tears into a business and not know if it's going to work. The more business leaders we meet, the more we realize that many of us are living out the same common tale.

We all started a business because we wanted more freedom. We wanted to have more control, to author our own lives, and to be able to invest full time in the places we really wanted to.

Then, as we began running our businesses, they started to tear at us—sucking up our money and time. Many of us discovered our personal gaps, encountered areas of business we didn't fully understand, and had to confront deficits in our leadership and management abilities. We tried to learn on the job as quickly as possible, but weren't sure where to turn for advice. Running a business was harder than we'd ever expected it was going to be.

Let's just get brutally honest for a second. True or false?

- You're feeling burned out.
- You sense you've gone as far as you can personally go, and don't know how to get any further.
- You're running a business you believe in, but aren't able to pay yourself, or earn enough to grow the company.

If that sounds like your story, we get it. That was our story too.

So, why is it so hard to run a financially profitable business, while maintaining a decent personal life and upholding your values? We think we found a big part of the problem while we were 30,000 feet in the air, flying across the Atlantic Ocean.

IN THE AIR AND ON THE STEPS: MICHAEL NARRATES

In the summer of 2012, after the dust had mostly settled with Half a Bubble Out,[2] Kathryn and I took our daughter on a trip to Ireland and Northern England to celebrate her high school graduation. On the plane ride, I started reading a book which had been on my list for a while: *The Coming Jobs War,* by Jim Clifton, who was the CEO of Gallup at the time.[3] (Gallup is one of the most respected and well-known public opinion polling companies in the US.)

---

2   Many people ask us the story behind our "Half a Bubble Out" name. In case you're curious, the name Half a Bubble Out is a metaphor from the carpenter's level. When something is slightly out of level, the "bubble" becomes "half-out." At HaBO, we view this as symbolizing two things. The first is represented by the half a bubble that is "out" and means thinking creatively, reminding us to look at our clients and their challenges with fresh perspective and not through the same old grid. The half a bubble that remains "in" represents the need to maintain a strong foundation in the quality and skills of our craft as marketing and business consultants.

3   Clifton, Jim. *The Coming Jobs War: What Every Leader Must Know about the Future of Job Creation.* New York, NY: Gallup Press, 2011.

Although I'm not a fast reader, I read almost the entire book on the plane ride. Clifton's research fascinated me. In his first chapter, Clifton explained that Gallup had endeavored to go after the question, "What's on the mind of the world?" In an attempt to answer that, Gallup conducted their first global poll, asking people all over the world to respond to a number of questions all related to that theme. Clifton wrote that the pollsters assumed they would get answers about world peace or climate change—but that wasn't the case.

Clifton writes, "Six years into our global data collection effort, we may have already found the single most searing, clarifying, helpful, world-altering fact. What the whole world wants is a good job."

"What the whole world wants is a good job." —Jim Clifton

Over and over again, the number one answer people gave was "a good job." That was the *most* important thing to people, across the globe. These respondents—representing the majority of people—said that the one thing that could shift humanity, and lift people out of depression, and poverty and help save families, was a *good job*.

The word "good" is key. The book explained that a truly good job describes work that is engaging, fulfilling, satisfying, and can provide a livable wage. However, Clifton pointed out that most people in America do not work in what they would call a "good" job.[4]

---

4   Clifton's full description of the qualifications of a good job are: 1. You have a good job—meaning you are employed full time for an employer and work at least 30 hours per week for this employer—rather than a subsistence job that does little to raise you out of poverty or contribute to your country's formal economic output. 2. You know what is expected of you at work, and you have an inherent capacity to perform your tasks at work. 3. Your boss takes an interest in your success and development. 4. Your opinion counts at work. 5. You feel that your job has an important mission and purpose.

According to Gallup's extensive research, it turns out that three out of four Americans are *disengaged* at work.[5] Gallup defines this disengagement as "sleepwalking through their workdays," lacking in satisfaction and fulfillment.[6] In other words, three out of every four people see their jobs as something they must endure just to survive and make money, so they can hopefully enjoy life outside of work. That's miserable!

Clifton's research deeply moved me. I was inspired by the book's description of a good job, and horrified by the plight of 74 percent of disengaged working adults in America. Clifton argued that this level of apathy has widespread economic implications—when so many employees are disengaged, it's harder to run a company, which means budgets are tighter and margins are thinner. Fewer new jobs can be created, and everyone's stress level rises. The net effect leads to less economic freedom, less opportunity, and less personal mobility, along with lower education and investment across the board. Clifton's argument made crystal clear that America is in trouble if we don't figure out how to create more *good* jobs. I took that point personally.

I wanted to be able to provide my employees with meaningful work. I knew personally what it was like to not have a "good" job, and I didn't want that for myself or for my employees—I wanted to give them work that was fulfilling, stimulating, satisfying, and provided a good wage. After a tumultuous few years, we were finally close to achieving that level of satisfaction and success.

---

5   This number reflects Gallup's finding at the time of the book's publication, in 2011, which was what we responded to. A more recent article by Gallup titled, "Employee Engagement on the Rise," published in May of 2018, reports findings that worker engagement has improved slightly to thirty-three percent. Unfortunately, this still means that roughly two-thirds of American workers are sleepwalking through their work day.

6   Adkins, Amy. "U.S. Employee Engagement Flat in May." Gallup.com. Gallup, August 8, 2019. https://news.gallup.com/poll/183545/employee-engagement-flat-may.aspx.

But Clifton's book made me realize that I wanted to do more. How could I help other business leaders provide their employees with satisfying work?

THE PERSONAL CHALLENGE FOR SMALL BUSINESS OWNERS

From past reading and personal experience, I knew that small business owners already experience enormous challenges just keeping their businesses afloat. Although 80 percent of startups manage to last a year, once you get into the second year, only somewhere between 45 and 51 percent of businesses manage to survive. One statistic reported by *Forbes* states that only one in three small businesses will last a decade.[7] As our family explored Ireland and Northern England on our trip, I couldn't stop thinking about these ideas. Was it possible that the business failure rate was linked to the fact that so many employees were disengaged?

When employees are doing the bare minimum, they're not contributing to moving a business forward. At best, they're maintaining the status quo; at worst, they're dead weight, dragging down your momentum. Part of our job as leaders is to evaluate our employees to make sure we don't have anyone on our team that's dead weight. When you have 74 percent of employees who are disengaged—that's a lot of dead weight.

But what happens when everybody is doing their part? What if people worked with passion, rather than apathy? What kind of economic, social, and global change could occur if more people were fully engaged and excited about their work?

---

7   Otar, Chad. "What Percentage Of Small Businesses Fail -- And How Can You Avoid Being One Of Them?" *Forbes* Magazine, October 25, 2018. https://www.forbes.com/sites/forbesfinancecouncil/2018/10/25/what-percentage-of-small-businesses-fail-and-how-can-you-avoid-being-one-of-them/#1fd06e3f43b5. What percentage of small businesses fail?

At the end of our trip to the U.K., we got to the city of York, where Kathryn was born and raised until age seven, and where her mother still lives. I took myself to one of our favorite places in the city: York Minster, a stunning and enormous old cathedral, which took over 250 years to build, and was finally completed in 1472. On the ancient steps, in the shadow of magnificent history, I opened up my journal and tried to think about the future.

Given that business leaders are the ones responsible for creating jobs—either good ones or bad—I determined that any change must first start with them. Over the next few hours, I began sketching out a vision of a model that would help equip other business leaders to develop thriving companies, ones that could achieve their financial potential while still providing leaders with a sense of purpose and meaning. I began noting strategies that could empower leaders to run their businesses smoothly, in a way that kept their stress down and produced the kind of fulfillment we all long for.

The whole idea began to run downhill like water. For the next few months, I brainstormed incessantly with Kathryn—I couldn't shut up about it.

We began identifying goals: we wanted to help other business leaders not only survive, but also thrive—and in the thriving, create a positive impact on society. We wanted to help entrepreneurs and leaders live out the desires of their hearts while building prosperous businesses. We wanted to help business leaders create more jobs in our communities that would honor people and help them become their best selves.

We wanted to help people learn from our hard lessons, and reignite their hope in their dreams.

BIG, HAIRY, AUDACIOUS GOALS: KATHRYN NARRATES

It's true: Michael couldn't shut up about it. That epiphany on the York Minster steps had thrown him headlong into generating what we fondly refer to as our "BHAG": our Big, Hairy, Audacious Goal. We'll talk more about BHAGs in our Vision chapter.

For as long as I've known Michael—and that's a long time, specifically since a grade school production of "The Hobbit"—he has been one to make Big, Hairy, Audacious Goals. In fact, when we first started dating, his goals frightened me. They seemed *too* big. I wasn't sure he had the tools he needed to implement them.

As a teenager, Michael had been a troublemaker who'd barely graduated high school. Even when we were dating, Michael still hadn't completed college, whereas I was about to complete a Master's degree. Just about every adult in my life raised their eyebrows when I told them I was dating Michael Redman—and I wondered if there was something to their skepticism. Was this someone I could trust with my life? Could this dreamer make his big ideas a reality?

Once, when I was agonizing over whether or not to move forward in my relationship with Michael, I had a weirdly vivid dream. I imagined myself as a toddler in a living room, gripping onto a coffee table. There were other kids around me who seemed to know something I didn't—they were walking around the room without any kind of support. But I couldn't leave that coffee table; I was too afraid to walk away from what felt safe.

Then, I imagined Michael—also in chubby toddler form—come up to me. He took my hand and started walking with me out into the living room. It was exhilarating and terrifying to leave the familiar support I'd been leaning on—but it was about to get even more intense.

In my dream, the two of us walked toward an open door. Beyond the threshold was a park with a playground. I realized: that's where we're going. That's what we're going to be able to enjoy at the end of this. And before I can climb, before I can slide, before I can swing—I have to walk. I have to leave the coffee table.

When I woke up, the dream made me realize that I had something to learn from Michael. I had always been one to play it safe, but in dreaming together, we would step into a life I wouldn't have otherwise found.

Still, Michael had something to learn from me too.

My contribution was needed with *implementing* the dreams. The execution, the pragmatism—those have always been my areas of strength. I was able to partner with Michael in ways that allowed us to dream those big dreams, but also get it down on paper. Together, we were able to craft ideas *and* bring them into fruition.

As the two of us have taught each other, we've both gotten better at dreaming big and making those dreams happen in reality. We've both poured ourselves into learning so that we can gain the skills and tools needed to accomplish the BHAGs.

I think a lot of business leaders have a great deal in common with the toddler Kathryn from my dream, who was stuck at the coffee table. I think many of us have made a great start, but our progress has plateaued. We've hit some challenges, we've lost our balance, and we're terrified to go any further lest the whole thing fall apart. We know that we need to develop as leaders, but we don't know how. We know we could expand our business or improve our operations, but we don't have the expertise we need to get there.

We need someone to come up, grab our hand, and help us walk. We need guidance in learning those needed new skills.

GUIDES ALONG THE PATH

When our business, Half a Bubble Out, was in such a crazy season of volatile growth, the two of us looked around desperately for someone to give us that guidance. We found mentors who could tell us how to run a profitable business, but their own family lives were in ruins. We found books that could tell us how to strengthen one area in our company, and effectively use one tool—but they couldn't tell us how to use that tool in conjunction with all the other elements of our business. None of the books seemed to consider the importance of values or maintaining a decent personal life.

Where was the book that would give us a primer on all the key areas of business? Where was the book that would help us run a successful company while still upholding our values and investing in our family?

The fact that we *couldn't* find that book gave us the impetus to sit down and write the one we'd always been looking for. After years of research, reading, and honing our message—and certainly after a great big boost of momentum from Michael's epiphany on the York Minster steps—we think we've got the whole package.

This book aims to offer you the dream *with* the means of implementation.

It will not offer you all kinds of easy fixes. It will not suggest the answer is easy, or that you can simply stumble onto a wide, smooth road to riches. We will not claim that there is one "silver bullet" technique or tool that, if only put into use, will transform everything. We don't think it's that simple. We will also not claim that our model is the only one that works; there are multiple models that can lead to successful businesses.

Here's a claim we will make: you do need *some* framework. You need something that will help guide your path and provide you with signposts for the journey. Our framework specifically involves a holistic model that focuses on building up competency in six core areas. We'll provide a clear explanation of the challenges leaders face in business, and an achievable plan to overcome them—one that has proven results. It's a framework that will help you be profitable, experience purpose, and build a legacy that reflects your Core Values: we call it the Passion & Provision strategy.

These are Big, Hairy, Audacious Goals. But they're not goals that promise blind hope. Blind, empty hope is not a strategy.

We're offering you a different kind of hope. We're offering you hope *with* a road map that will lead to the practical implementation of your dreams. This book will introduce you to strategies that will bring life back into your business, both personally and financially.

Our request of you? Take our hand and step away from the place where you may have gotten stuck. You're going to need to be motivated to take real steps of change. As you develop the competency to walk, we'll then push you to go further in your knowledge, so that you can eventually run, jump, and climb.

IT'S POSSIBLE, AND HERE'S HOW

It's possible to have a business that allows you to become financially successful and still be emotionally fulfilled. It's possible to get to a place where you don't have to sacrifice your marriage or your relationship with your kids for the sake of your business. You actually *can* have it all, and there's a way to do it.

In this book, we're going to first explain why **Passion & Provision both matter.** Both, in fact, are necessary to running a profitable, fulfilling, and enjoyable company. When you and your employees feel more passion in your work, the natural consequence is that the business starts to perform better. Similarly, when your business is providing you with enough profit and cash to alleviate stress, you're able to grow and develop in ways that lead to a sense of greater fulfillment and passion.

We're also going to urge you to stop doing "symptom management" with your company's problems. Many business leaders make the mistake of focusing their improvement efforts on one clearly visible problem, when the real issue goes far deeper. **Companies need to view their business through a holistic model in order to holistically thrive.**

The holistic model incorporates six areas of business where leaders need *minimum competency* to be effective leaders and business operators. You need this minimum competency in order to move beyond where you may have gotten stuck, and take steps toward mastery. In other words, we're going to teach you how to walk in each of these six areas, so that you can eventually run:

1. **Vision:** Without a vision that is clear, complete, and compelling, your company will always struggle to reach its potential. The business may languish in mediocrity, which is almost worse than failure. People perish for lack of vision and so do companies.

2. **Leadership:** Strong leadership requires robust health in two parts: your inner game and your outer game. A poor inner game will result in negative, reactive leadership; but a strong inner game will result in stable, strong, creative leadership, the kind of leadership that enables you to empower others.

3. **Management and Operations:** You need to understand how to put the right people in the right positions, and then empower them to live into their full potential; this requires that you hire well, train well, and fire well. You also need operating systems in place to efficiently run your business and effectively troubleshoot problems.

4. **Marketing and Sales:** Good marketing and sales will turn strangers into raving fans and customers. We'll teach you how to use marketing strategies to show customers that your product or service will solve their problem, and make them the hero in their own story.

5. **Money:** Business leaders need to learn the basics of money and manage it well, or they risk losing both passion and provision in a single step. We'll discuss necessary reports to review and how to read them. We'll also explain how to understand the art, analysis, and big picture of how your finances impact your business.

6. **Culture:** Everything thrives or dies in relationship to its culture. A poor company culture results in disengaged employees who punch a clock just to get their next paycheck. A positive culture results in employees that perform like rock stars for you. We'll discuss ways you can develop healthy culture, both in the physical environment and relationally.

WALK BEFORE YOU RUN

"Little by little, one travels far." —J.R.R. Tolkien, *The Lord of the Rings*

Here's what we're going to ask from you: Learn the fundamentals. Master the fundamentals. Understand the knowledge and apply these principles. Then, you'll need to have the patience and endurance to do the hard work required to make necessary changes.

It's never easy to make large-scale changes; it's far easier to continue to operate as you always have. But consider this: if you don't take the risk and do the hard work, not only will you fail to achieve your own dream, you'll also fail to give your employees the privilege of working in a place that stokes their passion *while* providing them a paycheck. You and your employees will fall into the 74 percent of people who are sleepwalking through their workday. On that track, you will feel increasingly exhausted and dejected—eventually leading to burnout. In the worst-case scenario, you'll end up shutting down the business after possibly compromising your values in an effort to save it—and potentially damaging your personal relationships in the process.

On the other hand, if you do it right, you and your employees can be some of the 26 percent of Americans that have fulfilling, engaging jobs. You will be able to deliver enough revenue and cash flow to alleviate stress about today and bring you the freedom to build for tomorrow. You will cultivate a workplace culture that decreases the things you hate and increases the things you love about going to work. You will have a work environment that attracts great employees who love coming to work and giving their all. You will attract, convert, and retain raving fan customers.

When you do the hard work required to create a Passion & Provision company, you will ultimately experience the freedom you dreamed of. You will make the impact you were created to make and leave the legacy you were destined for.

These are Big, Hairy, Audacious Goals. But they're *possible*—we've seen the transformation firsthand. We're offering hope—and a road map to go with it.

Let's dream big. Let's leave the safety of our comfort zones. Let's cross the threshold and learn some new skills.

Let's go *play.*

||||||||||||||||||||

PART ONE

The Why

*Our Case for the Passion & Provision
Strategy and the Holistic Model*

||||||||||||||||||

CHAPTER ONE

Passion

Passion does not produce commitment. Commitment produces passion.

ROY H. WILLIAMS

SEEING THE DIFFERENCE: MICHAEL NARRATES

My father worked as the branch manager of a loan company. As part of his job, he had to carry out debt collection, either collecting money from debtors or repossessing the items they'd purchased. Sometimes my dad worked on the weekends, so my mom, sister, and I all tagged along, sitting in the family car as Dad knocked on the doors of those poor indebted souls. As you can imagine, people were not excited to talk with my father. He was met with a constant barrage of negativity. He'd return to the car, slam the door shut, and slump in his seat. After a pause, he'd finally start up the car again to head to the next onslaught.

Dad was successful in his company and rose through the ranks—but he *hated* his job. The misery of his day-to-day work radically impacted his health, and he often found himself in the hospital with stress-related illnesses. He believed he was doing the right thing by providing for our family, but frankly, the misery wasn't worth the price.

In the midst of wrestling with his own turmoil from work, my dad saw me dreaming about something different. Trying to give me a dose of reality, he told me that trying to find any happiness at work was not possible. According to him, you just had to do your job, suck it up if you didn't like it, and get on with life. In his mind, misery and work would always go hand in hand.

My mom's dad, on the other hand—Grandpa Max— showed me something different. Grandpa was raised in the logging industry in Oregon. When my grandpa was old enough, he drove logging trucks until he was sent to the Pacific during World War II. Once he returned, he was offered a job as the foreman of all the drivers, but Grandpa had heard of something called a "pension" that would help take care of his family, long term. He thought this was a good idea, so he went to work for Greyhound. He drove a bus for thirty-five years and retired in his early sixties.

It was not the kind of profession that most people find impressive, but Grandpa loved his job. Driving was his passion and he loved interacting with all kinds of people. When I was a kid, I went on rides with him. I'd watch Grandpa lean forward with a smile to greet people as they came on his bus. He was incredibly kind to passengers and taught me that kindness isn't just good customer service; it's a good way of life. Grandpa lived to be ninety-eight years old, and pulled his pension for over forty years. Good decision, Grandpa! (And sorry, Greyhound!)

I went on to have my own experiences with terrible jobs, but—for better or worse—I couldn't endure the misery the way my dad had. I once worked at a shrimp factory and spent eight hours a day with my bare hands plunged into ice water, sticking gutted shrimp onto wooden skewers. I was smelly, freezing, and bored out of my mind. I lasted about two weeks.

It only took a few of these terrible jobs to confirm that I couldn't, and *wouldn't*, follow Dad's advice. I didn't want to land in a life-sucking career, just to get the bills paid. I wanted to earn a good living, be happy, and use my creative abilities in a meaningful and productive way. My dad had said that was impossible, but I'd seen my grandpa live a life that proved Dad wrong. Watching the results of their professional decisions gave me a taste of what I wanted and didn't want for my own life.

I wanted to feel passion *while* I was making a buck. I wanted to feel fulfilled. Was that too much to ask?

Kathryn and I think not; in fact, we think a sense of fulfillment is what we're meant for. We also think that's what most business leaders and employees are hungering to experience. So how do we get there?

"Success without…fulfillment is the ultimate failure." —Allistair McCaw

THE PASSION & PROVISION STRATEGY

How do we get there, indeed? The strategy that we'll spend this book discussing is the answer to that question. It's our road map directing us to a destination fueled by hope. This is the Passion & Provision strategy; it helps business leaders redefine their lives and their companies with passion and provision as foundational elements.

Here are some of the defining characteristics of a business owner who leads a Passion & Provision company:

- You're working in a business that allows you to use the natural gifts and talents you were born with, along with the skills you have worked hard to acquire and develop along the way. You have sufficient finances and resources to sustain your business, grow your business, and provide for yourself and your employees.
- You experience both creative and financial freedom.
- You have the freedom to contribute to your community, establish a legacy, and make the impact you know you were designed to make.

Many people simply don't believe this can happen. Even within our business now, which resoundingly fits the description of a Passion & Provision company, we're still constantly working to keep it thriving. There are many days we have to look at each other and remind ourselves that we can *retain* Passion & Provision. These fulfilling qualities don't just come with a magic wand. They're accomplished through many deliberate choices and discipline. It's hard work—but the rewards are literally life changing.

LABOR AND TOIL

As we start discussing "hard work," we want to make an important and necessary distinction between labor and toil. Labor partners with passion, but toil leads to burnout.

Think again of York Minster cathedral, which we described in our Introduction. Imagine ancient workers lugging stones, making bricks and mortar, bracing themselves against beams to erect the balustrades. The worker who doesn't have a sense of purpose toils away at the back-breaking work with nothing but his muscle to sustain him. In his mind, he's only building a wall. But the worker who *has* a sense of a greater purpose understands that he's building a cathedral. His work has meaning. He labors with the vision of a stunning, lasting legacy.

As a business leader, you're the master builder responsible for reminding your employees that they're building a cathedral, not just a wall. Running a Passion & Provision company means that it's your job to remind people that their job has purpose and meaning. We believe that if you're going to inspire others, you need to recognize the greater purpose for yourself. Our goal with this book is to give you *reasons* to trust in a better tomorrow; we want to give your hope fuel.

In fact, we'd say the main difference between *labor*—which is meaningful—and *toil*—which is meaningless—is purpose. In either case, the work is still hard; both York Minster workers would have produced an equal amount of sweat. But the difference in what motivates the work means everything. One works with a vision of hope; one simply lays bricks to earn his next meal. One smiles from behind the wheel of the Greyhound bus; one slumps in his seat while driving to his next appointment. One is labor; one is toil.

When you're leading a business, the work is often hard. Times of transition can easily produce feelings of confusion, frustration, and sap your motivation. You might feel doubt or restlessness. You might have an unexpected hiccup in your cash flow. You might have to deal with frustrated employees. Those challenges are going to come, regardless of what kind of state of mind you're in.

When you're *laboring*—working *with* a sense of purpose—you might confront all those challenges, but you'll trust that you can pull out of them. You have hope that there's a reward coming, and that your work will not be in vain. You're more resilient through difficult times. Eventually, the sense of purpose and meaning which defines labor will pull you forward out of the swamp of the challenges that confront every business leader.

Think of a woman who labors in birth. She experiences excruciating pain along the way, but there's purpose driving her through the pain which gives her hope to endure. At the end of a healthy birth labor, there's a baby. Likewise, labor in your profession feels purposeful when you believe in it, enjoy it (most of the time), and keep at it. That's the kind of work fueled by faith and hope; it's the kind of work that Michael's Grandpa enjoyed as a Greyhound bus driver, and it's the kind of work we're able to experience in our own company.

Toil—working *without* a sense of purpose—offers no help when you're confronted with challenges. In fact, it will pull you down as negative emotions keep piling on top of one another. There's a well-known Greek myth about a man, Sisyphus, who was cursed by the gods. As punishment, he had to eternally push a giant rock up a hill. Just as he neared the top, the boulder would slip and roll back down the hill, and Sisyphus would have to start the process all over again. There was never any meaningful progress. *That's* toil.

THE CONSEQUENCES OF TOIL: KATHRYN NARRATES

The two of us have experienced the misery of toil firsthand, when we felt like our work had no recognizable value. In fact, it's partly because of those awful experiences that we're so zealous about helping business leaders seek Passion & Provision instead.

Before we started Half a Bubble Out, we each had our share of mind-numbing jobs. Michael had his shrimp factory torture, and I spent one job doing nothing but filing. I was bored out of my mind! In another context, I worked as the executive assistant to the president of RSA Data Security. It sounds like an important job, but my boss had never had an assistant before and didn't know what to do with me. After I finished my first assignment (remodeling my office, check), he didn't know what else to ask me to do. I ended up spending two solid weeks playing Tetris all day.

I was hitting those Tetris high scores every single day. I also was a miserable human being! I would come home cranky, depressed, frustrated, and irritable—because I'd made zero contribution and had wasted the day. For me, that was toil.

When you are working outside of your gifts, talents, and skills for any extended period of time, you start to experience toil. That's the situation I found myself in, and it's what 74 percent of Americans experience in their day-to-day work. This experience of toil leads to disengagement and a lack of productivity.

Toil leads to disengagement and a lack of productivity.

As we discussed earlier, toil also occurs when you're working without a sense of purpose—even *if* you're using your skills. If you work out of guilt, shame, or mere obligation for any extended period of time, you're going to experience toil. When you feel like your work has no meaning, and there's no hope that it ever will—you get stuck in a negative downward spiral.

When you're working outside of your gifts, or working without purpose, your efforts cannot be sustained. You're going to head toward **burnout.**

BEWARE OF BURNOUT

There are real and profound consequences of burnout. Most of us have experienced them firsthand, or we have watched a loved one suffer from them.

Our friend, Dr. Terry B. Walling, recently introduced us to the work of Dr. Archibald Hart, a colleague at Fuller Seminary, who described **the Four Stages of Burnout:**[8]

1. **Stage One: Exhaustion/Depletion.** You experience physical exhaustion and loss of boundaries. Adrenaline, and its reserves, typically become one's main source of energy. *Typical Response: No acknowledgment; individual maintains current level of stress and allows for increasing amounts of activity.*
2. **Stage Two: Physical Symptoms.** You experience more physical exhaustion; adrenaline becomes further depleted. Physical symptoms manifest (fatigue, irritability, lack of sleep, nervous habits, etc.). One's results are diminished. *Typical Response: Denial of situation; individual makes excuses and justifications while they begin to compromise their standards and values for behavior.*
3. **Stage Three: Frequency of Sickness/Depression.** There's even more physical exhaustion and loss of boundaries; adrenaline is exhausted. Physical symptoms increase (loss of sleep, inability to rest, skin irritations, continued vulnerability to sickness and complete fatigue, etc.). *Typical Response: Extreme denial/compromise and lying to self and others. Individual begins*

---

8   Walling, Terry B. *Deciding: Clarifying Your Kingdom Contribution.* Leader Breakthru: 2017.

to drop their responsibilities, commitments, and even their involvement in close relationships.

4. **Stage Four: Physical/Emotional Shutdown.** Physical shutdown begins to occur. Hide and flight can be the response and/or norm. *Typical Response: Disengagement—complete state of physical depletion, inability to respond to others or offer contribution. Requires extended period of recovery and help from others.*

Notice the progression that happens in these stages: the worse it gets, the more detrimental the burnout becomes for an entire network of people. It's not just the one person experiencing burnout who gets burned—it's their spouse, and family, and closest friends. That's another terrible consequence of toil: **personal lives fall apart.**

There's a phrase we sometimes hear that makes us want to crawl out of our skin: "It's just business." This phrase is used to justify all kinds of negative choices and catastrophic behavior. It's also not true.

If it's just business, then why does work sometimes lead to people losing their marriages or relationships with their kids? You *can't* separate business from everything else in your life. Our experience at work has a noticeable impact on our lives at home.

Michael will tell you that when I was miserable at work, I was a miserable person in every other area of my life. When you're burned out, you're exhausted, depressed, physically sick, and you start to mistreat the people you care about. It's like you start indiscriminately dropping land mines everywhere you go, and you can't control where and when those land mines explode. Burnout leads to blowups—both in and out of the office.

As people, we are meant to contribute to a story larger than ourselves and to experience the joy of building a legacy. The Latin word *vocare,* which is where we get our word "vocation," means *calling.* Your work is meant to lead to a calling—to a greater contribution to the world, an impact, a legacy. It's why we believe Passion and Provision are so incredibly important.

So what do we mean exactly, when we talk about Passion and Provision? We're so glad you asked.

PASSION: ROOTS AND FRUIT

Passion is one of those fuzzy words that can be tricky for people. We hear a lot about "finding your passion," and people react to the word in all sorts of ways. Poets love it, songwriters embrace it, and romance novels splash it across their covers. Some people aren't so enthused about the word. Practical, methodical people say, "Passion-shmassion. Get your head out of the clouds, get your feet on the ground, and get something done." Others see the word as daunting, as though there's something that must be conjured up that's beyond their capacity.

Here's what we *don't* mean when we talk about passion. First, we're not talking about sexual passion. That's another book entirely, and our sincerest apologies if you thought that's what you were getting into.

Second, we are not referring to overwhelming emotions that spontaneously come and go, robbing people of self-control. The idea that we are "passionate" about something one day and then ambivalent about it the next is—in our opinion—a misuse of the word.

What we *are* talking about is twofold, and it involves both *roots* and *fruit.*

THE ROOTS OF PASSION

True passion has deep roots of conviction, values, and commitment. From those deep roots come the positive emotions that we often associate with the word passion, which we'll discuss more in a second. But it's important to understand that the positive emotions are the *fruit* that grow from the deep roots, and the roots need to come first. Many people want the fruit, but they don't consider the roots required to grow it.

> If you say you have a passion, but you wouldn't be willing to sacrifice for it, then it really isn't your passion.

One of the deepest roots of passion is the **willingness to sacrifice.** This concept is where we get the idea of the Passion of the Christ in Christian tradition. In this context, the willingness to endure pain and suffering to reach a desired destination is what passion is all about. If you say you have a passion, but you wouldn't be willing to sacrifice for it, then we'd suggest it really isn't your passion.

Passion must be rooted in your strong conviction that what you're doing matters. It must align with your values of what you know to be good and worthy. It requires your commitment and your sacrifice. Those are the *roots* of passion.

THE FRUITS OF PASSION

The fruits of passion are the positive emotions that we more often associate with the word, and they grow out of those deep roots. When you're working in your passion, you feel **satisfaction** and **a sense of contribution,** indicating that you're doing work that fits who you are. You believe that what you're doing matters, and you like doing it.

There are two main conditions which will lead to these positive fruits—think of these as the optimal conditions to nurture growth from passion's deep roots.

1. You are doing work which feels meaningful.
2. You are using your gifts, talents, and skills.

The absence of either one of these sets you up for toil. If you're doing meaningful work, but it's a bad fit for your gifts, you can easily become discouraged at your inability to make progress. On the other hand, if you're using your skills but the end goal feels pointless, you're headed toward burnout and misery. Generally, true passion comes most organically when you experience both purpose *and* the utilization of your abilities.

There is something about this kind of passion that deeply touches the soul and leads to real fulfillment—not a fickle "happiness," but a deep pleasure, sigh-of-relief, truly satisfied fulfillment, the kind of sensation that causes you to breathe deeply and conclude, "*It's all good.*" You feel like your gifts are being utilized, and you're doing what you're meant to do. This is what it's like to be fulfilled.

A new general manager hired by one of our clients recently said to us, "I've finally found my tribe." He told us he was in the right place, at the right time, and doing the right thing; he felt like he'd finally found his place. Those are the sorts of comments that characterize a person who's experiencing passion at work: it occurs when you're doing the things you're supposed to be doing, and you know that they matter. That's the sweet spot.

In his book, *The Happiness Advantage: How a Positive Brain Fuels Success in Work and Life,* Shawn Achor references research by Barbara Fredrickson, which identifies the ten most common positive emotions: joy, gratitude, serenity, interest, hope, pride, amusement, inspiration, awe, and love.[9]

When you work in your passion, you may experience a range of these positive emotions, often via different moods. Passion can lead to **fun,** when you're amused and delighted by the work you're doing. Passion can also look serious, like when it stokes your deep **interest,** commanding your attention and engagement. Passion can lead to a sense of **joy** and **gratitude,** like the kind of satisfaction you might experience when spending time with your kids. You may feel a sense of awe and **pride** in what you and your team accomplish. In any one of those contexts, someone could say truly, "I'm experiencing my passion right now." The fruits of passion can come in many forms, but more often than not, they'll be related to these positive emotions.

Passion also helps you **persevere** through the hard times, because you can remember the purpose behind your hard work. There will be many seasons where work is a grind, even when you're working in your passion—but it's passion that will enable you to persist.

Passion is doing the things you were meant to do, in the way you were meant to do them, and it enables your soul to thrive.

A FEW MORE DEFINING POINTS ABOUT PASSION

Before we define provision, there are three more noteworthy aspects of passion to mention as we lay the groundwork.

---

9   Achor, Shawn. *The Happiness Advantage: How a Positive Brain Fuels Success in Work and Life.* New York: Currency, 2018.

First, **passion doesn't come in paychecks.** Money alone cannot provide the satisfaction or fulfillment we need to sustain the long haul of business ownership. We experienced this firsthand in our miserable "boom" days with Half a Bubble Out, and Michael's father also experienced the emptiness of a life sustained only by paychecks, without passion.

We once heard from a successful lawyer who admitted that he earns incredible wealth but hates his job. At the suggestion of our client, he listened to our podcast on Passion & Provision and felt like we'd articulated many of the realizations he'd been having in his current job. "Thank you for making a podcast just for me," he later told us. It is possible to be well provided for, financially, but not have passion for your work; your experience in that case will be toil.

Second, having passion for your job doesn't mean that you enjoy what you do all the time. Most athletes will tell you that they love playing the game, but those 5 a.m. daily workouts are a beast! Similarly, there are aspects of owning a business that we don't love or that don't come naturally. We have to work hard at tasks we don't enjoy, because it is part of what we have to do to succeed as a company. This is true both for ourselves as business owners and for our employees.

Having passion for your job doesn't mean that you enjoy what you do all the time.

A helpful measure we use is what we call the **51 percent rule.** If you can say that you enjoy what you're doing at least 51 percent of the time, then it is likely that you've found a place of passion.

Fifty-one percent is a great starting place with passion, because that percentage can grow.

The third noteworthy aspect of passion to note is that **passion must be balanced.** There is great research on the concept of passion by Robert J. Vallarand, who proposes a Dualistic Model of Passion.[10] Vallarand finds there are two kinds of passion—Harmonious Passion and Obsessive Passion. His definition of Harmonious Passion is determined by five areas—psychological well-being, physical health, relational well-being, high performance in a main level of endeavor, and contribution to society.

Vallarand's research says Harmonious Passion is all about high performance, well-being, and contribution. That's exactly what we want to guide you toward as well, only we're using different words. When you use your gifts, talents, and skills, you're working toward achieving high performance. When you work with purpose and meaning, you experience more positive psychological well-being. When you seek to create a meaningful legacy, you're working toward making a contribution. That's what everyone wants, right?

But Vallarand's research also issues a warning: when these five areas are imbalanced and negatively affected by the amount of effort put into a company, passion moves from Harmonious to *Obsessive.* As you can imagine, Obsessive Passion is a dangerous passion that can destroy you and the people around you. It's important to remember that any attribute taken too far becomes a liability. In the realm of business, this kind of passion can result in something as simple as the notion of a workaholic, or as complex

10   Vallarand, Robert J. et al. "Les Passions De L'Ame: On Obsessive and Harmonious Passion." *Journal of Personality and Social Psychology* 85, no. 4 (2003): 756–67. DOI: 10.1037/0022-3514.85.4.756.

as a person who has to win at all costs and will break the law to do so.

TRUE PASSION

So: let's sum up.

True passion is a sustaining force which compels you to endure and even sacrifice, because you believe in the purpose of what you're doing. It's rooted in conviction, commitment, and values. True passion is also sustained by hope: the belief that what you're doing will lead to a better life—for yourself, for others, for the world. It leads to harmony and a positive legacy.

In order to experience this kind of passion, it's important to feel like your work is meaningful, and that it uses your gifts, talents, and skills. Working within your passion leads to the positive fruits of satisfaction, fulfillment, a sense of contribution, and a host of other positive emotions.

Sounds pretty wonderful, doesn't it? But there's a catch. Passion can't sustain itself without sufficient *provision* along the way.

CHAPTER TWO

||||||||||||||||

Provision

"Annual income: 20 pounds. Annual expenditure: £19.60. Result: happiness.

Annual income: 20 pounds. Annual expenditure: £20.06. Result: misery."

CHARLES DICKENS

We have a friend—we'll call her Rebecca. She sells a thing—let's say it's flowers.

Rebecca has always loved flower arrangement and has a natural talent for putting together stunning bouquets. For years, she's been told that she should do this as her career. She feels joy in the creation of beautiful things, and she likes coming up with new ideas for different occasions—weddings, funerals, holiday celebrations, and so on.

Rebecca decided to chase her passion into business and created a small florist startup. Let's do a quick passion checklist for Rebecca:

- She finds meaning in her work and believes that it genuinely helps others.
- She is using her talents, skills, and gifts.
- She has the deep roots: she's committed, ready to sacrifice, and is honoring her personal values.

Rebecca, therefore, is living out her passion.

Unfortunately, there's a problem. Two years into her startup she has enough money in the company to fund her operations, but she's not yet profitable. She isn't able to pay herself and isn't quite breaking even.

Although Rebecca's work taps into her passion, she feels an increased amount of stress every day. She has certain knowledge gaps in business skills and leadership development. She can't bring herself to look over her financial statements because they make her so anxious. She starts losing sleep at night. Tensions begin to build in her marriage as she depletes her family's savings account to keep the business operational.

Rebecca's living out her passion—but her passion is quickly being depleted by the burdens of maintaining her business.

If Rebecca continues on the trajectory she's on without taking new steps to shore up her professional practices, she's going to likely run into one of several unhappy scenarios:

1. Her business may fail.
2. She may burn out and decide to walk away.
3. She may pursue the business's success at the expense of her close relationships.

None of those situations are ideal. In fact—they're all miserable! Rebecca's trajectory makes something crystal clear: **provision is essential for passion to thrive.**

PASSION & PROVISION

Whereas passion makes a huge difference in your *quality* of life, provision makes a huge difference in *sustaining* the life of your business. When we look at the business failure rate, the most obvious commonality in those failing businesses is a lack of provision. Most often, that occurs financially, but insufficient provision can also be intellectual, like when business leaders lack the training and knowledge required to keep their business going. It can also relate to insufficient emotional strength if you're not able to endure challenges or burnout.

If you're in a business that's barely making it and feels like it could go under any given week, that is unsustainable. Passion for the business may carry you for a while, but in the end, provision is a required piece of the puzzle for you to achieve your goals and dreams. The provision piece is just as necessary to a fulfilling life as passion, because it's provision that enables you to bring to reality the life you envisioned when you started this great adventure!

We have experienced passion without provision, and we've experienced provision without passion. Either scenario is terrible. Here's our conclusion: Passion & Provision *must* go together.

In fact, passion can actually help provision to thrive. When people are doing their best work and contributing in a positive way to a community—whether through the arts, engineering, math, or marketing—they're attractive and inspiring to be around. We're drawn to people who are producing their best work, and there are often financial rewards for doing so. For that reason, we think it's important and necessary to discuss the two concepts together.

That doesn't mean that once you're living into your passion, you'll magically become profitable—Rebecca and other business leaders like her can attest to that fact. Getting to a place of sufficient provision requires strategy, understanding, and a lot of hard work. We're going to discuss much more about that in the chapters to come.

Still, before we go any further, we're asking for your buy-in on this fundamental point: **Passion without provision is unsustainable; provision without passion is meaningless.**

If business leaders are going to experience *thriving* in their workplace, they need the peace of mind to sleep at night. If business leaders want to experience the *freedom* they dreamed of, they need to be able to grow beyond the plateau where they've gotten stuck. If business leaders want to experience *fulfillment* at work and at home, they need to be able to pay themselves and their employees. They need provision.

Passion without provision is unsustainable; provision without passion is meaningless.

Let's get more specific about what we mean when we talk "provision." What does that actually look like?

HOW MUCH IS "ENOUGH?"

Imagine an ancient sailing ship getting ready to set out from its home port in England for a long trip across the Atlantic to the Caribbean. Nowadays, a ship could get a full tank of diesel in the Mediterranean and make it all the way to Florida in one stretch, but ancient sailing vessels didn't have that power. They had to bring enough provisions on board to sustain them to the next port, and carefully plan stops along the way to restock.

These provisions were calculated and in place before the journey began. The ship's captain would consider how many people were on board, where the ship would stop, and ultimately where the ship was headed. No matter what, it was critical to have gathered enough provisions to cover the needs of the crew from port to port if you wanted to survive. These provisions were for the day-to-day needs of the crew, so that collectively, they were equipped to pursue their end goals.

That, in a nutshell, is what we mean when we talk about provision. **Provision is having the resources you need to achieve your goals.** Pay attention to the last part of that sentence. Provision isn't having just enough to break even—it's having enough to achieve your *goals*.

Sufficient provision is more than just achieving the bare minimum to survive today. If a ship's crew was so borderline with their provisions, they would have no ability to focus on anything other than getting to the next port. They wouldn't be able to detour to avoid pirates or take advantage of a favorable wind and fly past a port town. They'd be nervous and hungry, working only to get to the next place they could restock.

Business leaders can also fall into this trap. They focus on having enough for today, enough for the next pay period, enough to cover this round of bills. But that doesn't allow you any space to pursue bigger dreams.

Sufficient provision, on the other hand, enables you to get through today *and* build for the dreams of the future. You have enough provisions to be solid and stable and to know you're safe. You can make payroll. You can pay the bills and you don't have to lay awake, stressed out every night. You have enough provisions to meet all your needs, and *extra* to make sure that there is a safety margin, as well as some to give away.

That's provision. *That's* what it means to have "enough."

INSUFFICIENT PROVISION

So what prevents business leaders from getting there? Why are stories like Rebecca's so common? There's a long answer and a short answer to those questions. We're going to spend the rest of this chapter giving you the short answer.

The long answer is the rest of the book.

In other words, it's complicated. A company's level of provision is connected to literally every aspect of the business, which means that business leaders need to build up their skills in the six core areas. However, as a starting place, we can identify some of the common ways insufficient provision can rear its ugly head. First and foremost, let's talk cash.

CONGESTED CASH FLOW

Most business leaders have heard the phrase: "Cash is king." It's a reality that business owners are all too familiar with. The level of cash flow that a company experiences will make or break it—even if the company looks profitable on paper.

Let's think back to our adventurous sailors, trying to get to their next port. Imagine you're the captain, and you know that it's going to take you thirty days at sea to get from your current location to your destination in the Caribbean. Once you get there, you're going to be able to sell your goods for a profit, and you'll have plenty of money to buy more rations. You assume everything will go smoothly and pack sufficient rations for thirty days at sea.

Then, reality hits. On day twenty-six, there's a storm. You're blown off course and it could take an extra week before you get to port. On top of all that, some of the food was thrown overboard to stabilize the ship during the storm.

At this point, your sailors are hungry. They're thirsty. They might be briefly appeased if you remind them that they'll have all they can eat and more by just waiting until you can get to port. But on day thirty-three, that rationale doesn't work anymore. The needs are pressing and immediate. On day thirty-five, you'll have a mutiny on your hands. On day thirty-six, you'll be thrown overboard. Your sailors are starving and dying of thirst, and no one cares that the payload is imminent. It doesn't matter what you're promised *eventually* if you don't have sufficient provision to get past day thirty.

So what does this look like in a business context? You might have experienced something like this firsthand, but in case you haven't, we'll paint the picture.

Suppose you sell coasters for a living. You buy them in ten

thousand coaster lots, at a dollar apiece. You can't buy less than that at a time, because you only get the competitive price when you buy all ten thousand at once.

But that's okay, because you have a buyer who has committed to buying all ten thousand coasters for a sum of $20,000. How perfect! How easy! You've got an immediate, profitable turnaround. It's every entrepreneur's dream.

Unfortunately, that extra $10,000 doesn't arrive immediately. You put the money out for the coasters, and the coaster company agrees to send them to you within thirty days. A month passes, and bills pile up on your desk. You manage to put together enough cash to pay them all, reassuring yourself that the big payload is coming.

When you finally get the coasters, your buyer asks you to ship them along, and send her an invoice. You get the coasters shipped and issue the invoice the very same day. Done! Now the $10,000 will roll in!

Except—your buyer has thirty days to pay you. Now you're looking at sixty days since you've put out $10,000, and you have a second month's worth of bills to pay. If you were on a boat sailing to the Caribbean, your sailors would be looking dangerously thirsty at this point. Still, you convince yourself you can hang on another month.

Then, there's another snag. Your buyer, bless her heart, had a rough month and she can't make the payment on time. Her company finally manages to pay you *ninety* days later. On paper, you've still made a profit of $10,000, but if you don't have enough cash to sustain yourself until that payment arrives—mutiny. Mutiny, and walking the plank. In other words: you're sunk.

Your cash flow is the single biggest factor that dictates whether you can survive or not. You could be a millionaire on paper but going broke in reality because you don't have any cash. That's what we mean when we say "Cash is king": if you have more cash in the bank than you have bills, you can survive and fight another day. If you *don't* have sufficient cash, your days are numbered.

To run a successful business, you need margin. Is there margin in your time? Is there margin in your plan? And perhaps most importantly: is there margin in your checking account? Think back to our Caribbean sailing odyssey. Remember how insufficient those thirty days of rations were? It's not enough to plan to *get by*. Provision isn't just about having the minimum; it's also about having enough to be able to handle the challenges that come along and take advantage of opportunities that come your way.

There are three important terms worth understanding when we talk about cash flow. **Breakeven** means that you're able to cover all your expenses *and* pay yourself a fair wage, with nothing left over. In numerical terms, you could say that it costs you a dollar to do everything you do in a given day, and you're making a dollar every day in profit. That's breaking even.

Negative cash flow is anything short of breakeven. It may cost you a dollar a day to exist, and you're only bringing in ninety cents in daily sales. You may not be able to afford to pay yourself a decent salary, or you may struggle to pay the bills. That's negative cash flow.

Positive cash flow means you're making more than breakeven. You're selling $1.10 every day, which is ten cents beyond what it costs you to exist. Your company's growing and there's some margin to play with, which can also help buffer you against unexpected challenges.

As a general rule of thumb, **we recommend a minimum target of 10 percent net profit.** That's going to give you enough "provision" for both survival *and* progress toward your goals.

FAILURE TO SECURE A LOAN

"Ah, well, this isn't that big of a deal," you might be thinking. "When I need help, I'll just go to a bank and get a loan. Then my cash flow issues will be fixed."

At least—that's what *we* thought when we were first getting started.

The two of us sat in front of a banker after two years of running Half a Bubble Out and gave her a dazzling description of all the reasons the small-business-friendly bank could believe in us and should loan us the money. She looked at our numbers and then gave us an apologetic look. "I don't know if this is going to work, guys." Then she looked at Kathryn, who had left a high-paying job to work in our company, and said, "You might want to seriously think about going back to your real job." Ouch.

That was a bad day.

Here's what we learned from the experience: it is really hard for small businesses to get a conventional loan until you've proven that you can be profitable and consistent with paying your bills for several years in a row. In many cases, if you don't have a minimum of two years' worth of consistently strong numbers, you're considered too big of a lending risk. It's ironic: you have to *not* need the money in order to get the money.

Some business leaders—even experienced ones—make the mistake of getting their loan from anyone who *will* take them on. We knew one gentleman who had been in business for over thirty-five years but ultimately ran his company into the ground. He made a series of mistakes, but his fatal undoing was getting buried in debt to loan sharks, trying to keep his business afloat. In spite of his prominent reputation and his well-established practice, he became indebted hundreds of thousands of dollars to multiple shady vendors.

FAILURE TO PROPERLY MANAGE EXPECTATIONS

So what's a business leader to do? We can start by trying to make sure we have a realistic idea of just how much we'll really need— and just how long it will take us to get there. Often, the problem isn't so much with the loan brokers; it's due to the **unrealistic expectations** that many business leaders have as they begin their companies. This isn't easy and it definitely takes some skill and experience to do it well. Good research, mentors and experience can help improve your accuracy. Too many entrepreneurs either don't count the costs and just jump in, or *think* they've counted the costs, but never got an outside perspective.

This, too, is a provision problem: it's insufficient provision of knowledge. We harbored our own unrealistic expectations early in our careers, and we can now identify other business leaders operating with the same inflated ideas.

We've encountered these leaders a number of times, when entrepreneurs have sought to hire us for a major marketing campaign. They often have big ideas and even bigger expectations—but low capital. We once had someone tell us, "I've got this great idea! It's going to cost $50,000. I have $10,000 right now, which I know isn't enough, but if you can do your magic for just the $10,000 right now, I can pay you the remaining $40,000 in six months.

Because by then, my idea will be working!" That's not a joke—we've had several versions of that conversation.

Entrepreneurs are characteristically optimistic, and that can often lead to exaggerated expectations. We think that a company will be easier to run than it actually is, faster to become profitable, and cost less money and time to get to the break-even point. We can't think of a single new businessperson who didn't struggle with these unrealistic expectations—including ourselves, two decades ago. All of us who are new to business have poor expectations. It's like the side mirror on your car: your expectations distort the distance between you and the object of your goal.

After seventeen years in business, we're able to see more clearly what getting a business up and running is really going to require. Here's an unfortunate truth: usually, getting a business to break even is going to take longer than you think and cost more money. You're going to have to invest in many different areas, including your own salary. If you're a new entrepreneur, be blatantly honest with yourself. If you're going to quit your job to start a company, how long can you live without taking a profit? You either need money in the bank, money coming in from somewhere else, or investment capital.

Almost everything takes longer than you think and costs more than you planned.

Setting up a company well and getting it on course with all the fundamentals is critical. If you plunge headlong into starting up a business without correcting unrealistic expectations, you're signing up for a brutal crash in the future. Your business could blow up, or you might give up from exhaustion because you can't afford to tread water anymore. You might lose your dream because you ignored some of the basic fundamentals of business.

Here's an example of what it looks like to do this well. We have a friend, Bill, who's a successful investment broker and came up with an idea to start a business in an entirely new market. It was a cool idea with lots of potential.

Because Bill is a seasoned business person, he had the realistic expectation that it was going to take a while before his business could breakeven, and that he was going to need to invest a lot of money. With those realistic expectations in place, he was able to prepare for the long journey ahead of him. In other words—he packed plenty of provisions aboard his ship.

It took *six* years for Bill to get his new company to the break-even point—longer even than his conservative estimate. But because of Bill's savvy preparation, he was able to pay himself a salary throughout those six years. He also managed to pay another person who he brought in as a partner. Once he finally hit break even at six years, everything started accelerating quickly. At seven years, his share of the company was worth $1 million, and his partner bought him out. It was a long haul to get there, but he had the realistic expectations to prepare for the duration, and as a result, was able to see the business through until it made him a major profit.

We want to encourage you to build an understanding of some of these business fundamentals so you can proceed with a clear view of what it's going to take. Rather than setting yourself up to crash, take the time to establish yourself well so that you can actually achieve your dream. We're going to do everything we can within this book, and in the resources we offer outside of it, to help you acquire those fundamentals.

INABILITY TO GET TO THE NEXT LEVEL

Plenty of companies fall victim to some of the insufficient provision problems we've just discussed and simply don't make it, falling into the business failure statistics. But insufficient provision can also affect established companies—even companies that most would consider "successful." Any business that has made it through the critical early years but is now **stuck in its current position, unable to grow to the next level,** is probably also experiencing insufficient provision in some capacity.

Plenty of business leaders have the basic provision stuff down. They can consistently pay the bills and turn a profit; they're leading a staff of thirty and paying themselves a six-figure paycheck. But they can't seem to generate the revenue to go any further. They keep hitting the glass ceiling and can't figure out how to get to their next phase of growth.

We knew one business leader in this position who said he felt like he was trying to fight an invisible beast that seemed to be holding him down, but he couldn't get his arms around it. There's frustration, confusion, and stress in this phase—the cash seems to be disappearing as you try to grow the company from one level to the next. That's also a provision issue.

Another common scenario that can happen even in established businesses is a profitable company that can't pay its owners a living wage. We see this often: a business owner steadily grows their company over five to seven years, maintaining a solid staff. They may have lots of customers for whatever they sell. They get to this place where they've done it all—but they haven't been able to pay themselves consistently. In one sense, they're successful, but not in what they take home. Once again—that's a provision issue.

CONSEQUENCES OF INSUFFICIENT PROVISION

If there's any doubt that passion must be supported by provision, let's consider the consequences of *insufficient* provision.

First: you're **stressed.** That's a given. You're lying awake at night, wondering if you can make payroll or pay your mortgage. Your **personal health may suffer.**

You're experiencing **toil.** You're nowhere near that 51 percent passion baseline; running a business is hard, frustrating, and exhausting. You often feel like you've come to hate your business.

The business is suffering. Your employees have **low morale** as they sense the instability of the company. Your own stress is rubbing off on them, and it's resulting in **lower productivity, less creativity, and poorer results**; everyone's shifted into survival mode. You also sometimes—secretly—feel **resentment for your employees** because you have to pay them. Every time you catch one of them slacking off, you feel a surge of anger. If your business is barely staying afloat or if you can't pay yourself—that can easily create animosity between you and your team.

You're **embarrassed.** Most entrepreneurs launch their businesses with a host of people cheering them on—their family, their friends, their wider community. In fact, many of those supporters may actually have helped invest money in the startup. You also care about your reputation with your vendors and community partners. You wonder: "How am I going to save face with all the people who believed in me if this doesn't work?"

You're **depressed** and **disappointed.** You're not able to live into the future or grow your company. You feel like the destiny you're meant for is out of your reach, and you're not going to be able to live into your dreams.

You're experiencing **family conflict.** There's a good chance your spouse, your parents, and/or your siblings and children are directly impacted by how your business does. Maybe they're financially tied in; they're certainly emotionally tied in. Maybe you tried to shore up your business by working longer and longer hours; weekends easily got sucked away too. You may have started letting down your spouse or missing your kids' sports games. Maybe your spouse has even accused you of not doing enough to provide for the family. As you experience stress, you may find yourself reacting more in anger and impatience.

There's also a critical **loss of hope.** Your desire to make an impact, to live a life of freedom, to experience fulfillment at work—it all can go by the wayside if you're feeling crushed under the burden of insufficient provision.

BENEFITS OF SUFFICIENT PROVISION

On the other hand, when there *is* sufficient provision, it feeds your business like oxygen. Having enough cash, enough resources, enough knowledge to handle each next struggle is like having a full tank of gas. There's **increased innovation** as people are more easily able to brainstorm ideas for growth, and there's **margin to invest in new tools.** Those new investments can lead to **more**

opportunities. You have better credit, a solid reputation, and you enjoy **respect** in your professional community.

Sufficient provision feeds your business like oxygen.

Sufficient provision means there's a level of **safety** in your workplace; employees know they don't need to worry about whether or not they're going to receive their next paycheck. **Morale is improved.** There's **more creativity** all around and less anxiety. You can feel **genuine appreciation for your employees** and hand them their paychecks with gratitude, not resentment.

Not to mention, *you're* a much healthier human being. You have **more energy** because you can sleep at night. You have more mental bandwidth and creativity. You're able to be **choosier with clients** because you're not desperate for every last dollar, which means you enjoy the people you work with more. You go home feeling satisfied after work. You're also making **healthier decisions** because you're not constantly operating from a place of desperate survival mode.

Sufficient provision also means **many of your internal personal needs are met:** emotionally, psychologically, even socially. More "fruit" for your labor (i.e., more cash) is validating, and it helps fuel your passion. You feel a sense of confirmation that the risk and labor you put into your company is paying off.

Your family is provided for—both financially and with your presence. When things are going well at work, you're able to be more **present and available at home.** It's easier to genuinely enjoy family time on weekends and vacations. When you take time off, you're more able to truly unplug, because you can trust the business is going to be okay in your absence. You're a happier and healthier human being, which means **you're a lot more fun** to be around.

A RAFT OR A SHIP

Provision is a scalable concept. If you're selling tacos on the beach in Mexico and it's only costing you $15 a day to exist, your provision needs are not going to be substantial. On the other hand, if you're operating out of a high-rise in Manhattan with enormous overhead costs, you're going to need a lot more provision for the journey. In either case though, you still need *enough* to sustain you for today and some extra to build for tomorrow.

The place of "enough" is going to look different for everyone. What's most important is that you *prepare* for the unique journey you're going to undertake. You may not be planning to embark on a sailing ship across the Atlantic; you may only envision a leisurely float down the river. If you can confidently anticipate low provision needs, then sure: take a raft. Pack a picnic lunch. Be home by supper.

The danger comes when your expectations don't align with the reality that comes. If you prepare for a calm river float, but then suddenly find yourself in rough waters—that's going to be a dangerous situation for yourself and your business. If you've done nothing to prepare for unexpected challenges, then you could easily sink. Your business could fail, or you may exhaust yourself trying to tread water. It's doubtful you'll manage to reach your destination.

On the other hand, if you've calculated the odds and have some gear along for the "just in case" needs—extra food, some life jackets, a tool kit for repairs—then you stand a much better chance of completing your journey. You'll be able to enjoy the ride, learn a lot, and prepare for bigger adventures.

Many people started businesses because they believed it was possible to become self-made. They had zeal and courage and a passion for their product. But they're often not equipped to handle the journey. Essentially, they try to set out across the ocean in a raft.

As a business leader, you're the captain responsible for ensuring that your crew is going to be protected, provided for, and that you have every likely chance to achieve your goals. You need knowledge and you need adequate preparation.

Achieving provision in the future starts with preparing well today. How do you do that? You learn. You learn about your future needs, and you learn what it will realistically take to meet them. How long are you going to be out at sea before you reach your next port? Are you heading into an easy field or a tough one? Will you need to be aggressive or can you sail along casually? As you gain knowledge and understanding, you're going to be far better equipped to handle the journey, while maintaining both passion *and* provision. Like our friend Bill, you'll have what you need to sustain yourself until you've met the goal you're aiming for.

In the chapters that follow, we want to give you a clear picture of the vessel you need for your desired journey. We want to help you understand that vessel, inside and out—which parts work together, how to take on repairs. We want to help you evaluate your leadership, choose the ideal destination, consider your operations, manage your sailors—er, staff. We want to help provide you with intellectual provision, so that you are better equipped to achieve financial provision, so that your passion can thrive.

If you're tired of sucking down water while you tread in place, barely keeping your head above the waves—let us help you get up *on* the water. Let's get you in the boat you need so that when the waves hit, you're ready to take them on.

||||||||||||||||||

CHAPTER THREE

The Holistic Model

"Learn how to see. Realize that everything connects to everything else."
LEONARDO DA VINCI

Early in our marriage, we bought a house in Colorado. During the home inspection, a large foundational crack was discovered in the basement. The current owners agreed to fix the crack, and it was taken care of before we moved in. Problem solved, we thought.

Some months later, Michael started doing some remodeling in the basement and pulled down some paneling. Hidden under dirt and behind the paneling, we found another massive crack—one that no one had noticed because it had been covered up.

We didn't realize how serious the crack was until our contractor began setting up posts underneath our house to prop up the walls. When we asked him why the posts were necessary, he said matter-of-factly, "Your house is in danger of collapsing. Quite frankly, I'm surprised your master bedroom didn't cave in."

Workers dug a huge trench on the outside wall to expose the

entire foundation. When they did, they discovered the full length of the crack: it was eighteen feet, end to end, and you could see light through it from the other side.

The crack had been hidden underground, covered up, paneled over. But this unseen foundational weakness had the power to bring our entire home to rubble.

IS YOUR FOUNDATION SOLID OR SHAKY?

There are foundational aspects to a business, and if that foundation isn't solid, complete, and level, you're in trouble. Without a strong foundation supporting your business, everything you've built up could potentially fall to the ground.

The temptation in business is to focus on one problem area, and ideally, fix it and move on as quickly as possible. Often though, that "small" problem may actually be grounded in a much bigger problem. For instance, you think your marketing is stale and decide you want new branding. But the reason your branding is stale is because your business lacks a clear vision. The reason you lack a clear vision is because you're in the weeds of running your business operations and have lost sight of the big picture.

A "surface" problem may connect to multiple, interconnected problems. If you try to fix one and ignore the other issues—the bigger, deeper issues—you may as well ignore a crack in your home's foundation.

When we started remodeling and Michael pulled off the paneling, it would have been easier and cheaper to just tack that paneling back up and pretend we'd never seen the crack. "The house has lasted since 1905," we could have reasoned. "What's a few more years?"

As a business owner, this temptation is real. You might be afraid to deal with the bigger problem you've discovered. Maybe you don't know how to deal with it, or you may not have the money to do so. It feels easier to tell yourself, "The business has been going along well enough. I don't fully understand the implications of this problem, but nothing has collapsed yet. Maybe we can keep moving and no one will ever notice."

We get it. Dealing with foundational issues can be expensive, time-consuming, and hard. But we didn't want our master bedroom to cave in, and we're guessing you don't want your business to collapse either.

There's a common saying: "You don't know what you don't know." How can you fix foundational problems in your business if you can't identify them? Even if you could identify them, how would you know where to begin to fix them?

This chapter aims to shed light on *what you may not know*. We believe there are six core competencies that make up the foundation of a business: vision, leadership, management and operations, marketing and sales, money, and culture. As a business leader, **you need a working knowledge of these six core competencies to ensure Passion & Provision can thrive in your company.**

Think of these core competencies as your foundation stones. To do that, you're going to want to think like an ancient builder. In modern day, most foundations are solid concrete, but hundreds of years ago, concrete wasn't available. Strong foundations were built through the careful selection of interlocking stones. When good-quality stones were properly placed and aligned with strong cornerstones, the foundation was solid. The structure on top was stable: ready to endure time, weather, and natural disasters.

We view these six fundamental skills as your interlocking stones. We're going to discuss them each briefly within the context of this chapter, and then describe each one in greater depth in the chapters to come. We'll teach you how to examine each stone, so that you can ensure your foundation is made up of good, quality, stable materials—able to withstand time and storms.

A WORKING KNOWLEDGE—NOT MASTERY

Before you panic about the idea that you need to master six areas of running a business, let us clarify: a *working knowledge* is different from *mastery*. You need to be "good enough" in six areas to be able to know what you don't know. By achieving a *working knowledge* of the pieces and parts of your business, you can help your employees do their jobs effectively, and you'll feel greater confidence and competency as a leader.

By our very nature as human beings, we tend to think in binary terms: yes or no; right or wrong; on or off. Business leaders can fall into the trap of using those same oversimplified terms when they think about themselves or their employees. Either you can do it or you can't. Either you're smart or you're an idiot. Your employee is awesome or they're awful.

However, that way of thinking is totally unproductive. First of all, it's not true. Second, binary thinking doesn't allow you to properly assess yourself or your employees' competency.

Rather than thinking in binary terms, consider yourself and your employees in terms of *minimum competency*. Do you have **enough** knowledge and skill to "*make it work*" and meet the minimum requirements—that's what we mean by "working knowledge"—

or do you need to educate yourself and/or your team to achieve those minimum requirements?

> "He who would learn to fly one day must first learn to stand and walk and run and climb and dance; one cannot fly into flying." —Friedrich Nietzsche

MINIMUM COMPETENCY

A working knowledge, (i.e., minimum competency) involves the following:

1. You understand relevant vocabulary and terms.
2. You have the ability to ask intelligent questions.
3. You have the basic skills and capacity to DO what's required.
4. You have an idea of where to go in order to learn more.
5. You have the necessary humility to get help when you need it.

Once you have a working knowledge of each core area of your business, you'll better understand where you have gaps. From there, commit yourself to growing and learning in the places where you discover that you have significant weaknesses.

Here's an example. Let's say that you want to learn how to ride a bike. Your point of minimum competency is going to be when you manage to get up on that bike, balance without training wheels, and push the pedals down to carry you forward. Before you hit that point, you're not going anywhere: you're stuck with a bike you can't ride. A concept like "gear shifting" would make no sense to you, because you can't even balance upright. Once you hit the point of minimum competency, you *can* ride a bike.

You start understanding the right questions to ask about how to position your body and the bike's mechanics. You can start spotting other cyclists who seem to really know what they're doing and you can learn from them. You've got the skill and knowledge required to hit the road and begin a long journey of growth.

At the level of minimum competency, you've still got a long ways to go before you can bomb around town, ride up hills, take sharp corners, and so on. You've got even further (like, way further) to go before you're a master cyclist, taking on the Tour de France. But you have the *minimum* skills required to ride a bike, and you can get better and better from there.

That's the goal with minimum competency in each area of your business. You're trying to get to a level where you can take yourself forward and the company forward, steadily building toward further mastery.

Here's another way you can think about it. Imagine that you're looking at a white board, and we draw a vertical line with "zero" at the bottom and "100" at the top. "100" describes total mastery in your area of expertise: you've been at it for a decade or more, you have more than 10,000 hours of experience, you could test brilliantly in your knowledge, your skill is well practiced, and you understand the nuances of your particular field. You're a true expert, a bonified master: that's 100.

Zero means you know nothing. You got no skills, no knowledge, no nothin'. You're an idiot—no offense.

Somewhere around the middle is where we'd identify "minimum competency," and the specific point of where that minimum competency is will change for every role. For instance, your accountant is going to need strong competency in the area of accounting to successfully carry out her job; on the spectrum, maybe she needs to come in with a competency level around 70 or 80. As her boss, you need a *working* knowledge of accounting so that you can effectively manage her, ask her the right questions, and ensure she's working toward the company's Vision. But you don't need the same level of expertise that she does; your level of minimum competency might sit more around the 50 or 60 range.

In the range of minimum competency, you know *enough* to effectively carry out your job and pursue further growth. Your skills are good enough that you can ask the right questions and determine what you don't know. You have the basic skills required to manage your employees, do your accounting, create a marketing plan, and so on.

As you come to better understand the core areas of your business, you'll also be in a better position to oversee others on your team and set clear goals for *their* growth in those areas. What knowledge is necessary for them as they begin? What do you hope they learn as they go? If you're clueless about the work your employees do, you can't evaluate or motivate them. However, when you have minimum competency, you'll know enough to do both.

If you fall below that minimum, then you don't have enough understanding to effectively run your business. You won't have the basic skills required to manage your employees well. Even worse, you may not even *know* you have blind spots; too many people think they have minimum competency in an area when they don't. Our goal with this book is to get you to a level of minimum competency in each fundamental area of business, and then provide you with tools to go from there.

And we do recommend that you *go* from there. As you develop as a professional business leader, you want to pursue steady improvement in each area. It's fun to ride a bike in an empty parking lot, but it's way better to have the skills to go on much longer rides, on more challenging terrain. Likewise, your business will have more flexibility, strength, and success as you continue to strengthen your skills, practice, knowledge, and experience. Determine which areas you most need to improve in, and seek out learning there first.

Many of us had minimum competency in enough areas that we were able to get our businesses started, but the business failure rate attests to the fact that many of us encountered knowledge gaps and challenges along the way. If we were to actually administer a test in the six areas of core competency, we're guessing most business leaders would struggle to pass them all. When you have two-thirds of businesses failing within a decade, that's a sign that business leaders need more help along the way.

Even the third of businesses that succeed would likely benefit from a boost. Most successful businesses benefited from a winning combination of having smart people who learned on the go, a lot of hustling, and luck. Quite frankly, those three characteristics describe the two of us: we hustled, we learned on the go (acquiring some painful lessons in the process), and we got lucky.

If a business doesn't benefit from these posts to prop it up, it's either going to collapse underneath you and you'll end up in the basement, or you're going to get so tired of the stress, you'll give up. It has all taken too long and you have seen so little progress, and you're too tired—so you shut it down.

That's where we want to intervene. We believe the knowledge

that we've compiled in the chapters that follow will help business leaders achieve that critical "learning on the go."

"And so it is: **experience** is not sufficient, but it is necessary. It is the only possible beginning, and ultimately the most urgent part of the long process of learning." —Paul Goldberger

This is not a full-time master's program that will require you to step away from your work. This is an education for someone who is in the trenches now, who needs enough information that will lead to success in real life and needs further resources to build on from there. We're going to address your leadership, your development, your maturity, and help you flag your areas of deficit. We'll also provide next steps and resources so that you're not left alone with your questions, but rather can continue in your training with support.

I'LL JUST GET SOMEONE ELSE TO DO IT

You might be reading this thinking, "Surely this advice is a bit extreme. I don't need a working knowledge in *every* area of my business. I could probably bump up my expertise in the areas that I deal with, but not finance—our finance director takes care of all that. And not marketing—we've already got a great marketer."

We don't want to get too doom and gloom on you, but we've seen that kind of thinking lead to many a successful business's downfall. How, you ask? Here are a few examples, which may or may not be hypothetical.

Let's say you're the executive director of an organization and you've fully entrusted your finance director with all of your business accounts. You hate dealing with the money stuff, so you just don't; it's all been put in the hands of your trusted finance director. The only question you ever ask about money is, "Are we still doing well?" Frankly, you don't know what questions *to* ask, much beyond that.

When you talked yesterday with your trusted finance director, you were told that you had $800,000 in the bank. Then today, your finance director comes in, ashen-faced. He confesses that you have less than $20,000; he's been making up figures for months because he didn't want to worry you. You're totally broke, and you had no idea.

Example number two: you're the new owner of a decades-old company that has extraordinary national success. You have great clients, great cash flow, and the business is widely respected. However, after recognizing that there's been a concerning level of turnover, you discover that the company's culture is eating your employees alive.

The more you look into this issue, the worse the picture gets. Your employees feel disconnected and see no purpose in their work. Their morale is in the tank. Everybody's protecting their own little slice in the company, and attempts at collaboration are treated with hostility and suspicion. No one is working together. People go into their offices, close the doors, and don't talk to anyone.

The negativity is rapidly draining the company's effectiveness. The turnover rate is causing money to hemorrhage. Opportunities fall by the wayside because no one wants to bother to go after them. In spite of your company's nationally recognized success, you realize that you may not survive the next five years.

Maybe, as a new owner, you ask a senior leader how it got this bad. He shrugs. "There was enough money coming in, and our CEO didn't want to change anything."

Examples may or *may not* be hypothetical. This stuff really happens.

It turns out, you need to know something about your product *and* your finances. You need to know something about leadership *and* culture. You need to know something about managing your employees *and* providing them with a big-picture vision. In short, you need minimum competency in each core area of business, and you need to understand that they all holistically connect to one another.

We want to help you succeed and thrive—not just in one area, but in all areas. We don't want to just target a symptom; we want to focus on holistic health.

THE CASE FOR A HOLISTIC MODEL

We think the holistic framework makes a lot of sense, but a holistic approach is not a popular one in our country. In two of our largest and most respected fields—medicine and higher education—we like specialists.

If you have a medical ailment, you go to the doctor. You tell them what's wrong with you, and they send you on to a specialist. If that specialist can't figure it out, you go to another specialist. If you have multiple symptoms, affecting multiple parts of your body, you go see multiple specialists. But rarely do all these specialists get together and talk about what might be happening in your body on a holistic level. This is puzzling to us.

Here's another puzzle, related to education. From kindergarten through twelfth grade, most kids are educated using an approach called scope and sequence. Curricula determines the *scope* of what students should learn, (i.e., the depth and breadth of a subject) then, a *sequence* is built so that one lesson can be layered on another, until students learn the full scope of knowledge that they supposedly need. Multiple lessons all come together so that kids can build a fuller understanding about a whole subject. This seems like a good model. It is, in fact, a holistic model—it acknowledges that many pieces of knowledge must come together to produce full understanding.

However, at the university level, scope and sequence is tossed out the window. It's replaced—once again—with specialization. Students go to various classes that may or may not have the same professor, so there's little or no continuity. Professors have the freedom to teach what they think is important. Even when a program is put together with required classes, rarely are students given help connecting a new class to their previous class, and there's no one connecting it to the next class they'll take. Individual skills and knowledge packets are taught in a siloed fashion. There's no scope and sequence, and therefore no holistic perspective.

We often get interns working for us at Half a Bubble Out who make this point painfully clear. They'll come to us after spending years in their business or communication programs, but invariably, they tell us, "I learned more here in three months than I have in my entire college education." We're not providing these students with any earth-shattering information—we're just helping them connect the dots, seeing how one area of business impacts another.

Still, connecting the dots is not a major goal among business leaders. As in medicine and higher ed, the general opinion in the business world is that specialists are better. Specialists make more money, and that must be for good reason, right? The business leader might think, "If I'm going to hire people, I'm going to hire somebody who's a *specialist*. I don't care if they know anything but that one thing—at least they'll be an expert in that one thing!"

Don't get us wrong—specialists can provide amazing expertise in a given area. But we think this expertise can actually end up leading people astray if it's not viewed from within a *holistic* framework.

Here's an example. Let's say you want to pay for a financial consultant, because you're concerned about your level of cash flow. An outsourced CFO guy comes in. He's trying to help you solve your financial problems, approaching it from a financial grid. He's got ideas about accounting and ratios and running your numbers. However, he can't speak to the efficacy of your marketing, which would surely impact your profit. He can't speak to the efficacy of your management and operations, which could be creating a huge drain on your resources and efficiency.

Perhaps he'll touch on those issues—"Maybe you could get your employees to work harder. Is there a way you can get your payroll down? Is there a way you could get more customers for the same amount of money?"

But when you ask him for suggestions about making that happen, what will he say? "I don't know. That's not my specialty."

So, let's say you bring in a marketing consultant next. She's full of advice: "You need to build this plan and you need to spend money on awareness. Buy ads, buy more services, build more blogs!" Your marketing consultant lays out an elaborate marketing plan but doesn't get specific about how much it will cost. She can't speak to how fast it's going to increase profits either, based on the fact that you'll have to spend a bunch of money to make it work. After all—that's not her specialty.

Maybe you think you need more customers, so you hire a specialist to help you drum up new clientele. But what if your biggest problem with customers is poor customer retention, because your disengaged employees are providing terrible customer service? Or what if your measly profits are a result of not understanding which products or services are really making you money, because you don't understand your finances? Or what if your financial drain is due to the fact that your team doesn't have clarity on their roles, due to your poor leadership or inefficient systems?

Each specialist comes in with solutions to grow your business, but if they're not looking at *all* the aspects of your business, your foundation's going to get lopsided. While there's value to expertise, knowledge, and experience, every recommendation must still come with an understanding of how *this* part affects the *rest* of the business.

"Aha!" you might be thinking. "What I need to do is get a room *full* of specialists and get them to all talk to each other!"

Let's consider this best-case scenario. First, let's assume that you have enough spare cash to hire six or seven different specialists at once, one for each fundamental area of your business. Then, let's say they manage to all be available at the same time, and you're able to bring them into the same room. Pretend that you're able to train them with some common vocabulary to talk to each other effectively, so that they can each comprehend what the others are saying and communicate well. Then, let's say you're able to filter all their advice through your clearly expressed common vision, with a common Core Purpose, common Core Values, and a common Big, Hairy, Audacious Goal on where you're going.

If you could work that out—then, yes. That would probably be ideal.

However, most business leaders could never afford this best-case scenario. (You probably already know this.) Additionally, even if you could afford it, *you* still need minimum competency in each area of business to know what advice to prioritize first and determine the next step. In order to lead your people, you need a basic grasp about what it is each of them do.

Even big corporations can fall victim to the inefficiency of siloed solutions. Corporations build huge departments, each with their own leader, each functioning independent of the other departments. Marketing doesn't talk to Sales, which doesn't talk to Research and Development. As a result, you've got people in Research and Development creating products that the Marketing people can't market and the Sales people can't sell.

In sum: you need minimum competency in each area of business—that's basically non-negotiable. You also need someone to connect the dots for you, and you need that information in a vehicle that won't break the bank.

Ta-dah! It's this book!

Here's how we're aiming to equip you: small businesses need to get help in multiple areas, preferably simultaneously, or at least in close succession. That way, you're propping up each part of the business and growing it a little bit, then moving to the next area, and then the next area so that your foundation doesn't get lopsided. Our aim with these chapters is to give you the knowledge necessary to build minimum competency in each area, in relatively short succession, so that you can begin that process of simultaneous improvement.

Businesses need to operate, not in silos, but in *symbiosis*. They are holistic organisms, and each area impacts the others. Everybody needs to help everybody else.

"Synergy—the bonus that is achieved when things work together harmoniously." —Mark Twain

INTERTWINED AND INTERLOCKING

When we look at the real world, the natural world, we find something much different than silos. We see everything intertwining. Plants grow from a combination of good dirt, clean water, sunshine, and protection from threats. A fresh loaf of bread is made from a combination of ingredients, must be kneaded to rise, then experiences a chemical reaction from the yeast, baking powder, and heat before it finally emerges as done. The finished product is a masterpiece of intertwining elements that synergize together.

Likewise, Passion & Provision must go together. Their interaction causes the sum of the parts to be greater than the whole—and you want that synergy. To get there, you need a holistic model that can address multiple facets of your business at once. Our framework provides a "big picture" reference point, containing the fundamental areas of running a business.

Imagine you're doing a jigsaw puzzle. You're not going to make much progress on that puzzle if your method solely involves studying each tiny puzzle piece for ideas about where it's going to fit best; you need to reference the picture on the box, which gives you a vision for how all the pieces fit together. Then, you go back and forth between studying the puzzle pieces and then studying the picture. You focus on one area at a time, build it up, then move to another area. That's similar to how you're going to want to take on the puzzle of your business: you intentionally take on one area at a time, building it up a little, then building up another area, always keeping the big picture in mind.

We think it's a fool's errand to focus on one area of improvement in your business and neglect all the others. The best way forward is to take in the big picture and then examine how the pieces work together within that larger framework.

The holistic model is like the top picture on the box of a jigsaw puzzle. Using this framework, you're going to be able to figure out the edge pieces, and the sky pieces, and the barn pieces, and assemble them in a way that collectively works to aid the whole picture coming together.

Business leaders can easily get so distracted by working "in" their business, they forget to work "on" their business. They're so deep down in the weeds of their daily operations or product development, that they forget to be strategic. Essentially, they're only staring at the little puzzle pieces, and they never understand how all those pieces relate to the others.

By working within a holistic framework, you're able to work not just *in* your business, but also *on* it. You're empowered to work strategically. And, by building up your minimum competency in each core area, you're not limited in your scope. You can freely engage with the different areas of your business because you know what questions to ask, or where to go to learn more. When you have a working knowledge of each core area, and understand how they work in connection to each other, you're empowered as a leader. You'll become capable of propelling your business forward in ways you haven't been able to before.

THE SIX CORE COMPETENCIES

So, what are the six core competencies? You get a gold star if you remember that we touched on these briefly in our book's Introduction. We're going to go over them again here, focusing not only on why each one matters, but also at how they impact the other areas.

VISION

Vision is at the center of the wheel because it holds everything else together. Vision requires that you know who you are, what you do, why you do it, and where you want to take your business in the future. It's critical to have a compelling Vision to help guide today's decisions and future decisions; if you don't know where you're going, then you risk never getting there.

Your Vision as a leader will determine how you motivate your employees—your "non-negotiable" values, your style of management—and will help you focus your operations. The Vision will inform your marketing, focus your financial decisions, and directly impact your culture. It's the hub of your wheel and the very first thing you need to accomplish as a leader.

LEADERSHIP

Leadership springs directly out of Vision; it's about doing the right things, at the right time, in the right way. A company cannot grow beyond its leader, which means the strength of your leadership will ultimately determine the success of your company.

Good leaders must have a strong "inner and outer game." Your "inner game" relates to your own integrity and motivations; leaders with a strong inner game are able to empower their employees from a position of creativity, not reactive anxiety or fear. Your "outer game" refers to your ability to relate and communicate effectively, as well as get the tasks of your business accomplished.

As a leader, you must know the Vision for where your company is going. You need minimum competency in the areas of running a business and cultivating healthy relationships. Good leaders inspire their employees, protect them, and hold them accountable. That, in turn, leads to thriving employees in every area of business. Don't suck as a leader. It's bad for everyone.

MANAGEMENT AND OPERATIONS

Management and Operations relate to getting the right people in place, and getting the right things actually *done*. You must help your business effectively and efficiently deal with the detailed, day-to-day operations of getting work accomplished. These are the processes that go into producing your product and delivering it to customers. Your style of management will be informed by your effectiveness as a leader and by the vision-oriented direction you give your employees. Your employees' response to your management—their morale and goal achievement—will significantly impact the efficacy of your operations, and therefore your bottom line. See how everything is connected?

MARKETING AND SALES

Marketing and sales touch every part of your business. Marketing is not just about finding customers; it is about everything that happens once they become a customer. Every interaction with every employee is part of your marketing. It's about making sure that your company can keep the promises it is making in your marketing.

"The purpose of business is to create and keep a customer." —Peter Drucker

In a Passion & Provision company, your goal is to solve the real needs of real people. You must help people who are unaware of you become aware of you, then get them to purchase your product, then convert them into a regular customer, and ultimately turn them into raving fans.

When you market and sell your product, you're helping take people from the "before" state of their challenges in life, and showing them that your product and service will lead them to a gratifying "after." You're helping solve their problems so that you can take them from being the victim in their story, to being the hero.

Your marketing and sales will be a huge generator of income and customer allegiance. Good marketing requires a clear vision for what your company is all about, and there needs to be solid systems in place to capitalize on effective marketing.

MONEY

Money is the lifeblood that enables a company to survive. You need to be able to make revenue, turn a profit, and create steady cash flow in order to thrive. When you're not managing your money well, your expenses are higher than they need to be and your profit is less than it could be. Failure to pay attention to your financial health could result in bankruptcy creeping up on you like a giant monster; you could be taken out, without ever knowing that you had a problem. You must not only understand the fundamentals of finance, but also know how to strategically manipulate different levers of finance so that they work to your advantage.

We've already discussed in this chapter some of the ways that a company's money can be impacted by other areas of business. Although an increase in revenue is most often the "symptom" that business leaders may want to improve, the financial state of a company may often have its root in one of the other areas.

CULTURE

Culture is about creating an environment that nurtures and rein-forces the behaviors, attitudes, and beliefs that will lead to the fulfillment of your company's Vision. It's about cultivating creativity and positivity. It's about honoring your employees' dignity and contribution. It's about making work an enjoyable place to be.

Your company's culture will impact your employees' motivation and output. It will help you, as a business leader, remain focused on what really matters, according to your Vision and values. In our part of the world, where farming and agriculture abound, we think of cultivating your culture as a kind of fertilizer to the soil. Imagine bigger vegetables and multiple harvests a year, compared to smaller vegetables and one harvest a year. Good culture is going to make everything *grow better.*

THE LEVER, THE FULCRUM, THE FOUNDATION

Think of a simple lever and fulcrum.

Imagine the lever as a long stick with a big object on one end, resting on a little fulcrum in the middle. When you put the fulcrum and the lever in the right place in relationship to one another, you're able to move that heavy object. By changing the length of the lever and the position of the fulcrum, you can move bigger and bigger objects.

The ancient scholar Archimedes showed mathematically that a lighter, smaller object can move a much larger, heavier object, given the right circumstances. His findings determined that effort and results are not linear; we can put in less effort and get better results if we have the right tools and apply them the right way.

"Give me a lever long enough and a fulcrum on which to place it, and I shall move the world." —Archimedes

When you understand how the six core areas of business relate to one another, you're able to achieve more than you might think you're capable of. Why? You're bringing the lever and fulcrum *together*. If you handed someone a giant stick and told them to move a boulder, they wouldn't be able to get started. Similarly, if you handed someone a fulcrum with only a small stick, they wouldn't be able to move the boulder. The lever and the fulcrum can't operate independently of one another. But when they work together, a synergy happens.

By leaning into the holistic model within your business, the pieces become synergistic. They become the embodiment of the saying, "The sum of the whole is greater than the sum of its parts."

We've had to learn something about methods of construction

over the years—both in terms of avoiding a housing collapse and in terms of running a business. In both areas, we've realized that it's the *interconnectedness* that matters.

In Colorado, the holistic model looked like props leaning against the walls, while cracks were being repaired underneath; it was the holistic model that kept our master bedroom from falling into our basement. In business, the holistic model looks like building minimum competency as a leader in the six core areas of business and embracing their interconnectedness. *That's* what will help lead you to a work experience that provides you with increased Passion and Provision across the board. *That's* what will take you from a crumbling structure to a building that can stand.

The York Minster cathedral towers over Kathryn's hometown of York, England. The incredible, masterful craftsmanship catches your eye everywhere you go. It's why Michael sought it out as a place of inspiration when we were first laying the groundwork for the Passion & Provision strategy, and it's why we still think of it often as a place of hope, fulfillment, and an example of what humanity is capable of when they work collaboratively toward a common goal that stretches far into the future.

It's the craftsmanship *above* ground that gets everyone's attention—but the bigger magic might actually be what's below. This church has offered refuge for over 1,380 years. The reason it has lasted when so many other buildings have fallen is due to its incredibly strong foundation. Every ancient stone that was cut, shaped, and placed beneath the massive structure above was done so with the care of a master craftsman.

Without that foundation—without ensuring that every stone was strong, and sound and positioned exactly right—this building would have crumbled to the ground centuries ago. But *with* its foundational strength, everything else can rise up.

Every building needs a foundation of strength. You may have ambitions to create a company on the scale of the York Minster cathedral, or you may envision something equivalent to a modest little barn. Regardless of how large you hope to grow, the foundation is equally important for longevity and strength. That's what holds everything together. That's what enables the rest to rise.

||||||||||||||||||||

PART TWO

The What and the How

Build a Working Knowledge of the
Six Core Competencies

CHAPTER FOUR

||||||||||||||||||||

Vision: The High Horizon

The best way to predict the future is to create it.

PETER DRUCKER

Time to get behind the wheel.

Let's imagine you're a police cadet, and you're about to train for high-speed car chases. Before training begins, the officers in charge bark at you to pay attention. "This information is critical!" they say. "If you don't want to get yourself killed or kill anyone else, listen up." First, they explain, when you're driving at high speed, the dangers go up exponentially. It takes you far greater distance and time to stop than if you were driving at normal speeds, which means the potential you have for harming yourself or others radically increases.

Your trainers are going to talk about the temptation to focus on the *low horizon* (i.e., looking right over the edge of the hood). Imagine a serious and somewhat intimidating sergeant explaining this to you: "When you get going ninety, one hundred, 110 miles an hour, you can get scared. You start looking at what's right in front of you. But if you do that, you're going to end up killing someone. Your reaction time can't keep up with the speed you're going, so if you're trying to navigate around what's right in front of you, you're going to swerve all over the place. You're going to overcorrect and flip your vehicle, or you're going to smash into something, or veer into oncoming traffic. The *low horizon is not your friend*."

EYES ON THE HIGH HORIZON

This low horizon danger is just as real for business leaders. Especially when you get stressed, or when the speed of business picks up, you start solving the problems right in front of you. You focus on putting out fires, or you swerve every time you see a new opportunity or threat. You make quick decisions that don't consider your Core Values or your Core Purpose; they just seem like the right decision for the immediate future. But that's dangerous driving, and it's not going to help you reach your ultimate goals. The low horizon doesn't work well in a high-speed chase, and it doesn't work well in business either.

Let's go back to our sergeant. Imagine him taking off his aviators and giving you a piercing stare. "If you want to stay safe, you need to keep your eyes on the *high* horizon. Keep your eyes way out in front of you. *That's* where you're searching to make corrections. When something comes into your vision on that high horizon in the distance, you'll see it in time to course correct, and your corrections will be more subtle. They're smoother, and you're going to be able to avoid the obstacles in your path more effectively. Everybody's safer, and you have a chance of actually catching the bad guy."

Business constantly requires that you adjust to varying factors that are outside of your control. Without a clear idea of where you're going, how are you going to know whether to turn left or right? If there's an obstacle that forces you into a detour, how are you going to make sure your course correction is moving you toward where you want to go? When you spot an appealing new opportunity, how will you know if that road will take you in the direction you're aiming for, or if it's just a distraction that will take you off course?

Consider the complications presented by speed as well. In our "boom" days at Half a Bubble Out, our business doubled nearly overnight. The sensation was like jolting from sixty miles per hour—which felt fast, but manageable—to 120 miles per hour, which felt downright dangerous. Even with two new hires (which, as we've explained, we hired at a reckless pace which didn't work out well), we could barely keep up. All we could focus on was clearing the next thing off our plates, and our eyes dropped to the low horizon.

If your phone starts ringing off the hook and your customer workload explodes, or if there's one fire after another you're trying to deal with— *that's* when it's going to feel most tempting to look down at what's immediately in front of you—but that's also when it's *most* important to keep your eyes up on the high horizon. Businesses have failed because of explosive growth; think of a restaurant that gets an amazing review and gets too famous too quickly. They can't keep up with their influx of customers and people end up having a terrible experience—the food takes too long to come out, it's undercooked, and the service is bad because the servers are overwhelmed.

The best way to help yourself when your speed radically increases is *to identify the high horizon vision ahead of time.* If you already know where you're going and how you want to get there, an increase in speed isn't going to jeopardize your entire journey—it will accelerate it. Granted, the pace will feel dangerous for a while, but you won't make the same mistakes that you would have if you were only operating with a low horizon view. If you can maintain the high horizon view as your pace increases, you'll learn to adjust to your new speed of business; for instance, we now feel comfortable operating at "ninety miles per hour" at Half a Bubble Out, even though that would have felt impossible in our early "sixty miles per hour" days. No matter how fast you're driving: you always need to keep your eyes up.

And what exactly are you looking at, when you keep your eyes up? What exactly are you focusing on, on that high horizon? That's what this chapter is going to explain.

"If you want to build a ship, don't drum up the men to gather wood, divide the work, and give orders. Instead, teach them to yearn for the vast and endless sea." —Antoine de Saint-Exupery

The first core competency we're going to discuss, and the one at the center of the wheel, connecting to all the other competencies, is Vision. **Forming a clear, complete, and compelling Vision for your company and then navigating by it is the equivalent of keeping your eyes on the *high horizon*.** By forming a Vision for your company, you're going to help yourself in the short term, the long term, and at every step along the way.

- **Short term:** Your Vision will help you make decisions and understand what opportunities to say yes or no to. It will help you survive your current challenges in a way that maintains your Core Values and keeps you on course. The Vision will help you form a Strategic Plan that will provide your employees with clear quarterly and annual goals, enabling them to work efficiently and productively.
- **Long term:** The Vision will also identify your long-term goals and describe how achieving those goals will impact the world around you. Your Vision will give you a clear idea of your purpose and hoped-for legacy, which will enable you to keep yourself and your employees motivated during hard times. You'll maintain your Core Values, ensuring that you get to your destination in a way that you can feel good about.

A clear, complete, compelling Vision answers the questions: Why are we doing this? What's the point? What is it we're actually trying to achieve? And what will our life and company look like when we get there?

Here's one low horizon answer to those questions: "I'm just trying to make money." We know from experience *that* answer won't give you clarity about how to direct your company. It won't give you or your staff the hope or passion needed to persevere during the hard seasons. A high horizon answer, on the other hand, is going to include a clear Vision that helps guide everything that you do as a company.

While there are several models for Vision forming out there, we love the model provided in Jim Collins's book, *Good to Great*.[11] Collins's book studied what separates a "good" company from a "great" company, and the development of a clear, complete and compelling Vision was a critical piece. We believe it brings clarity in a world of confusing terminology and it helps you as a leader communicate with and inspire your team. We have been using this model with our clients for a long time and have seen from experience how powerful it is to bring together these four elements instead of just trying to shove things into a single statement.

Collins divides Vision into two halves that each contain two elements:

1. Your Core Ideology, which is made up of:
   A. Your Core Values
   B. Your Core Purpose
2. Your Envisioned Future, which is made up of:
   A. Your BHAG or "Big, Hairy, Audacious Goal"
   B. Your Vivid Description

Once you have your clear, complete, compelling Vision, you'll have the clarity needed to form a practical Strategic Plan, which will direct your quarterly, yearly, and three-year goals.

THE IMPORTANCE OF VISION

Figuratively speaking, operating without a clear vision can lead to

---

11   Collins, Jim. *Good to Great: Why Some Companies Make the Leap...and Others Don't*. New York, NY: HarperBusiness, 2001.

a disastrous car wreck. It can pose dangers to life, limb, and property. But what does this actually look like in a business context?

When Walt Disney formed his famous company alongside his brother, Roy Disney, his primary goal was to make people happy. His shows, his movies, his theme parks—they all mainly worked to bring happiness via wholesome entertainment that promoted wholesome values. Because of their work and their output, the Disney Company enjoyed widespread public trust.

After the deaths of the Disney brothers, Roy Disney's son, Roy E. Disney, took a large leadership role within the company, seeing it through multiple CEOs and serving on its board of directors. He consistently advocated for its promotion of family values. However, Roy E. Disney seriously clashed with the Disney Company's CEO through the '80s, '90s, and early 2000s: Michael Eisner.

Two years after Eisner took over Disney as CEO, the company created a subsidiary production company, Touchstone, through which it produced its first R-rated movie, *Down and Out in Beverly Hills*—a major change from the G and PG movies Disney had always been known for.[12] Eisner also focused on building up Disney's theme parks in Europe and Hong Kong, but did so—Roy E. Disney claimed—"on the cheap."[13]

Eisner saw opportunities to expand the Disney Company's control and make more money, but Roy E. Disney believed Eisner was doing so by ignoring the company's Core Purpose

---

12   Robinette, Eric. "Disney Has Released More R-Rated Movies Than You'd Expect." Showbiz Cheat Sheet, July 17, 2019. https://www.cheatsheet.com/entertainment/disney-has-released-more-r-rated-movies-than-youd-expect.html/.

13   "Roy Disney's Letter to Michael Eisner." *The Guardian*. Guardian News and Media, December 2, 2003. https://www.theguardian.com/media/2003/dec/02/broadcasting.citynews1.

of producing wholesome entertainment. As far as Eisner was concerned, his expansions were serving the company. For Roy E. Disney, the expansions felt like a betrayal of everything his father and uncle stood for.

After a steady build-up of animosity between the two leaders, Roy E. Disney ultimately resigned. He published an open letter of resignation to Eisner which laid out, publicly and plainly, his belief that Eisner had taken the Disney Company far off course from where his uncle, Walt, had wanted it to go. One point in his letter says this clearly:

> "The perception by all of our stakeholders—consumers, investors, employees, distributors, and suppliers—that the Company is rapacious, soul-less, and always looking for the 'quick buck' rather than long-term value...is leading to a loss of public trust."[14]

Roy E. Disney essentially argued that Eisner had moved away from the Core Purpose of what his father and uncle sought to create, focusing instead on the low horizon concept of making money. He claimed that Eisner's leadership had led to low morale, infighting, stagnant growth, and a major decrease in public trust.[15]

After Roy E. Disney's resignation, he started a grassroots campaign to oust Eisner, which was ultimately successful. Walt's nephew regained a position of leadership in the com-

---

14 Ibid.

15 This, of course, is one side of the story. Eisner's leadership was widely considered to have overseen successful growth at Disney, albeit through controversial means. Regardless of who you view as the Disney villain, it's clear that there was disagreement on the company's high horizon Vision, which lead to turmoil.

pany and a consulting contract.[16] Disney once again began to realign itself with one of their Core Values of providing wholesome entertainment.

VISION IS VITAL

Even the biggest and most famous companies can experience the turmoil of a loss of Vision. When the "soul" of a company is neglected or lost, it's a clear sign that the Core Values and Core Purpose of a company are being neglected. Either those values and purpose are missing completely, or they've been put away in some dusty drawer and forgotten by the folks doing the day-to-day work. The ultimate result, as Roy E. Disney points out, is a loss in customers, frustrated employees, and reflects directly on the bottom line.

Let that sink in for a second. Neglecting your Core Values and Core Purpose can lead to every business leader's nightmare:

- You lose customers.
- You lose employees.
- Your profits dive.

We want to make something incredibly clear: Vision isn't just a "soft" part of business. It is a crucial piece of successful businesses.

Vision isn't just a "soft" part of business. It is a crucial piece of successful businesses.

---

16   Verrier, Richard. "Feud at Disney Ends Quietly." Los Angeles Times. Los Angeles Times, July 9, 2005. https://www.latimes.com/archives/la-xpm-2005-jul-09-fi-disney9-story.html.

In fact, research conducted by the *Harvard Business Review* found that companies that historically have maintained a Core Purpose and Core Values, while flexing their strategies in changing business environments, "have outperformed the general stock market by a factor of 12, since 1925."[17] In other words, the companies that thrive and beat out other competitors hang on tightly to their Vision, even while adjusting their strategies to achieve their goals.

Your Vision for your business should be at the center of all you do: it's the center of the wheel, the fuel, the GPS. It's the first thing a leader needs to define.

But so many of us don't. Why not?

Business leaders often fail to articulate a Vision early on for two reasons. First, the majority of business leaders are impatient; they want to throw themselves in and just start getting things done, solving the problems right in front of them—but without a clear idea of where they're going. This doesn't work well in the long run. Business leaders in this category may end up solving problems that simply take them in a circle, ending up back where they started, rather than problem-solving in a way that takes them straight ahead.

The minority who don't plunge in commit the opposite problem: they don't want to do anything *but* sit and plan. They never get started because the plan never feels done. But that's counterproductive also. The Vision, by itself, is not your business; it's just a *picture* of where you want your business to go. You still ultimately need to get your vehicle started and get driving.

---

17   Collins, James C., and Jerry I. Porras. "Building Your Company's Vision." *Harvard Business Review*, September 1996.

Our recommendation is probably obvious, but even so, it's not often put into practice: get a Vision articulated, including your Core Identity and your Envisioned Future. Then, get to work.

Why is this so important? We recently sat down with our friend Ryan to record a podcast; Ryan shared a story when an employee of his came to him and asked, "Why are we doing what we're doing?"

The only answer he had at the time to give her was, "Well...we're making payroll." As soon as he said the words, he realized that his answer was inadequate. That wasn't going to inspire his employees. He needed a bigger purpose—he needed a high horizon.

When you're trying to figure out how to sustain your business over the long haul, you need a source of inspiration for yourself and others. There's no question that you need to inspire your customers, but equally important to the thriving of your business is the need to maintain your own inspiration and inspire your employees. Without that fire in your bellies, employees will rotate through your door, costing you thousands of dollars that could have been saved by their retention; likewise, you will struggle to maintain the energy you need to effectively lead your company.

On the other hand, inspiring people saves you money *and* makes you money. The Vision is where you articulate the inspiring principles that are going to sustain you through the hard times, and help you motivate your employees. It will help you flex your strategies from a long distance off, as though you're looking at the high horizon while driving over one hundred miles an hour; you'll be able to make the adjustments confidently, safely, and with nuance. The Vision also will help you maintain the values that will define your company, your career, and your legacy.

"Having the big picture in mind enables us to overcome the day-to-day routines that attempt to distract us from pursuing our dream."
—Assegid Habtewold[18]

ELEMENTS OF A CLEAR, COMPLETE, AND COMPELLING VISION

A clear, complete and compelling vision has two parts: the Core Ideology and the Envisioned Future.[19] The Core Ideology spells out *who* you are, describing your character as an organization, by specifically looking at *why* you're working toward that particular goal, and *how* you're going to behave along the way. The Envisioned Future spells out *where* you're going, your big goals and dreams. It also provides clarification about how you'll know when you get there and what life will be like for you and your company once you arrive. Collectively, this Vision allows you to live in the present with hope. You're able to remember the reason you're working so hard and why it matters.

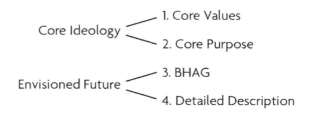

4 Elements of a Clear and Compelling Vision

Core Ideology
1. Core Values
2. Core Purpose

Envisioned Future
3. BHAG
4. Detailed Description

---

18 Habtewold, Assegid. *The 9 Cardinal Building Blocks for Continued Success in Leadership*. Success Pathways, 2014.

19 Our deepest thanks to Jim Collins for providing these terms and recommendations in his book, *Good to Great*.

You must first and foremost run a company out of *who you are*; that's a foundational aspect of being a Passion & Provision company. That sense of identity is defined through your Core Ideology.

CORE IDEOLOGY

Your Core Ideology defines the heart and soul of your business. It answers the questions:

- What is your character as a company?
- What core principles and values will you hold on to tightly as you grow and change?
- What's non-negotiable about how you operate your business?
- What are you doing as a business? (Phrased as a simple, straightforward statement.)

Many areas of business must change and adapt over time, but your Core Ideology should anchor you in the midst of those changes. These principles should never change, even if it means you have to abandon your market or decline to step into an area of possible growth because it conflicts with who you are as a company.

You have to define your Core Ideology first before you envision a future. Why? Because identity needs to be formed before direction is chosen if you want the best and most efficient path to a Passion & Provision company.

To understand the importance of starting with identity, imagine a team of people who want to create an entertainment company. Now, imagine that they skip the Core Ideology and go straight to their Envisioned Future, picturing themselves on the Vegas strip. They start making calls and doing the legwork to set up that location for their business. Then after all that work, imagine that they get around to forming their Core Ideology and realize that they have a value for wholesome entertainment. There goes the Vegas Strip BHAG, right down the sewer.

The Core Ideology provides boundaries for your company to help direct and fuel its growth. It's made up of two components: your Core Values and your Core Purpose. When taken together, the Core Values and Core Purpose will form the crux of your business leadership: they'll provide the ideology that directs every move.

You can think of those two boundaries—the Core Values and Core Purpose—as the two banks of a river, funneling your direction forward and channeling your power. Historically, when engineers have *strengthened the boundaries* of rivers prone to flood by building up levies, the surrounding communities have experienced more prosperity, more efficiency, and greater usefulness of their resource.

> The Core Values and Core Purpose are like two banks of a river, funneling your direction forward and channeling your power.

We can testify to this personally: several years ago one of our elderly neighbors told us that he remembers when there was a foot of water at our house, decades earlier, because of the Sacramento River flooding. We live ten *miles* from the river. Flooding isn't an issue in our neighborhood anymore because of the engineering changes that have been made to raise the banks of the river.

The boundaries create more power, safety, and allow for more development. The same is true when forming the boundaries for your company described by the Core Ideology.

The boundaries of your Vision's Core Ideology are formed by your Core Values and your Core Purpose. When implemented properly, they can enhance your business's efficiency, prosperity, reputation, longevity, and power. They keep the right things in, and they keep the wrong things out. Let's take a closer look at both.

Core Values

A few years ago we had a doctor as a client and had recently rebuilt his website. One day the website's traffic completely disappeared. He called up our office manager and began railing against her. He accused us of being incompetent, untrustworthy, and unethical. "I don't know what you people are doing out there," he raged, "but you are wrecking our business!"

Our office manager got off the phone with our client and her face was white as a ghost. She'd felt attacked and shaken by his accusations. Normally when a client experiences an issue like this, there's a first step of looking into the problem: was it an issue with Google? Can we manage an easy fix? What happened? But this client had jumped straight to the assumption that we were incompetent and untrustworthy, and he yelled as much into the ears of our office manager.

Trust is one of our Core Values at Half a Bubble Out. If this client didn't trust us, then we didn't have anything to build on. The client had also violated a second Core Value of ours: kindness. He'd gone after trust, and he'd done it in a mean way. For us, that was a deal-breaker.

Within an hour, we'd shot him an email and explained we would no longer be working with him. We told him that his treatment of our employee was completely inappropriate, and we wouldn't allow anyone to treat our staff in that way. Therefore, we concluded, we've determined our business partnership is no longer a good fit for either one of us.

Did that mean a loss in revenue? Yes. He was a significant client, and we had come to rely on the income he provided. But despite what we gained from him in profit, we knew that his breach of our Core Values would lead to a negative net value in working with him. So, we fired him.

This particular story has a happy ending: our client called us after receiving the email, apologized, and acknowledged that he'd flown off the handle. He said he hadn't meant what he'd said and asked us if we would take them back. We agreed and we were able to repair the relationship as well as his website. We dug in and discovered that the website issue was due to a surprise update that Google released that rocked the internet world at that time. And ironically, his traffic loss was because he had engaged another company before us who actually had been unethical in their SEO practices. The update that Google released effectively uncovered this and shut his website down. We were able to have several more years of a fruitful business relationship—during which, our client never again violated our values of trust and kindness.

Your Core Values articulate the deeply held principles that guide your business's operations. In that way, they also act as boundaries; they form one side of the river's banks when creating your company's Core Ideology.

Without Core Values in place, a situation like what we just described with a lucrative client could have led us to make all kinds of unhealthy compromises. What if we hadn't had the clarity of our Core Values and decided that we couldn't risk losing this client? How would our office manager have felt if we did nothing to push against the treatment she'd received? How would that have impaired our trust as a staff? And what kind of treatment would we have continued to endure from the client if he hadn't been put in his place? We would have continued to make money—but at a serious loss all around.

We learned how crucial Core Values are when we let clients walk all over us during the "rapid growth" days of Half a Bubble Out, described in our Introduction. In those early days, it was just scary to think about losing any business, but as we solidified our values that began to change, we got more selective about who we wanted to work with. When we hold ourselves, our staff, and our clients accountable to uphold our Core Values, *everyone's* happier doing business together. Our employees understand that we will protect them, which helps them thrive in their roles. Customers like working with us, because they trust us. And we, as the leaders of our business, can feel good about how we're operating.

When we decisively fired our client, our employees got a clear picture of just how important our Core Values are. This story has become lore in our company, with every new employee learning about it fairly early in their tenure. Our staff knows that not only will they benefit from our Core Values, they're also expected to live into our Core Values. And what are those Core Values? We've already mentioned the first two.

- **Trust,** because it helps people perform with greater competence and character. Trust also increases the speed of decision making, and decreases the *cost* of decisions, allowing us to do more with less resources. When trust goes down, it bleeds money from the company, causes discord, and creates all kinds of other problems.

- **Kindness,** because kindness matters. We want to honor the dignity of those we work with and we believe they should honor our dignity as well. Kindness helps everyone's morale, leading to greater creativity and productivity. Plus, it makes work a nicer place to be.
- **Competence,** because we believe in quality and personal growth. If we want our business to thrive and be profitable, we need competence in ourselves and the people on our team.
- **Authenticity,** because we want to make sure we stay true to who we are both personally and professionally. We sometimes refer to this as WYSIWYG, a term from the early days of computers—what you see is what you get!
- **Fun,** because we love to laugh. We spend most of our waking lives at work, and we want to enjoy ourselves while we do it.

When defining your Core Values, you're looking for three to five values that are so critical for you, that if they were to be violated, you would rather close the door of the business than keep moving forward. (We recommend no more than five Core Values, otherwise it gets too hard to remember them all.) For instance, if we determined that we couldn't uphold our value of kindness, and that the only way we could succeed in our target market was to be cutthroat and bash our competitors, we would decide to step away from the business entirely. If we had to sacrifice that Core Value, it wouldn't be worth it to continue.

When you define your company's Core Values, you provide crucial clarity for yourself, and for everyone you work with. Think of the Core Values as drawing a line in the sand: you draw a clear boundary which says what behaviors are acceptable and what are unacceptable. These values will help you form the rules of engagement as you interact with your staff, with your clients, and with your vendors.

Once you've defined them, you should hire, train, and fire to your Core Values:

- You *hire* people who live out your Core Values and embrace them.
- You *train* to help people grow in your Core Values and improve in their roles.
- You *fire* people who show a pattern of transgressing your Core Values.

Hire, train, and fire to your Core Values.

Without articulating your Core Values, you operate with a major blind spot. If you don't know what your values are, and write them down so that others can see them and know them, you and your team can begin violating your principles without even realizing it is happening. An employee could start violating your values, but you may not want to fire them, so you let them continue to trample on what you believe to be right. That leads to a toxic work environment and compromised productivity.

On the other hand, when you know your Core Values, you remove that blind spot. You and your team know the "rules of the road." If we go back to our driving analogy, your Core Values are one piece of helping you keep a high horizon and avoid the hazards and obstacles in the road. These values increase safety for yourself and your employees, especially as you get busier and are moving faster. They will ultimately help you be more successful in reaching your end goal.

Core Purpose

Your Core Purpose is a clear articulation of *why* you're doing what you're doing. It is the reason your organization exists, and it goes beyond your product or your target market. A Core Purpose is about the soul of your company—about your reason for being beyond just making money.

Here's our reason for being: we equip business leaders with education, coaching, and services so they can build companies full of profit, purpose, and legacy. We call that Passion & Provision. That's our Core Purpose.

The Core Purpose is not something that depends on current market conditions or cultural trends. Ideally, this statement is something that should be able to last a hundred years, through multiple leaders.

In the 1991 movie *City Slickers*, Billy Crystal's character, Mitch—a "city slicker"—and his two urbanite friends decide to work on a long cattle drive as a way to deal with their midlife crises. They think the cattle run will help them become "real men" and find out who they are. In one scene, Curly the old grizzled cowboy—played by Jack Palance— who's been leading the cattle drive has a conversation with Mitch. Mitch admits that he's been struggling with an identity crisis, and the cowboy says, "Do you know what the secret of life is?" He holds up one finger: "This."

Mitch asks, "...Your finger?"

"One thing," Curly replies. "Just one thing. You stick to that, and everything else don't mean shit." When Mitch asks him what the "one thing" is, Curly replies, "That's what you've gotta figure out."[20]

The Core Purpose is the one thing that helps you determine your reason to exist. In a business, if you have that one thing, you're able to make decisions with clear direction. You know what you're about, you know why your company exists, and you know why you're doing what you do.

Having your Core Values and Core Purpose established helps you take the next step in the Vision process, which is figuring out where you are going.

ENVISIONED FUTURE

Let's say that you've recently done some soul searching on a personal level, and you've been able to think about who you want to be and what you want to be known for (psst—that's a sign that you've done some work on your Core Values and Core Purpose.) Out of this soul searching, you decide you want to do something remarkable with your life. You decide you want to run a marathon—and not just any marathon; you want to run the most elite marathon in the US: the Boston Marathon.

To run the Boston Marathon, you have to qualify by completing a *different* marathon at a fast-enough pace. It's a major undertaking—but it's your dream. Completing the Boston marathon becomes your Big, Hairy, Audacious Goal.

So, you start training. In the hardest moments—when you're

---

20   *City Slickers*. Columbia Pictures, 1991.

nursing blisters or running through sleet or pushing up a hill on your seventeenth mile—you push yourself to imagine what it's going to be like when you complete the Boston marathon. Your family and friends will all be there, cheering. You'll collapse on the ground, but you'll be filled with indescribable joy. You'll have a new understanding of your own capabilities, a new zest to take on challenges and dreams. Surrounded by famous historical landmarks and old brick buildings, you will embark on a brand-new phase of your life. It will be incredible. It will be life changing.

That Vivid Description of what happens *after* the finish line is going to keep you motivated during the hardest times. In fact, it's the picture of what will happen once you *complete* your BHAG that drives you to actually accomplish it.

Both pieces—the BHAG and the Vivid Description—are key in helping you realize your Envisioned Future. Let's talk about both in greater detail.

BHAG (Big, Hairy, Audacious Goal)

Where do you want to go? That's the question you're answering when you form your Envisioned Future and identify your BHAG: the Big, Hairy, Audacious Goal.

The Big, Hairy, Audacious Goal: it's your dream, your world-changing idea, your life-changing legacy. If you want to get really starry eyed, you can call it your destiny. The BHAG should establish a goal between ten and thirty years into your future. The BHAG should be short—just one or two sentences. It's easy to remember, easy to reference, and easy to splash across your wall in a motivational poster—if that's your style.

When you accomplish the BHAG, that's when you'll know you've made it: it's the finish line. Ideally, accomplishing that first BHAG will set you up to form *new* BHAGs—BHAGs you wouldn't have even thought possible before accomplishing the first one. Like a runner who's just completed her first half-marathon and now dreams of doing more, crossing one finish line inspires you to find new goals—new world-changing ideas, new life-changing legacies to pursue.

As you can imagine, your Core Values guide your BHAG a great deal. If you have a grandiose BHAG and a Core Purpose that outlines why you believe that goal matters so much, it could be tempting to try to get there any way you can. You might say, "I want my business to be *this* big, and make *this* much money, and reach *this* amount of people. And I'm going to *cheat, rob, and steal* to get there." No! Your end goal is not going to be worth reaching if you trample your values to get there. You need to define how you're going to operate, on the way to accomplishing the BHAG. That's one reason why it's so important to outline your Core Ideology first.

When you start dreaming up your BHAG, think decades out. Give yourself plenty of time to do your world changing. If it's too short term, you're going to be looking at the low horizon, not the high horizon. Imagine that you tell your staff, "In the next eighteen months, we're going to land a client!" Your employees are not going to get goosebumps of enthusiasm over that goal. And also, what happens once you land the client? It's too easy and too short term to give you any operational clarity about what happens next. A high-level BHAG, on the other hand, is going to provide clarity about where you're going and motivation to get there.

Here is another bad BHAG that is more common than any of us

probably want to admit: "In thirty years, I will have made a pile of money, and I will be sitting on the beach drinking mai tais."

Drinks on the beach are fine—if we're only talking about you. But for everyone else in your company, and even for yourself, deep down—that is not a big enough dream. Nobody is going to want to follow you if that's your dream, because it's mainly selfish. You're also not going to be able to sustain your own efforts on those worst days by simply thinking of your favorite cocktail. You need a deeper cause to live for.

A good BHAG, on the other hand, is going to be something you and your staff can believe in. Why does it need to be "Big, Hairy, and Audacious"? It needs to be **big** because you want it to inspire others. If it's not big enough, it won't inspire people. It also needs to be **hairy** and **audacious** because it should scare people a little. There should be a chance that you might not be able to do it. The BHAG is not an easy target; it should be difficult. It should be *possible*—but it might be a little bit impossible.

It's that little-bit-impossible part that provides the spark for the fire of inspiration. People lose heart when they're not stretched, but when you're asking your company to dream bigger and go further, you give people the opportunity to step into their purpose. You offer them a calling.

Good teachers manage to find the sweet spot between too hard, and not hard enough. They make the lesson hard enough that it keeps their students interested, but not so difficult that they get frustrated and check out. The BHAG should fit somewhere in that same sweet spot, perhaps erring on the side of too hard.

When John F. Kennedy announced his goal to land a man on the moon, that was a BHAG—and he even said as much: "We choose to go to the moon in this decade and do the other things, *not because they are easy, but because they are hard,* because that goal will serve to organize and measure the best of our energies and skills..."[21] The moon-shot BHAG inspired a nation and continues to inspire people to identify their own moon-shot goals.

A Big, Hairy, Audacious Goal holds people's attention. It gives people the opportunity to live for something bigger than their day-to-day work—to choose to throw themselves into a project that they believe in. For JFK, that was landing on the moon. For the workers who formed the foundation and walls and buttresses of the York Minster, the BHAG was to build a cathedral that would outlast their lifetimes.

For us, the BHAG is to help 10,000 leaders build Passion and Provision companies filled with Passion and Provision jobs, so we can impact the lives of 100,000 workers, who will then impact their families and community.

What would happen, if we actually managed to accomplish that BHAG? That could lead to 100,000 transformed lives; 100,000 people shifting from sleepwalking through their work days, to doing work that helps them be their best selves, fully engage, and thrive. A hundred thousand people who go home to their families energized and optimistic, not drained and depressed! Ten thousand companies is a lot and we might not make it, but that's the point. If you choose a goal that's not big enough, it will fail to inspire as only a magnificent dream can.

21   Kennedy, John F. "John F. Kennedy Moon Speech - Rice Stadium." NASA. NASA. Accessed September 2, 2019. https://er.jsc.nasa.gov/seh/ricetalk.htm.

> "We will only grow as big as we dream. That's why we must dream big." —Gabrielle Williams[22]

But wait—we're getting ahead of ourselves. What we just described starts to get into the **Vivid Description,** which is the final piece of forming a clear, complete, and compelling Vision. The Vivid Description is where you describe what will happen if you manage to accomplish your BHAG.

Vivid Description

The Vivid Description paints a detailed picture of how the world will be different if we achieve our goals, helping us better understand what it will look like to have arrived. Essentially, it's a longer narrative that elaborates on your BHAG. It is a written document that provides, in one or two pages, an emotional description about why that future matters. When you read a well-written Vivid Description, you might find that you and your team get misty-eyed. It touches a place so important to you, that it is difficult to suppress the emotions you feel when you allow yourself to really go there.

Imagine inviting your staff to consider this question: "If we do [this], and we do it well—how will that change the world?" That's what you describe in the Vivid Description. Bring situational experiences to life—think about the real people your accomplished BHAG might impact and how their lives will practically look different. Describe the emotional impact of those changes.

---

22   "Ministers & Members Search - THE HON. GABRIELLE WILLIAMS (DANDENONG)." Member Profile - The Hon. Gabrielle Williams, August 13, 2019. https://www.parliament.vic.gov.au/about/people-in-parliament/members-search/list-all-members/details/22/15.

By the end, you will have an incredibly compelling picture of why it matters so much to press on toward the finish line.

When you have these discussions with your staff, the hope and inspiration that builds up is palpable. *Those* are the thoughts that keep the two of us going! We've also experienced receiving our team members' help in holding us accountable to achieving the BHAG. Sometimes they'll offer up a comment: "If we're aiming for the BHAG—will this move help us get there?" Our employees have told us that they love being part of making the dream a reality.

Conversations like that highlight not only the inspirational quality of a BHAG, but also the clarification that it provides, as spelled out in your Vivid Description. Every decision can be weighed against the high horizon goal. You're able to form your immediate, intermediate, and long-term goals in terms of how they'll help you achieve this Envisioned Future.

QUICK REVIEW

A clear, complete, compelling Vision includes your Core Values, Core Purpose, BHAG, and a Vivid Description.

When taken together, these elements of Vision create your business's identity. The stronger your identity as an organization, the more you attract your employee tribe and client tribe. A well-formed Vision acts as a calling card as you communicate your message: "This is what we stand for. This is what we believe. This is how we will behave. This is where we are going and how we will change the world. Are you interested? If so, then come this way." Your Vision becomes a kind of siren song, drawing people to you who are attracted by everything you're about.

STRATEGIC PLAN

Every Vision needs a Strategic Plan to go with it. Think back to our Boston Marathon analogy. Of course it was valuable for you to identify the BHAG of completing it, and it's motivating to consider the Vivid Description of what life will look like when you get there—but you still have to *get* there. You need gear, you need to enhance your nutrition, and most of all, you need a training schedule. You want to run the Boston Marathon in two or three years; that means, you need to first qualify as a contender at a different marathon. You give yourself a year to train for the first marathon, and then figure out a weekly training schedule.

Through identifying practical, time-stamped, incremental goals, you plot your route to achieve the BHAG. That's the Strategic Plan. It's the blueprint of how you'll actually make progress toward the BHAG. Note the difference: the Vision is a *picture* of who you are, how you'll behave, and where you're going. The Strategic Plan is a specific list of time-stamped goals that directs your efforts for the immediate and near future.

A Strategic Plan allows you to deal with what the Vision doesn't address: specifically, the when and the how. A Strategic Plan is written with a specific time frame, for instance, the next three years of work; some people say one to three years, others say three to five. The bottom line for a Strategic Plan is that it should be written in such a way that you can plan with reasonable accuracy what you and your team need to achieve in the immediate and not-too-distant future.

Within those three years, consider: what needs to happen by year three to help move you toward your BHAG? What does that practically look like, in terms of operations and sales and growth? And, if that's what needs to happen by year three, then what needs to be accomplished in year two and year one? Finally, you develop quarterly goals for the upcoming year. Once you articulate your Vision for the future, you determine specifically how it will look to put one foot in front of the other over the next three years.

Remember: your Vision should remain *unchanged*; your Core Purpose, your Core Values, your BHAG, and your Vivid Description should all remain fixed. The Strategic Plan, however, *can* and should change to adjust to an ever-changing world, just as you might decide to adjust your marathon training schedule if you were to get injured. If your market changes or issues come up with your manufacturer, you can alter the Strategic Plan to work with those changes while still upholding the core principles of your Vision. Likewise, if an opportunity comes up—you have a friend who encourages you to do a triathlon with him—you have the flexibility within your Strategic Plan to accommodate that new opportunity, so long as it still helps you move toward the BHAG.

Maybe you think the Strategic Plan sounds like overkill. Surely an experienced or confident business leader could move their company toward the BHAG without mapping out these short-term targets. Is a Strategic Plan really that necessary?

We'd say yes. Our imaginary friend, Fred, will help us explain why. Let's say Fred sets out to build a shed in his backyard. Fred might have a clear Core Purpose for the shed—he knows *why* he wants to build it. He's got his Envisioned Future; he can mentally picture his *end goal* of how he wants this shed to look and can come up with a *Vivid Description* of how his life will be better once he has it. He's got power tools to make it happen—you can think of those as the Core Values, since that's *how* he's going to carry out this project. But Fred never stops to draw up a plan with measurements. He thinks he can build a shed without putting together a cut list or planning it out step-by-step. It's just a shed, after all. How hard can it be?

So Fred tries putting this imagined structure together. The result is a disaster—it's a messy amalgamation of different ideas. Fred's shed is ugly, missing pieces, and can't stand up to the wind. He wasted money on materials because he didn't bother measuring. He wasted time by undoing mistakes and making multiple, unnecessary trips to the hardware store to get items he forgot he needed. The envisioned shed had seemed like such an easy project when Fred started out—he thought it was going to work. How did it turn into *this*?

When you set out toward a goal without clear, specific planning, you set yourself up to waste time and money. You also may seriously jeopardize your chances of actually achieving your goal.

Your Vision is the picture of where you want to go or what you want to accomplish. When your end product looks exactly like the picture—you're done. The shed is perfect. You crossed the finish line. You made it to the Boston Marathon.

If your company is turning out to be anything like Fred's shed though—then you're *not* done. You need to keep building. When running a business, you need to measure your success against the picture provided by your Vision, and you're not done until you get there.

The Strategic Plan is *how* you get yourself efficiently from point A to point B on the way to the BHAG.

HOW TO FORM THE STRATEGIC PLAN

It's not hard to form a Strategic Plan. In a nutshell, here's how you could form your own:

1. **Write out the BHAG:** where do you want to be in thirty years?
2. With the long-term target of the BHAG, consider: **what goals do you want to accomplish in the next three years?** Figure out what you're going to *measure* to determine whether or not you accomplished your three-year goals, such as revenue, number of customers, number of projects to complete, and/ or number of employees.
3. With the three-year goals in mind, **identify your annual goals: what do you need to do in the *next* year to move yourself toward the three-year goals?** Again, figure out what you'll measure to evaluate your progress. Your annual goals should be even more detailed than your three-year goals. We recommend choosing three annual goals; three is ambitious without being impossible.
4. **Break your annual goals into three to five quarterly targets.** "By March, we will have accomplished [this]; by June, we will have accomplished [this]..." Assign team members to those quarterly goals so that responsibilities are clear as to who's going to accomplish what, and keep the goals measurable.
5. **Make sure that each team member has the resources they need** to accomplish their quarterly goals. Also, **list out all the potential challenges** that you might run into that could end up being a big deal. Consider how you're going to solve those challenges, and give your staff support for problem-solving—a point person to troubleshoot with, or a contingency plan. Then, release the troops with their marching orders. They should know what to do and have the resources they need to do it.

6. **Meet with your staff regularly and evaluate your progress.** Are you on target? Are you behind? Are you ahead of schedule? **Reset quarterly goals as needed and debrief on lessons learned.** At the end of each quarter, create goals for the following quarter. When you complete a year, check how your progress measures up against your annual goal, and your three-year goal. By keeping all the goals measurable, you'll be able to see clearly when you've crossed the finish line.

Many of us know that this process works, just like many of us know the importance of eating healthy—but that doesn't mean we actually do it. It takes time to sit down and map out a Strategic Plan, and time often feels like a luxury you don't have when you're running a business. But remember Fred's shed; failing to plan is going to end up wasting your time and money, and could jeopardize your success.

"If you want to be fast, go slow." —Lao Tzu

Your Strategic Plan will be a living document, and you'll regularly make adjustments. But remember, those adjustments should always still point you toward the BHAG. Keep your eyes moving back and forth between your Strategic Plan and your high horizon.

VISION'S ROLE IN A PASSION & PROVISION COMPANY: KATHRYN NARRATES

Last year, the two of us were creating our Half a Bubble Out Village course, a resource for other small business leaders.[23] The

---

23   See our appendix for an explanation of what the Half a Bubble Out Village is, and what it provides to our members.

process involved crafting and building a series of instructional videos, and it was grueling. We'd set a goal and had a clear sense of why we wanted to complete this course—but it was still a grind.

One morning, I'd woken up tired. I was grumpy and I didn't like how my hair had turned out. I didn't want to go on camera. I didn't want to be responsible for saying anything intelligent. I said as much to Michael on our drive to work: "I really don't want to get in front of a camera today."

But then I began to think about the *reason* we were doing the videos in the first place. What could happen if we actually got our Passion & Provision strategy in the hands of 10,000 leaders in the future—or even just one hundred by the end of the next year? What could happen in the lives of people if they could live into this new paradigm? How could lives be changed and transformed if people began to see their work as meaningful? What could happen if that many business leaders could inspire themselves and their employees, and revitalize their struggling businesses?

The thought inspired *me!* Excitement began to rise up in me for *why* we were doing it, and by the time we got to work, I was actually excited to film that day. The Vision changed my entire attitude. It was the thought of the potential impact our work could have that gave me the energy and enthusiasm I needed to dive back into the grind.

Vision can make your work matter to you, whatever the Vision is. The *why* behind your work can sustain you, energize you, and remind you why you're in the fight. It provides your day-to-day work with a sense of bigger meaning and purpose, helping you continue to push forward. The struggles you experience today are placed in a larger context; you can remember that there's a worthy goal that you're working toward, which makes the temporary problems mere blips on the screen.

Your Vision also helps you work *in* and *on* your business—both of which are necessary. One of the best compliments we ever received was from one of our long-term clients and friends who recently passed away. He was an incredible man that we both respected greatly; he was constantly looking to improve and grow. He said to us several years ago, "One of the things I value most about you two is that you can both live in the weeds of the day-to-day details, but you can also come back up and look at the high-level picture. You can go back and forth." What he said that day gave us the ability to put words to something we didn't realize we were doing and helped us understand how powerful it was.

As a leader of a business, that's your role: you need to be able to go back and forth between the horizon—looking at the big picture, thinking about the goals and direction, working "on" the business—and also get into the weeds with your employees, working "in" the business. Then, you need to help your staff connect their daily work with the long-term Vision of where you're headed. That's how you'll keep everyone motivated to work toward the larger goal.

How do you effectively move back and forth? How do you have the clarity needed for the high horizon, along with the specific awareness needed to accomplish the goals in the near future? You form a clear, complete, compelling Vision, and you follow up with a well-formed Strategic Plan.

You're the leader: you're the one with your hand on the wheel. You're the one with your foot on the accelerator and the brakes. By forming your Vision and Strategic Plan, you embark on a journey that has the power to take everyone else in your vehicle to an amazing destination. You're the one responsible for keeping everyone safe. You're the one who's going to have the most influence on morale. You're the one who decides when to stop and stretch, how to guide the car to the best attractions, when to forge ahead and encourage your passengers to power through.

The leadership is on you, and it's an awesome and terrifying responsibility. That's why leadership is such a critical component for effectively carrying out your Vision, and that's why we're talking about leadership right...*now*.

TIME TO CRAFT YOUR VISION AND STRATEGIC PLAN

- Go to **fulfilledthebook.com** to download resources that will help you craft your Vision and Strategic Plan.
- Either alone or with a team, brainstorm your three to five Core Values.
- With those Core Values in hand, craft your Core Purpose.
- Now it's time to dream and create your BHAG and Vivid Description.
- With all that in hand, start working on your Strategic Plan.

CHAPTER FIVE

||||||||||||||||||||

Leadership

"Leaders are developers, team builders, imaginers, culture caretakers, roadblock removers, and inspirers. Their success depends on enabling the success of others."

ISABELLA DIAZ

In the Upper Napa Valley, there is a castle. It sits in the midst of one of California's oldest vineyards, surrounded by lush trees, a stream, and a lake. If you were to wake up anywhere on the grounds, you would think you'd been transported to thirteenth century Italy. And that's exactly what Dario Sattui, the creator of this castle in the Upper Napa Valley, wants you to feel when you visit his Castello di Amorosa—translated, *labor of love*.

Dario Sattui is a fourth-generation Italian American vintner, obsessed with medieval architecture. He was determined that his Castello di Amorosa would be perfectly authentic. The castle was made with nearly one million thirteenth-century stones shipped to California from Italy, and he only allowed ancient building techniques to be used to build the structure. Sattui filled over 200 shipping containers with antique furnishings from Europe to fill the rooms of his castle. He even transported medieval torture equipment for the dungeon. Sattui explains on his website, "In my mind, everything had to be authentic, or it wouldn't be worth the effort. Faking it in any way might be all right for others, but I would know the difference, making it a failed attempt to explore my passion."[24]

We have visited the Castello di Amorosa several times for wine tastings, and it is an *epic* experience. The level of detail Sattui pursued to achieve his dream of perfect authenticity is jaw-dropping. He even hired painters and muralists to replicate well-known pieces of art from ancient Italy in each of the rooms. During one visit, we purchased a wine tasting, which included a tour of the castle. We sipped the wine that had been poured for us out of barrels and took it all in.

In the castle's enormous Great Hall, our attention was arrested by a three-paneled mural called *The Allegory and Effects of Good Government*. Our tour guide explained that Sattui had the mural replicated from its original six-paneled work *The Allegory and Effects of Good and Bad Government* by Ambrogio Lorenzetti.

---

24 "History Of Castello Di Amorosa Winery & Dario Sattui, Founder." Castello di Amorosa. Accessed September 9, 2019. https://castellodiamorosa.com/explore/.

Apparently, the artist had been originally hired by the town council of Siena to paint a mural in the Council Room that would remind them of their responsibility of leadership. Our tour guide didn't say much more, but he'd said enough. Our interest was piqued. When we got home, we dug a little deeper and learned more.

Lorenzetti's mural is one of the most powerful illustrations of leadership we've ever seen. The first three panels—the ones we'd seen in the castle—feature The Allegory of Good Government, where different figures represent different ideas.[25] The chief figure in the first panel of this mural is Justice. She fairly administers both punishments and rewards to people while she looks above her, to the figure of Wisdom. Below Justice sits Harmony, who stands at the head of a line of the people of Siena, who are orderly and protected. Above them sits the largest figure—the Ruler of the realm. He's surrounded by personified virtues: Fortitude, Prudence, Magnanimity, Temperance, and so on.

Peace sits at the end of the bench of this row of virtues. She's reclining—kicking back, looking completely casual. Her cushion sits on top of a pile of armor. It's there for her to use, but she doesn't need it. The implication is that with so many other virtues and elements of good leadership in place, Peace can take off her armor and actually be peaceful. This is the picture of Good Government: justice is administered with wisdom, harmony is in place, rulers are ruled by virtue, and there is peace.

The second and third panels show the *results* of Good Government.

25   Harris, Beth, and Steven Zucker. "Ambrogio Lorenzetti, Palazzo Pubblico Frescos: Allegory and Effect of Good and Bad Government." Khan Academy. Khan Academy. Accessed September 9, 2019. https://www.khanacademy.org/humanities/renaissance-reformation/late-gothic-italy/siena-late-gothic/v/ambrogio-lorenzetti-s-palazzo-pubblico-frescos-allegory-and-effect-of-good-and-bad-government.

People are shown dancing on the city walls of Siena in rich clothing, indicating there is prosperity and joy. There's commerce and safety; windows are open, and everything is pristine, clean, and cared for. Beyond the city walls, there are scenes of thriving agriculture. People are tilling the land, and there are large herds and abundant produce. That's the *yield* of Good Government.

We were able to view those first three panels in the Castello di Amorosa, but when we looked up the second set of panels afterwards, we learned about the Allegory of Bad Government. In the first of those three panels, the largest figure is Tyranny, and he's surrounded by vices, instead of virtues—figures like Avarice, Cruelty, Pride, Fury, and Fraud. Justice is shown bound up at the base of the fresco, like she's been overtaken by Tyranny, and the architecture surrounding the figures shows that they are in the midst of war.

The panels showing the results of Bad Government display the results of tyrannical leadership. The city walls have holes in them, and windows are broken. The streets are dirty, people are cowering—there's no dancing. Out in the country, the fields are burned and houses are on fire. Everyone is fleeing. There's an incredible sense of fear and trouble—everything is wrong. In fact, the word "Terror" is written at the top of the landscape. Nothing is safe, and there's nowhere to run.

The murals give vivid imagery of the power of leadership to shape people's lives. Leaders are responsible for the experience of all the people below them; they have the power to lead people into terror and war—or thriving prosperity.

LEADERSHIP STYLES: BENEVOLENT RULE OR TYRANNY?

If leaders understood what could result from their leadership style and set out to create a prosperous entity with "benevolent rule," they could create a stunning legacy. But if they rule like a tyrant, motivating their people with fear and threats, they'll leave destruction in their wake.

Granted, there have been many tyrants throughout history who were able to accomplish incredible "success"—Napoleon, the Roman Caesars, Genghis Khan—but what surrounded them? They left a trail of destruction. The Mongolian Empire, for instance, conquered more land than any other empire in history, but they did so by raping women, pillaging towns, stealing land, and murdering anyone who stood in their way. There are also plenty of publicly traded companies that have been led by leaders who could arguably be described as unethical if not tyrannical: they're successful, and their companies are successful, but their employees are miserable.

What do we make of this? Do evil people thrive and virtuous people suffer? If we want to be prosperous—do we have to act like tyrants? Can good leadership actually lead to the thriving, happy prosperous pictures shown in the Allegory of Good Government? Can leaders enable their employees to experience both Passion & Provision in their work? Or can large profits only be accomplished off the bent backs of employees?

"There are only two ways to influence human behavior. You can *manipulate* it, or you can *inspire* it." —Simon Sinek, *Start with Why*[26]

---

26   Sinek, Simon. *Start with Why: How Great Leaders Inspire Everyone to Take Action.* London, England: Penguin Business, 2019.

The "tyrant" leaders who have found success have often done so through fear-based techniques. As a result, many of them end up being ousted for corruption or other scandals; many have imploded their marriages. There are countless unhappy stories from employees at some of these companies. In our opinion, the manipulative leadership method may work for a time—think of it like lightning in a bottle—but it can't endure, and it will ultimately be corrosive.

Consider what kind of leader you want to be. Imagine yourself nearing retirement and reflecting back on your leadership. How would you want to answer these questions?

- Over the course of my career, have I grown in kindness?
- Are my relationships intact?
- Has my marriage grown in health and love over the course of my career?
- Are my relationships with my children strong?
- Have I been able to inspire my employees to do great work?
- Have I been able to maintain decent health?

Do you want to answer yes to most of these questions? Of course you do.

Still, it's almost easier to think of business leaders who went the opposite direction—who divorced, who dealt with major health issues or psychological struggles, who became estranged from their loved ones, and who left embittered employees in their wake. But it doesn't have to be that way.

When we talk about leaders finishing well, we're talking about a "both/and" scenario. Here's the goal: you will build a profitable business and will take care of your family and employees financially. You will *also* leave a meaningful legacy in your community and hold intact your health, your marriage, and your relationship with family and friends. That's the "BHAG" when it comes to leadership.

You can still be a "successful" leader and ignore relationships. You can accomplish the tactical strategies that are needed to lead a group of people, even if you manipulate people to achieve your end goal.

However, we want to suggest that the true measurement of success isn't just about your business—it's about your humanity. It isn't just about the *doing*; it's about the *being*. We want to help you *be* a leader that inspires others. We want you to be healthy, both physically and emotionally. We want you to be a loving, present member of your family. In other words, we want *you* to experience Passion & Provision in life.

> The true measurement of success isn't just about your business—it's about your humanity.

If you want to be a leader of a Passion & Provision company, **you not only have to learn the strategic, tactical points of leadership, you also have to deal with people in a caring, vision-oriented way.** We want to address both halves of leadership in this chapter, and in the chapters that follow.

THE DEFINITION OF GOOD LEADERSHIP

Some people think that inspirational leaders just happen—they're a product of personality and circumstance and talent, and there's no way that anyone who doesn't have that magical combination could conjure up that inspirational quality. But we don't think that's true.

Inspirational leadership can be developed through intentional, thoughtful work on both your inner game and your outer game. Your inner life—your psychology, your thinking, your emotional reactions—needs deep and healthy roots. If you have a healthy "inner game" with deep, healthy roots, those roots give you the stability and the strength needed to lead others in an inspirational way. Your outer game refers to your observable competencies—how you interact with others, communicate, and perform the tasks of leadership over the company as a whole. We're about to talk more extensively about both.

But before we do, there's one crucial element of strong leadership that if you don't have it will make the rest of this chapter a complete waste of time. What are we referring to? Recognize your need for continued growth.

AVOID SYNDROME TWENTY-SEVEN: MICHAEL NARRATES

When I was twenty-seven years old, Kathryn and I had been married about a year and a half. One afternoon, I was walking across the parking lot from our car to our apartment, and I was feeling great. I had a skip in my step. Life was good. I thought to myself, "What can I be doing differently? What area do I need to grow in?" Almost immediately, I came to the happy conclusion: "Nothing. I'm good. There is nothing I need to improve."

About ten seconds later, I had a new thought—a troubling one. It occurred to me that not being able to recognize a single area for growth was...probably...an area in need of growth.

Among our friends, we've come to refer to my twenty-seven-year-old mentality as "Syndrome Twenty-Seven," which describes the perception that you've got everything together, you have nowhere to grow, you are all that and a bag of chips, and everyone around you should consider themselves fortunate just to have you in their lives.

Strong leaders are often confident, optimistic people—which can make them particularly susceptible to Syndrome Twenty-Seven. Hopefully, you grow out of it. It is to your peril if you don't.

Syndrome Twenty-Seven is a liability to your leadership and your success. The mentality that you don't need to grow creates a false humility that produces enormous blind spots in your leadership and organization. A lack of self-awareness makes you vulnerable. You don't know what you don't know, and that blindness can ultimately be fatal to your organization.

As you take a good look at your style of leadership while reading this chapter, expect to recognize areas where you need to grow—and *congratulate* yourself for being able to recognize needed growth! If you can spot those areas of growth, you do not have Syndrome Twenty-Seven.

Our friend, Terry Walling, also works as a leadership expert, consultant, and author. He introduced us to the book *Mastering Leadership*, by Robert J. Anderson and William A. Adams, which conducted doctoral-level research on what it takes to grow as a leader.[27] They administered a massive survey of adult development work, researching the ways others have tried to quantify and measure aspects of leadership and how people grow. They finally combined

27   Anderson, Robert J., and W. A. Adams. *Mastering Leadership: An Integrated Framework for Breakthrough Performance and Extraordinary Business Results*. Hoboken, NJ: Wiley, 2016.

all their discoveries into one integrated model. The research is amazing, but it is also dense and complex, so we're going to do our best to break down the major points for you here. Their recommendations boil down to growing your inner game and your outer game.

INNER GAME

Think of an iceberg. Above the water sits a large block of ice—but under the water, there's a bulk of ice that's far bigger than what's visible from the surface. The *deep* stuff is what moves the ice that's visible above water.

We can all observe a leader's life—their behavior, their choices, their decisions, their style of communication—and that's the outer game. In a sense, that's what's visible above water. The *inner* game of a leader is unseen, but it's the bulk of what leads to a leader's observable behavior; it's everything that's happening underneath the surface.

How do you know if you have a strong inner game? If you can answer yes to the following questions, chances are you've done some good work in this area. If the answer to most of these questions is no—then congratulations, you've discovered your first area of needed growth.

- Are you building self-awareness?
- Do you understand what motivates your decisions?
- Can you name your Core Values?
- Do you understand why certain things trigger strong emotional reactions and why others don't?

Everything under the water determines what shows up above water; the bulk beneath also informs where the visible ice moves, and what it does. Similarly, your emotions, your maturity, your character, your psychology, your past history, your values—all of the hidden qualities that make you, *you*, will significantly impact your style of leadership in either a negative or positive way.

Let's talk about some of the ways your inner game can manifest itself, and ideally, develop into strong leadership.

REACTIVE VERSUS CREATIVE

There are essentially two types of leaders; one is more effective and one is less effective. The research described in *Mastering Leadership* identifies those more effective, healthy leaders as *creative* and the less effective, unhealthy leaders as *reactive*. Adams and Anderson outline eighteen behaviors grouped into five categories for the creative leader, and eleven behaviors grouped into three categories for the reactive leader. Did we mention it is dense? Let's try to simplify a bit.

Whether you are creative or reactive, leadership plays out in two main areas. The first area concerns **tasks:** leaders are in charge of getting stuff done. They need to put together a system that works for their business, with multiple moving parts that involve different people in different roles. They need to be strategic, understanding what the business needs to grow, understanding money, culture, management, and any number of other task-related issues.

But leaders also need to deal with people, which means the second main area where we evaluate creative versus reactive leadership is **in relationships.** Business leaders need to deal with employees, vendors, investors, partners, and so on. Said simply, strong leaders are good both *relationally* and with the business of getting *stuff* done.

Strong leaders are good both *relationally* and with the business of getting *stuff* done.

Reactive Leaders

The **reactive leader** functions from a place of insecurity and fear-based decision making. Their reactions are informed by their own self-interest and self-protection. These reactive leaders tend to respond in three different ways:

1. They **comply** with others to a fault, letting others dictate decisions that should be made by the leader, because they are afraid of being misunderstood, or not liked. They play things safe and just try to keep everything calm.
2. They **protect** themselves at the expense of other people. This can look like keeping themselves distant, or being arrogant or critical of others.
3. They **control** others, through fear, manipulation, or other methods.

Often, a combination of two or even all three of those responses can play into a reactive leader's behavior, especially when dealing with relationships. Have you ever worked for a leader who was passive-aggressive? They don't say what they are really thinking but somehow expect you to understand them and get angry when you don't. That is a sign of reactive leadership.

Relationally, the reactive leader views others as adversaries. They have a win-or-lose mindset, and they seek out wins at any cost. If anything goes wrong, they blame others and deflect responsibility so that they don't have to accept that they "lost." Mistakes are never their fault.

This mindset is informed by their deep fear of losing control. Reactive leaders are trying to preserve themselves and maintain a tight grasp on their leadership power. The business's success becomes all about them—their success, their survival, and how they're going to use the people around them to maintain their power and get more if possible.

Reactive leaders can be ambitious, driven, perfectionists, and autocratic. For those reasons, they might be amazing at executing the *tasks* of their business. However, even if they're incredibly good at getting stuff done, they do the tasks out of a desire for self-promotion—they're not healthy relationally, at all.

Often, reactive leaders succeed in getting promoted, which means they have an immense amount of control over people who work underneath them. They have the power to *react* with an iron fist, which can mean employees are scared of their wrath, will jump to appease them, and may hide mistakes. If there's any kind of conflict, it's nasty. There's no possibility for healthy conflict with a reactive leader—because, remember, they'll always win, and anyone else will always lose.

Let's take a second to consider the best and worst-case scenarios of what could happen for a reactive leader. Best-case scenario: your business grows to the level of Amazon. You're an impressive, impossible, incredible success story—and *no one likes you*. You're remembered as a shrewd, cutthroat dealer who wouldn't let anyone stand in your way—including your spouse, children, parents, and closest friends, who may or may not still have relationships with you.

Worst-case scenario: your business fails, and still, no one likes you.

A reactive leader does not have the ability to cultivate a Passion

& Provision company for their employees or for themselves. Passion & Provision employees are inspired, feel empowered, feel trusted by their leaders to use their gifts, and seek to grow the company in the best way that they can. A controlling, reactive leader cannot accommodate the level of trust needed to afford employees those privileges. Likewise, the leader can't genuinely enjoy work, because of the underlying fear that acts as their main driving force.

Creative Leaders

A Passion & Provision company can *only* be accommodated by a leader who has enough faith in their employees giving them ownership over their roles. The leader has to be secure and confident enough to roll with the punches as events unfold. There may be more failure that way, but everyone who works at a company like that will feel more excited about what they're doing, and ultimately produce better work.

This kind of secure, positive leader is described by Anderson and Adams as the **creative leader.** The creative leader operates with a purposeful vision and leads with love. Yes, we said it, "love." The term sounds scary in the business realm, but "loving people" simply means the leader has genuine care and concern for others. Rather than operate with a self-focus, they're outward-focused on the success and well-being of others.

> The creative leader operates with a purposeful vision and leads with love.

Creative leaders can be distinguished by their hallmark attributes, which Adams and Anderson identify as:

1. **Relating:** Creative leaders show an interest in meeting other people and learning about them. They are collaborative rather than controlling. They foster team play and actively mentor and develop others.
2. **Self-awareness:** They know their strengths, weaknesses, and potential triggers. They are working to grow in needed areas.
3. **Authenticity:** They demonstrate integrity and are courageously genuine.
4. **Systems awareness:** They are able to do the right things at the right time to keep the company going. They ensure there are systems and planning in place to support the big picture, and they can work both *in* and *on* the business.
5. **Achieving:** They're able to accomplish needed tasks and achieve results. They can create sustainable productivity.

These creative leaders are not only strong relationally, but they also have some solid chops in the task area. They're purposeful and visionary but make a point to bring others along with them in a positive and encouraging way.

When Adams and Anderson were doing the research for *Mastering Leadership,* they hired outside companies to test their model, to either validate or invalidate their conclusions. The outside researchers found that there is a direct correlation between creative leadership and a company's profits and success. **Creative leadership consistently has been shown to result in more profits and more success than companies led by reactive leaders.** In fact, the top 10 percent of high-performing companies in over 500,000 companies surveyed had leaders that scored in the top 20 percent in leadership effectiveness. In contrast, the bottom 10 percent of companies had leaders that scored in the bottom 30 percent of leadership effectiveness.[28] The conclusion: better leadership leads to more profitable companies, full stop! From employee retention, to a return on equity, to the numbers on both finance and people, creative leadership brings about better numbers with greater overall success.[29] And what produces a creative leader? A healthy inner game.

The research in *Mastering Leadership* is thorough and complex; we highly recommend it to anyone looking to grow in their abilities as a leader. However, since we can't get into all the specifics of their research, we're going to move forward by simply highlighting several leadership qualities that leap out to us as key characteristics of a Passion & Provision leader: inspirational, emotionally intelligent, and persevering. Let's look at each of those attributes of leadership more closely.

INSPIRES OTHERS

A leader with a healthy inner game moves others through *inspiring* them. There are some famed military generals with amazing reputations as inspirational leaders. Supposedly, when General Patton visited his World War II troops at the battle lines, he inspired wholehearted adoration among his soldiers. The Bing Crosby movie *White Christmas* features a character supposedly based on General Patton and his soldiers sing, "We'll follow the old man wherever he wants to go."

When workers love, honor, and respect their leaders, there is a natural and healthy devotion that follows. People will go to the

---

28   Ibid.

29   Ibid.

end of the earth for you if they know you care about them. They'll care about what you care about, and they'll "follow you wherever you want to go." They'll give you their best, and they'll be happy about doing so. In order to be a leader worth respecting, you need a healthy inner game.

You can build your inner game in this area by solidifying your Vision. When you genuinely believe in your Core Values, your Core Purpose, and your BHAG, your enthusiasm will be infectious, and others will come along with you.

EMOTIONAL INTELLIGENCE AND TRUST

Leaders with a healthy inner game are also emotionally intelligent. They not only can identify other people's feelings, but they can identify their own feelings. Emotional intelligence manifests itself in two main ways: internal and external. Once again, we're dealing with the inner game and outer game.

Internal **emotional intelligence means you have inner awareness and inner self-control.** If you're triggered by a circumstance that brings up pain from the past, you're able to identify that you're triggered, and practice self-control to keep yourself objective and calm.

External **emotional intelligence means you have a sense of how to relate well interpersonally.** You can practice appropriate behavior in your relationships and build others up.

Consider these questions to evaluate your **external** emotional intelligence:

- Can you interact with others in a positive way that builds trust?
- Can you sense what another person is feeling, and respond appropriately with empathy?

Emotional intelligence is hugely important because it will either help or hinder your ability to create an atmosphere of *trust.* Trust is huge; it has a direct impact on your speed of business and costs. It's like the oil on the gears of a well-running machine.

The Speed of Trust, by Stephen M.R. Covey, presents fascinating research proving that high trust correlates directly to high speed and low cost.[30] When businesses operate in an atmosphere of trust, communication is smoother, more productive, and more efficient. Mistakes are communicated and resolved quickly. There's more collaboration and less infighting; as a result, business goes faster and operations are cheaper.

Low trust, on the other hand, correlates to tasks taking much longer, costing more money, and there's a proliferation of mistakes.

As a leader, emotional intelligence enables you to build an atmosphere of trust. You want to have employees that are working top notch for you and doing their best work. To have that, they need to work in a trusted team.

Trust is important outside the office as well. You want to build trust with your investors so they'll be willing to loan you more money at better rates. Vendors are also important to establish trust with, because of the constant negotiation of terms. Someone

---

30   Covey, Stephen M. R., and Rebecca R. Merrill. *The Speed of Trust: the One Thing That Changes Everything.* New York, NY: Free Press an imprint of Simon & Schuster, Inc., 2018.

who has poor emotional intelligence may be able to manipulate someone on the front end to get a deal, but it won't take long for a negative reputation to follow with other vendors. You run the risk of running out of vendors who will work with you, or you'll end up getting heftier charges because of your bad reputation. Less trust equals more money you'll have to pay.

Strong emotional intelligence will improve the Passion & Provision experienced for everyone in your company—that's reason enough to prioritize growth in this area. But it's also good for business: it will improve your bottom line, lower your stress, and increase your company's efficiency.

Growing in the area of emotional intelligence starts internally— and it's part of your job as a leader. You can grow in this area by reading books, working with a counselor or personal life coach, taking classes, and/or generally pursuing more understanding about how you tick. As your emotional intelligence improves on the inside, you'll see a direct correlation with an improved ability to be more emotionally intelligent on the outside—and that's good for everyone.

"I know of no more encouraging fact than the unquestionable ability of man to elevate his life by conscious endeavor." —Henry David Thoreau

PERSEVERANCE: MICHAEL NARRATES

When I was twelve years old, I signed up to go on a fifty-mile backpacking hike with my Boy Scout troop, through the back country of Yosemite Park. This was a questionable decision on my part. I was a roly-poly kid who watched a ton of TV and ate a lot of junk food. But my troop, Troop 31, was the coolest in town, and I was determined to keep up with the cool kids. Plus, I wanted the special patch.

I borrowed an old backpack and loaded it up. It weighed forty pounds, which was slightly less than half my size at the time. This was not a recipe for success.

Half a mile into the first day, I started whining. Then I started complaining. Eventually, I started crying. I lagged back into the rear of the group and my scout master, Bob, hung back with me.

Not surprisingly, Bob got frustrated with my attitude. Finally, he ordered me to put my pack down, and we walked the rest of the way to camp. One of the older boys hiked back on the trail to get my pack for me.

On the second day, we began trekking up a hill, and my whining and complaining started up again. Bob finally turned and lit into me. "Michael, this is day two of seven days," he said. "You have forty-five miles left in front of you. What are you going to do? Are you going to behave like this the whole time?"

Something about Bob's charge shifted my attitude. Within an hour, I had managed to grab hold of my emotions and set my mind on the fact that I wasn't going to be miserable, and that I was going to *do* this hike.

Toward the end of the day, Bob made a comment out of sheer shock. "What happened Michael? Your emotions just shifted 180 degrees. You went from a whiny baby to this happy-go-lucky kid, but your situation didn't change a bit." I remember him telling me he was proud of me—and surprised that I was able to accomplish such a monumental mindset shift.

I was able to finish the rest of the hike and had a phenomenal time. Even after I stumbled and smacked my face on a rock on day six, I was able to keep up a good attitude. I'd somehow concluded that I couldn't go back. I'd *started* the journey; Bob's speech reached me in the *middle* of the journey; I made up my mind I was going to *finish* the journey—so I might as well enjoy it.

I didn't realize I'd made a monumental mind-shift, but now—at age fifty-one—I think about the power I found on that hike on a regular basis whenever we're confronted with challenges. I also saw the power of a leader like Bob to call something out in me that I didn't know I possessed. It changed how I perceived myself and I learned that by changing my mind, I'd been able to persevere and could do it again in the future.

Perseverance is a willingness to set your mind with the determination that you *will* accomplish what you set out to do, and you'll do it with a positive attitude. Here's some honest (though not entirely dignified) communication: running a business is freaking hard. It can often feel like the equivalent of hiking fifty miles as a chubby kid with a pack on your back that's nearly half your weight. You're going to hit obstacles on a regular basis; challenges will come in all shapes and sizes. If you're going to survive, thrive, and grow a Passion & Provision company, you're going to need to make some choices to persevere.

Perseverance is the strength of character to push through when you would rather just close the door, cash it out, and go get a drink. Successful business leaders push through the hard times. That perseverance takes enormous courage. Without it, your business can easily run into trouble and collapse.

To help maintain perseverance, keep your eyes on the high horizon of your Vision. That's going to help carry your business through the day-to-day challenges. By raising your eyes to your high horizon, you won't trip over what's in front of you and effectively implode your business.

In fact, there's a kind of magic that comes when you choose to persevere. Perseverance doesn't just help you stay in business—it also functions as a magnet for opportunity, because people like grit. The phrase "fortune favors the brave" alludes to this—you can create your own luck by persevering.

You persevere by staying prepared, so that when opportunity comes up, you're ready to jump on it and see it through. You persevere by constantly building your skills and learning. You persevere by getting the foundational pieces of your business in place and honing them. When good fortune comes your way, you're ready to pounce and make the most of it.

WHY THE INNER GAME MATTERS

We once worked with an amazing leader—we'll call him Dylan.

Dylan mentored both of us; he even performed our marriage ceremony. When he moved to Colorado and asked us to follow him in a new job, his influence on us was strong enough that we did. Everything observable about Dylan was impressive: he was charismatic. He led great workshops. He was a compelling speaker. He was a phenomenal musician and singer. He was incredibly athletic in college. Anything Dylan did that was performance based, he excelled at. And he had great skills as a mentor—both of us would credit Dylan for helping us ultimately become who we are.

But Dylan was also a pathological liar. One day, we discovered that most of what we knew about him—everything from his education, to the state of his finances, to his earlier cancer diagnosis—was a lie. He never graduated from college. He was stealing money from two different companies. He never had stage-four Hodgkin's lymphoma, and his supposedly miraculous recovery had been invented.

Dylan had a rotten inner game. He had managed to succeed with an impressive outer game, but only up to a point. Eventually, the truth caught up with him. Because of how totally he neglected his inner self, relying instead on a hollow shell of his outer skills, Dylan caused massive damage to the people he worked with and all the people who trusted him. He lost his job. He lost his marriage. He lost his relationship with his four kids. He annihilated his life.

Your inner game *matters*. Think back to our iceberg illustration. The part underneath the water determines where the visible iceberg goes. If that bulk under the surface melts or breaks apart, the part seen above the water will likewise disintegrate—just like we experienced with Dylan. You can't sustain a floating berg on top of the water if there's nothing substantial underneath.

Conversely, if you work to build up your inner game, and actually *grow* the part underneath the water, then the visible berg will also grow. It may move or change shape or get lifted up higher out of the water. The more growth that happens *underneath* the surface, the more you see positive visible changes above the water.

The inner game is much larger than the outer game, and it's the inner game that directs the outer—not the other way around. For that reason, we need to do significant work *internally* before growth can be seen in our habits, reactions, and treatment of people.

Think of an outer game competency like decisiveness. A competent leader needs to make strong, decisive leadership moves. But a quality like decisiveness is radically impacted by your inner game. Are you secure or insecure? Are you anxious? Do you make decisions out of fear? All of those *inner* characteristics will have an impact on your *external* leadership qualities.

The more you as a leader choose to invest in your inner game, the better your leadership is going to be. The guy who solves some of his anger management issues is going to be much better to work for and have a better shot at having a Passion & Provision company. The woman who deals with her insecurity or her need to be the smartest person in the room, is going to be able to trust her employees more and empower them to step into their full potential. Your investment in your inner game will lead to enormous rewards.

> The more you as a leader choose to invest in your inner game, the better your leadership is going to be.

The inner drives the outer, but that doesn't mean we disregard the outer game completely. These two work in tandem, and there's a skillset and competency level associated with your outer game as well.

OUTER GAME

The outer game describes the observable competencies of Leadership. Someone with a strong outer game knows how to articulate Vision: they know what they want their team to do, and why, and they know how to structure operations so that the team can carry out their goals. They're strategic, capable of coming up with both great ideas and the means of implementation. They can carry out their objectives and bring people on board.

In a nutshell, the outer game refers to your competency in the observable behaviors of relating well to others and getting tasks done. When most people think of an effective versus an ineffective leader, they're usually thinking of the leader's outer game—their communication, management style, strategy, decisiveness, and so on.

Many of us have sat under incompetent leaders who have been promoted past their capacity—people we would think of as having a weak outer game. Often, the widespread, unspoken conclusion about that leader is that they don't have a clue what they're doing, and they're leading everyone in circles.

We don't want that to be how people perceive you—so let's dig a little deeper into a few of the traits of a leader with a strong outer game. In this next section we outline four of those traits. The first two—decisiveness and collaboration—are discussed in Adams & Anderson's list of eighteen behaviors or competencies.[31] The following two—communication and empowering/protecting—are ones that we have observed to be critical components of an effective outer game and are inferred from the eighteen behaviors.

---

31   Ibid.

DECISIVENESS

The ability to make decisions is a pretty important ability that we'd like to give a moment's attention to. It's also one of the eighteen behaviors of a creative leader, as discussed in *Mastering Leadership*. Strong, decisive leadership impacts nearly every area of business that a leader touches.

A lack of decisiveness can cause many leaders to stumble; in fact, it's one of the most common complaints about leadership we hear from employees during our consultations. These leaders might be afraid to make the wrong decision, so they refuse to make one, delay the decision, or conclude they simply *can't* decide what to do on a given issue. This can be incredibly frustrating for employees and makes your business vulnerable.

We're not advocating for shoot-from-the-hip decision making, because that can be dangerous too. **Strong leaders should take sufficient time to weigh evidence and arguments about what to do—then move forward with decisive action.** So how does a leader strengthen their competency as a decision maker?

Once again, we're going to come back to the importance of Vision. (We told you it was connected to everything!) The Core Values, Core Purpose, and BHAG identified in your Vision make a huge difference in decision making. If you know where you're going, it's easier and faster to make decisions about how to get there. You're able to build a Strategic Plan that helps direct everyone's moves within the company, including your own.

The Vision and Strategic Plan help to clarify choices. They take some otherwise appealing choices off the table, and enable you to focus on the best path forward. From there, you have to take it to the next step: determine how you're going to focus your strategy to achieve the Vision, achieve results, and deal with potential obstacles.

COLLABORATION

There's a well-known saying, usually said to be an African proverb, which says, "Go fast, go alone. Go together, go far." Statistics support the wisdom of the proverb: empirical evidence proves that teams go farther in business.

"Go fast, go alone. Go together, go far."

Many business leaders would prefer to not deal with employees at all. They'd rather be a "solopreneur" and go fast. Employees cost money, and they can be hard to manage—and there are plenty of horror stories about business partnerships that crashed and burned.

By going it alone, you're able to pivot fast, make changes, and have control over everything. Still, at some point, especially if your business does well, you may decide you want to go *far*. It's too exhausting to do so many little sprints; you want to be able to go the distance. At that point, you need to bring other people on board.

Almost every great company out there has had a team behind it, which often began with a partnership. Microsoft's Bill Gates had a partner: Paul Allen. Apple's Steve Jobs had a partner: Steve Wozniak. Hewlett and Packard, of Hewlett-Packard, were partners. Walt Disney partnered with his brother, Roy Disney—one of the most successful partnerships in history.

When you study each Disney brother's biography, it becomes clear that there's no way either one of them could have accomplished a trillionth of what they did alone. Walt was the visionary, or "Innovator," but his brother had the business acumen to bring Walt's dreams into a reality—he functioned as the "Integrator." The power of the Innovator/Integrator partnership is the subject of the book *Rocket Fuel*, which discusses just how powerful an effective partnership can be.[32]

Tips for Partnership

So, let's correct a myth here: partners are *not* a bad thing. True, there are some legitimate stories about partnerships that went wrong—but those horror stories can be avoided. **Enter a partnership wisely by establishing rules and game plans.** Most often, when partnerships fail, it's because a partner broke those rules or they never existed in the first place.

Resist the temptation to do it all on your own. You'll be able to go much farther if you team up with a skilled partner whose gifts complement your own. Here are a few recommendations that will help you enter into a partnership successfully from the start:

- Make sure you and your partner align with your Core Values.
- Establish the ultimate end point for your company. For instance, are you building it to sell? Or do you want to stay with this business for the long haul?
- Identify and clarify your domains of leadership. Who will fulfill what role?
- Articulate rules for how you're going to handle disagreements, so that conflict doesn't threaten the whole partnership.

---

32 Wickman, Gino, and Mark C. Winters. *Rocket Fuel: The One Essential Combination That Will Get You More of What You Want from Your Business*. Dallas, TX: Benbella Books, 2016.

We highly recommend a great book called *The Partnership Charter*, by David Gage, for further reading on how to optimize your business partnership.[33] It provides a framework for having a discussion with your potential partner ahead of starting a business to determine if you're a good match or not. That discussion can form the basis of an agreement you form with your partner; as time goes on and circumstances get hard, you can return to those initial agreements, using them as a reference point to discuss where you might be now. It doesn't make the hard times less hard, but that early alignment can give you an agreed-upon framework to navigate with and make the hard times more *bearable*.

David Gage's wife was originally in a business partnership with two other women that easily classifies as a partnership horror story. The failed partnership ended up costing over a hundred thousand dollars in legal fees, and then—without resolution—the three women all just walked away. All the pain, all the hurt, and all that cash, was essentially flushed down the toilet. However, instead of saying, "We'll never do this again," Gage came at it from a different angle. He knew that great companies have partners, so he decided he needed to figure out how to do partnerships better.

Business entrepreneurs don't always have the foresight to be this intentional from the start. More often than not, partnerships form almost by accident, which is probably a major contributing factor to the high business failure rate. Mark Zuckerberg famously started "the Facebook" out of his dorm room as a kind of hobby. His business partner, Eduardo Saverin, was a fellow Harvard classmate; they thought they were simply making "something

33   Gage, David. *The Partnership Charter: How to Start Out Right with Your New Business Partnership (or Fix the One You're in)*. New York: Basic Books, 2004.

cool."[34] Long before they had thought to establish any kind of partnership "rules," their business blew up into a huge success—which ended badly for the two partners. Zuckerberg effectively ousted Saverin, resulting in lawsuits and plenty of bad blood.

Gage's book highlights what business partners should do *as soon as they realize* they're effectively partnering in a business together. Whether you're just getting into a partnership or struggling to improve the one you're in—sit down, have some intentional conversation, and work on it.

Partnership is like marriage. Even if you made a poor decision about who you committed to in the beginning, do your best to come to alignment through counseling (yes, counseling) or seeking out resources like Gage's book. If you don't, the whole enterprise could dissolve. Divorce happens in marriage and divorce happens in business partnerships—but if you fight to save the relationship, you could end up reaping the benefits for the rest of your life.

We can speak to that personally, as business partners *and* spouses. When you work at a partnership with someone whose gifts complement your own, everyone wins. In our own partnership, Kathryn is more skilled with project management and tasks—call her the Integrator. Michael is more skilled with strategy and vision; he gets the Innovator title.

If you were to draw our different skillsets as a Venn diagram—all the task stuff in Kathryn's circle, and all the visionary stuff in Michael's—then, in the beginning, there was only a tiny bit

---

34   Carlson, Nicholas. "EXCLUSIVE: How Mark Zuckerberg Booted His Co-Founder out of the Company." Business Insider. Business Insider, May 15, 2012. https://www.businessinsider.com/how-mark-zuckerberg-booted-his-co-founder-out-of-the-company-2012-5.

of overlap. However, as we've learned from each other over the years, we've not only balanced each other out, we've also developed much more overlap in our skillsets. Kathryn's much more creative than she used to be, and Michael is better at getting stuff done. We've grown as a result of our partnership, and now we're both more effective at leading our employee.

GOOD COMMUNICATION

A strong leader communicates truthfully, in a way that honors others' dignity. They address honestly what needs to get done and how to get there. Their communication is delivered clearly, appropriately, and in a healthy way—in other words, the communication doesn't come in the midst of an emotional reaction.

A leader's strength of communication can be seen when they're trying to motivate people. Leaders seeking the healthier option of inspiring their employees (versus manipulating them) will try to help their employee understand the importance of their task. They'll encourage their staff, and give a resounding pep talk: "Go get 'em!"

But a leader's communication abilities will be seen even more clearly when something goes wrong. When people do something wrong that costs you money or time, you're squeezed. Pressure and tension push on your insides, like blood being pushed out of a wound—and the greater the pressure, the faster the bleeding. That bleeding comes out in the way you communicate.

Are you harsh? Are you a people pleaser? Are you sharp? Are you condemning? Do you yell? Do you use isolation and distance to protect yourself and manipulate others? Do you shame and humiliate? That's poor, reactive communication.

Or do you stop? Do you have a calm voice? Do you take a moment to try to determine what's going on and how it happened? Do you set about solving the problem and analyze where you went off base? Do you ensure that learning happens along the way, so that everyone ends up stronger after surviving a major mistake? Do you honor others' dignity as you discuss where they went wrong? That's positive, healthy communication.

> "The challenge of leadership is to be strong, but not rude; be kind, but not weak; be bold, but not bully; be thoughtful, but not lazy; be humble, but not timid; be proud, but not arrogant; have humor, but without folly." —Jim Rohn

It's also important to accept responsibility for where *you* may have gone wrong. Perhaps you set goals incorrectly or communicated unclearly. Perhaps you failed to hold an employee accountable for their task or created an atmosphere of distrust. By showing a willingness to acknowledge your own errors, you'll encourage your staff to own theirs.

More than anything else, your communication style in the midst of a mistake has the power to establish trust or dismantle it. If you communicate in a restorative way, the atmosphere of trust will be powerfully strengthened. However, if you communicate in a punitive way—in a way that shames and punishes—you will do more to create a culture of fear.

One of our friends, a successful business leader, once had an employee who made a *$20,000* mistake. Because of the company's size, that $20,000 hit our friend, the CEO, significantly. We actually heard this story from the employee who made the mistake. He told us how profoundly he'd blown it—what a dumb mistake it had been. He told us that he expected his boss, our friend, to respond in anger. He anticipated that his boss would yell at him, force him to pay back the money, fire him—or maybe do all three.

Instead, our friend came into his employee's office. He said, "Okay, let's take a second and breathe. I don't think you did this intentionally, and I'm not going to fire you. What happened? Let's figure out how to prevent this from happening again." He reassured his employee that he didn't believe he was an incompetent, horrible person, and he kept the focus on moving forward.

Together, they owned the problem. Nobody tried to skirt the fact that the employee had made a mistake. But because the CEO approached the employee in a gracious way that honored his dignity, he enabled everyone to grow past the mistake. Essentially, he said, "Yes, you blew it—but this moment is not going to define you." He held his employee accountable for what he'd done, while communicating productively to solve the problem and ensure it never happened again.

Mistakes happen to all of us. As leaders, we need to be ready to deal with them. When mistakes happen, show strong leadership through *productive* communication:

- First, do what you need to do to regulate your own emotions and get to a calm, level-headed place. Then—and only then—proceed.
- Respect and honor your employees.
- Treat the mistake as a competence issue, not a character issue, and work to strengthen the competence of the person who messed up.

- Honor the dignity of your employees by giving them the benefit of the doubt, trusting their good intentions.
- Correct the mistake(s) and figure out how to get things back on track. (Reference our guide on troubleshooting in the next chapter for more specific ideas on how to do this.)

EMPOWERING AND PROTECTING

Caring for your employees goes beyond simply communicating well; strong leaders also empower and protect their employees. That sense of security is going to help your employees give you their very best work.

When we think of the importance of empowering your employees and protecting them, we think of the townspeople in the "Allegory and Effects of Good and Bad Government." With good, just, virtuous leadership, the people are protected. As a result, they can thrive. They can freely engage in commerce; they're able to farm and cultivate the land; they prosper and enjoy themselves. Productivity and joy flourish when leaders protect the people below them.

When there's no sense of protection—when there's war, and no reliable justice, and no predictable help to be found—everything contracts. The land suffers. No one can conduct business. People shift from a position of giving to one of taking, in an effort to survive. The town no longer attracts anyone to it; instead, people look to escape.

Good leaders **empower and protect their employees.** In doing so, you enable them to thrive and your company reaps the benefits.

You **empower people by giving them everything they need to**

be successful. You ensure that they have all necessary resources, training, and clarity to do their best work. That is good for you, and it's good for them. You also empower your employees by *inspiring* them. You help your employees see that what they're doing matters and inspire them to raise the bar. Effective empowerment also relies on clear goal setting and communication, which we'll discuss in greater depth in the following chapter.

You can **protect your employees by identifying the rules and boundaries of how work is done.** You help clarify, "This is the way we play the game: these are the rules of how we behave; this is how you decide what and what not to do."

Our experience in York, England reminds us that ancient cities protected their citizens with fortress-like walls. Although most people usually lived outside the city's center, if there was ever an enemy approaching, all citizens could find refuge behind the strong walls of their fortress city. Imagine being a farmer out in the field and hearing a rumble. Is it thunder or is there danger afoot? You could look at the walls of your city and know you're protected. The guards would signal you to either hurry inside or remain at work.

Those walls were the boundary line; they were a symbol of safety and protection. The walls were where you went to hide, and it was where the army fought from to defend the city. For the most part, those walls kept the enemies and thieves on the outside, which enabled virtuous, prosperous life to thrive on the inside. Families could move at will, children could play in the street, and commerce could continue. Protected people are empowered to thrive.

Your Vision's Core Values will help you protect your employees in this critical way. For example, you might make sure that you align yourselves with vendors, clients, and others who have similar values and won't berate your staff. You may choose not to hire someone who could undermine your culture. You might ensure that, when someone makes a mistake, you deal with it quickly, safely, and in a way that honors your employees' dignity.

In a conversation with one of our employees during her annual review, we asked her, "Do you feel like your opinion is respected here?"

She responded with a story about a conversation she'd had with some of her other coworkers while the two of us had been away. It was a watercooler conversation—it had more to do with politics and society and general life than it had to do with work. Apparently, the conversation had prompted people to share a wide variety of opinions.

Our employee said, "I felt like, even with the difference in opinions, everyone respected everyone else. It was an enjoyable conversation because we could share different ideas and thoughts—but everyone was respectful." She added, "I experience that kind of respect in work here on a regular basis."

We were able to tell her honestly that if respect *hadn't* been shown, there would have been serious consequences for anyone who'd been disrespectful. That would have been a violation of our Core Values, which would have demanded swift attention and action.

"I know!" she said enthusiastically. "And that makes me feel good, and safe, and comfortable here. It's one of the reasons I've been here for eight years, and want to continue to be part of this team."

We've learned that the safer our employees feel, the more they are empowered to do what they need to do. As leaders, it's our job to create those strong walls of refuge. It's our job to inspire our staff to thrive and let them know that we've got their backs along the way.

THE LENGTH OF YOUR SHADOW: MICHAEL NARRATES

When I was twenty-three, a mentor told me something I'll never forget. "Michael, I see people following you," he said. "There's no question about whether or not you'll become a leader. You *are* a leader. But the question is: *where* are you leading people?"

At the time, I was still in a pretty irresponsible place. I was dating Kathryn seriously but had no clear picture of how I would support her. I created new business cards about every other week, as new business ideas came to mind—but rarely followed through with them. (The truth is, I suffered from a lack of knowing how to take what was in my mind and turn it into reality.) I was also helping lead a church youth group part time, but I hadn't bothered to seriously pursue training or education.

My mentor's question made me wake up. I realized that I needed to get serious about my life. Nobody had ever helped me recognize the responsibility that I had—one which I hadn't necessarily asked for, but which was still mine. The question prompted me to really consider the direction of my life and my intentions about everything I wanted to be a part of in the future.

I needed to get serious about my training and my education—and I needed to get serious about my relationship with my future wife. I was basically heading in the right direction, but I wasn't exactly heading in a straight line. I needed to decide to get in the game and fully engage, so that I could lead people in a *good* direction.

Here's the truth: if you're leading a business, then you *are* a leader. The question is: where are you leading people?

Are you a reactive leader, leading others toward fearful behavior and hiding mistakes? Have you created a climate of fear and distrust? Have you neglected your inner game, at the expense of your outer game?

Or are you a creative leader, with a secure inner game, who focuses on the well-being of others? Are you creating a climate of collaboration, safety, trust, and creativity? Are you building up your outer game competencies with diligence, so that your business can excel?

Business leaders change the temperature of the room. If they're encouraging, creative, and empowering of their staff, the business is going to thrive. People are going to like being at work, and they'll perform well. But if a leader is manipulative, indecisive, and belittles their employees, the production and energy within a business will be constrained.

Think of this spatially. Imagine that every leader casts a shadow, defined by their maturity and capabilities. A business can't grow beyond the length of a leader's shadow. If a leader is immature and won't recognize their weaknesses, they'll cast a small shadow. A company may be able to sprint and grow beyond that leader's capability for a time, due to lucky circumstances or a great opportunity. However, the company will eventually retract back down to the length of its leader's shadow. A leader with a small shadow is going to lead a small company.

However, you can grow your shadow as a leader by working on your inner and outer game. Grow your inner game by building up your maturity, emotional intelligence, and inner health. Grow your outer game by building up your competencies. Seek out training. Seek out help, education, and mentorship.

If you stay stuck in Syndrome Twenty-Seven and don't pursue growth, you won't be able to recognize or capitalize on opportunities. They'll wash over you like a wave, and you'll find yourself in the same place you've been stuck for years. However, by strengthening your games, you'll increase your maturity and capabilities, which define your impact: your leadership shadow will actually grow.

As your company's leader, it's critical that you pursue growth in all the necessary competencies of running a profitable and healthy company. As you deepen your maturity and expand your competencies, you're better able to create an environment where your employees can thrive. You'll care for people better. You'll be better at getting tasks done. Your business will become a place that's emotionally healthier, more personally fulfilling, and more financially profitable.

You allow Passion to flourish, which leads to more fulfillment. You allow Provision to grow, which leads to more success.

Are you willing to do the hard work to have that?

Or would you rather settle for less?

If you're up for the challenge, then it's time to further grow your shadow. Let's get deeper into the holistic model, so that you're equipped to oversee the different aspects of your business and get them humming along.

CHAPTER SIX

||||||||||||||||||||

Management and Operations

"The conventional definition of management is getting work done through people, but real management is developing people through work."

AGHA HASAN ABEDI

BILL WALSH 4EVAH: KATHRYN NARRATES

When Michael and I got married, we made a deal: I had to learn to like the drums, so that I could fully appreciate my husband's percussive skills, and Michael had to learn to like football—specifically, the NFL. I fell in love with the NFL long before I fell in love with Michael. I'm a 49ers fan first but root for Green Bay on the back end.

Michael thinks I got the easier part of the deal. Drumming seasons come and go, but the NFL is relentless.

One of the great stories of the NFL—especially for 49ers fans—is a story about how Coach Bill Walsh turned the struggling 49ers around with his leadership and management during the late '70s and '80s. Humor me for a second—I just have to geek out a little.

Bill Walsh took over the 49ers in 1979, after a brutal season when the franchise had only won two out of sixteen games. During Walsh's first season, the 49ers once again went two and fourteen. As far as most people could see, Walsh wasn't off to a great start.

The team's 1980 season began so badly, Walsh didn't think he'd survive it: they lost every one of their first five games. Walsh reported later in a memoir that he was sure he was going to get fired.[35] He'd wanted to be an NFL coach for his entire life, but the fall of 1980 made him think it was about to be over in a blink of an eye. Things were *bad*.

But then—the team started to pick up their game. The 49ers ended their 1980 year with a six and ten record—a slight, but noticeable improvement from their last two seasons, and enough to provide Walsh with a bit of job security.

---

35   Ranadive, Ameet. "3 Leadership Lessons from Bill Walsh (Former 49ers Coach)."
      Medium. Great Business Stories, September 29, 2016. https://medium.com/
      great-business-stories/3-leadership-lessons-from-bill-walsh-former-49ers-coach-24e544e8013.

In 1981—after two failing seasons under Walsh's leadership—the team showed dramatic improvement, ending thirteen and three. Their transformation was so jaw-dropping, in fact, that Walsh was named the 1981 NFL Coach of the Year.

In 1982, Walsh's team ended up taking on the Dallas Cowboys in the playoffs, a franchise that had dominated the NFC East for over a decade, winning seven division championships and appearing in five Super Bowls in the 1970s alone. In a famous moment at the end of a playoff game, with less than a minute on the clock, the 49ers' wide receiver, Dwight Clark, made a leaping grab in the end zone to catch a game-winning touchdown pass from his quarterback, Joe Montana. This moment became famous in NFL history, known simply as The Catch. It transformed the 49ers from a losing team into a dynasty. They went on to win the 1982 Super Bowl and became known as one of the NFL's most formidable forces.

By the end of Walsh's tenure with the 49ers, they had won six division titles, three NFC Championships, and three Super Bowls. In 1993, Walsh was named to the Pro Football Hall of Fame.

It took time for Walsh to turn the ship around—but those initial losing seasons weren't wasted. Walsh spent that time building a foundation that would later enable the team to succeed as dramatically as it did. So how did he do it?

Bill Walsh's amazing leadership and management was all built on the premise that the team needed to work together as a *community*. He worked to manage the culture of the 49ers, bringing them into a team mentality even as he juggled management of the day-to-day pieces that supported his players' individual growth. He became famous for that community mindset. Before

Walsh took over, many teams operated with the assumption that a team's effectiveness was due to the individual competency of its players—but Walsh focused more on *community* competency. Through helping his players put aside their egos and participate in a community identity, the power of their playing was transformed.

A MODEL MANAGER

We love Bill Walsh's example of management because he succeeded in pushing forward a transformative Vision, even while he continued getting the day-to-day stuff done. In a Passion & Provision company, management and operations work to effectively handle the daily tasks of business in a way that moves your whole franchise toward the high horizon Vision. It's community oriented, even while it prioritizes efficiency and achievement.

Like Walsh experienced, it takes time to transform your business into a Passion & Provision model—to solve, adjust, and grow the identity of your business into something new. The bigger your company, the more time it will take. Small companies can shift more quickly, but if you're leading a large company, it's going to feel more like turning an aircraft carrier in the ocean. You might need three to five years to change your culture on every level, until you're on your new desired course with everyone's buy-in.

Still, there are strategies and fundamentals you can put in place immediately to set your people up to succeed. In this chapter, we're going to discuss five core characteristics of management, along with effective hiring practices. We're going to give recommendations for improving your Standard Operating Procedures (SOPs), along with a particularly effective SOP for troubleshooting. Implementing these recommendations can provide you with some quick wins and fast results, even as the more profound changes take longer to get fully established.

We're going to keep things big picture. There are dense, detailed books which can give you further ideas about resource management, improving efficiency, and how to revolutionize your manufacturing and systems. If you decide after reading this chapter that you're ready to plunge in deeper, we've referenced several resources for further reading.

However, we're focused on getting you that *working knowledge* first, so that you have what you need to build a Passion & Provision company. These recommendations have been hard learned and hard earned through our own experience of growing as managers.

Here's what we can assure you, after our own implementation of these concepts: when you apply these ideas to your people and your company, you will radically increase your peace of mind, your profit, and the value of your company.

SUCCESS WITH PEOPLE AND THINGS

Our past two chapters related to big-picture planning, staying on course, and effective leadership. This chapter is where we're going to start to discuss the day-to-day operations of *getting stuff done*.

We believe you need to separate out two major categories of what goes into getting stuff done: people and things. When it comes to day-to-day operations in your business, your goal is to manage all of the people stuff and the non-people stuff in the best way possible to create your product or service in a way that many people would call "efficient."

> Management deals with people; operations deals with things.

When people see the word "efficient," they generally think it means how to get things done the fastest way possible. We think that definition should be expanded a bit. When we define efficiency in the context of operations, here's what we mean: 1) **The right things** are done in the 2) **right order,** 3) in the **allotted time,** 4) to the required level of **base-line quality,** 5) within your **specific context,** which all must lead to the end result of being 6) **within budget.**

When your management and operations become more efficient, you achieve many of the following benefits:

- Make fewer mistakes, creating less waste.
- Improve the quality of your products or services, which can lead to higher revenue.
- Create more margin, which can lead to more profit.
- Create more widgets per hour which gives you more opportunity to sell more in a given period. Again, this leads to more profit.
- Create more cash flow so you're not only making more gross revenue, but you have more cash to spend on other things.

So, let's connect the dots from our previous chapters. You've identified your Vision, which you then translated into a stellar Strategic Plan with annual and quarterly goals. You're working on your inner and outer game as a leader, so that you can inspire your employees to work toward that Vision with purpose and passion.

Now, how do you get them to effectively *do* the things they need to do, to make that Vision happen? How do you maximize efficiency, so that all the lovely results just described actually take place?

Start by building up your minimum competency of management and operations. (And after that, grow your proficiency into Super Bowl-level mastery!)

MANAGEMENT: THE FIVE FUNDAMENTALS

Most people have experienced bad management, and we could all probably come up with a list of frustrating management behaviors: indecisive leadership, micromanaging, passive-aggressiveness, and so on. As we discussed in our previous chapter, those behaviors are usually connected to a leader's weak inner game, and that management style will lead to unmotivated, unhappy employees.

A *great* manager, on the other hand, can breathe new life into a struggling business just like a great coach can turn around a failing NFL team franchise.

"Managing is not a series of mechanical tasks but a set of human interactions." —Thomas Teal[36]

Some of our readers will be doing the heavy lifting of management themselves. If you're running a small company, it's likely that all your staff reports to you and the material in this chapter will be personally relevant. Leaders of larger companies, on the other hand, will have employees working as managers of different teams. In that case, we recommend you read this: a.) for ways you can improve in managing your managers, and b.) for concepts to pass on to your managers, for *their* improvement.

---

36 Teal, Thomas. "The Human Side of Management." Harvard Business Review, August 1, 2014. https://hbr.org/1996/11/the-human-side-of-management.

So, what does it look like to have minimum competency in the area of *good* management?

Good management means you understand and create the systems needed to optimally manage your people. In other words, **you know how to put the *right* people in the *right* positions, and then you effectively empower them to live into their potential.** You equip them to experience Passion in their work! The net result of that good management means you deliver on the promises you've made to your clients—which, in turn, leads to higher Provision.

A good manager is able to work with people in such a way your business's reach and effectiveness is broadened. A good manager also *cares* for people. The two of us believe that people are not cold, faceless resources to be calculated and manipulated like pieces on the chessboard. A Passion & Provision company believes people are important and valuable parts of a company.

Still, you're not running a support group; you're running a company. It must survive and make a profit, or there's no financial security for anyone. Somehow, you've got to care for your people in a way that still empowers them to do their jobs *well*.

Everything we're about to discuss will directly impact your team's ability to **effectively** and **efficiently** get work done. We heard recently that the definition of "elegance" is to be effective and efficient. We love that picture of mastery.

There are five key areas of management that will help you achieve this *elegance* within your business. The first four are fundamental pieces that need to exist in every management process. The fifth area takes the foundation you build on the first four and then multiplies the benefits. Let's begin with the first four.

1. GOALS

Let's say that you want your company to grow 25 percent this next year, and you put that in your Strategic Plan as your annual goal. Next, you need to evaluate what you'll need to sell and how many sales you'll need to make to meet that 25 percent growth. Then, those goals are divided into four parts, which you associate with four quarters of the year. You've got your Strategic Plan; now, you need to move to management strategies so that everyone can effectively achieve those goals.

In order to thrive in their jobs, your employees need to know exactly what you're asking of them, and how they're going to be evaluated. For that reason, good management starts by identifying clear goals. Nobody is ever efficient or effective unless they have clear, achievable goals. When goals are well crafted, you can examine them, study them, and reference them in employee evaluations. You also will have more clarity about what kind of resources your employees need to achieve their goals, which is critical to empower their success.

> Nobody is ever efficient or effective unless they have clear, achievable goals.

There are several methodologies around what makes a good goal. The one we use, and probably the most well known, is the SMART goal methodology. The acronym "SMART" lists the characteristics of a well-crafted goal. The letters stand for Specific, Measurable, Attainable, Relevant, and Timely.

Let's say we want our salesperson, Greg, to drum up more sales so that we're making progress on that 25 percent growth. A *bad* goal would lack all the SMART qualities: "Greg, make contact with more potential clients and sell more stuff." A goal like that isn't going to help Greg do much of anything. It's too vague, there's no way to hold him accountable to it, and there's no indication of how he's supposed to get there.

A SMART goal for Greg might be a goal worded like this: "Respond to all new leads coming in with an acknowledgment phone call or email within one hour of getting notified during business hours."

Let's check that goal with the SMART criteria:

Specific—Greg needs to respond to all new leads.

Measurable—He has to do so with an acknowledgment email or phone call, which we have the ability to measure and track.

Attainable—Yes, he knows exactly what he needs to start building relationships with potential new clients, and it's within his power to do it.

Relevant—Yes, it contributes to improving his sales performance.

Timely—He needs to do this within an hour.

When employees know exactly what they're aiming for, have a clear timeline, and have the resources they need to achieve their goals, they're empowered to improve in the way you're looking for.

2. COMMUNICATION

Here's the thing though—SMART goals will still be ineffective goals if they're not communicated in a way that lands with your employees. English is not a literal language and contains many abstract terms. For instance, think of the challenges of interpreting the following phrases:

"Wow, that's hot." Is that a reference to the temperature of a beverage? The weather? An experience of good luck? Someone's physical attractiveness?

"Wow, that's cold." Do you need a jacket? Was someone rude to you? Does your water have too much ice? Are you discussing a color spectrum?

Plenty of words are fuzzy and need context for clarification. Our tone of voice and body language can be communication game-changers too. If a manager says, "You must have worked so hard on this!" while nodding enthusiastically over an employee's work and smiling—well then, the employee must have done a great job. If a manager furrows their brow, frowns at the employee's work, then looks up and says sarcastically, "You must have worked hard on this"—well then, the employee's about to have a bad day.

Communication doesn't just break down between two people though—it can also break down across departments. People may miss meetings, deadlines, or key information because there simply wasn't an effective system of communication set up to ensure all relevant people had all necessary information.

Here's an example. Recently, we had lunch with a friend, Shane who told us an amusing story that testifies to how common these communication breakdowns can be. Shane had been sent off to a conference by his boss, but his boss had never informed his direct supervisor, Julia, where he was going. Julia called Shane, annoyed, wondering why he wasn't at work, and Shane had to explain to her that their boss had sent him on a business trip. The story seems laughable, but those sorts of communication slips happen all the time.

So what do you do about it? We have two recommendations. **First: commit to grow as a communicator—both personally, and as a company.** Communication is fraught with challenges, so do your best to approach it with humility. Messages often need to be repeated—be willing to say it more than once. Push yourself to keep learning new communication skills and new strategies. Your company will require this continued growth, because as you continue to innovate as a company, you'll have to continue to update your systems of communication to keep up with it. As you try new things, you'll catch new communication misses. That's okay; those misses are an invitation to more improvement, which is something to embrace.

Secondly: grow in documentation. In the second half of this chapter, we're going to discuss the importance of Standard Operating Procedures, and you should certainly get those in place for establishing effective communication within your company. Create procedural checklists to ensure necessary communication is carried out. It's hard to improve systematic processes of communication if there's no written guide to reference, but if you *have* a checklist, you can adjust and improve it. Write things down as much as possible and seek out helpful technical tools for communication.

As your company's leader, you need to model good communication and encourage its growth. Part of how you do that, as we discussed in our previous chapter, is by ensuring *safety* for your employees. Employees need to trust that they can point out communication inefficiencies with the safety and protection of their leader—not get penalized. By creating a safe, trusted environment, your employees will be able to help your company communicate more smoothly across the board.

Those are some suggestions for improving communication as a company—but what about improving personally as a communicator? Managers need to communicate *clearly*, so that employees will understand what they need to do and act accordingly. If your employees don't clearly understand what you're asking of them, you won't be able to evaluate them properly, which is a crucial step in good management (and our next key area to discuss).

The Five Steps of Communication (Plus One)

Typically, effective communication occurs in a five-step process. Here are the five steps, along with tips about how to maximize the effectiveness of what you want to communicate. We've added a sixth "bonus" step to the communication process to help you avoid problems that could crop up during the first five:

1. We **think** about what we want to say.
   A. *Tip:* Get your thoughts clear before communicating. If you're not clear yet on what you *want* to say, you're not going to be able to communicate clearly!
2. We **voice** our message somehow, saying it verbally or putting it into written form.
   A. *Tip:* Watch your words, tone, intention, and rhetoric. That last one is a fancy way of describing figures of speech, like metaphors. We speak in them all the time (as you may have observed, reading this book); sometimes, when we're asked to explain what we mean with one metaphor,

we're guilty of responding with another metaphor! Use step six to help you improve in this step.

3. The message is **transmitted** through a myriad of potential distractions and noise in the world.

    A. *Tip:* Do your best to reduce the "noise" between you and the listener. That noise could be literal noise making it hard to hear, in which case you should find a different location to meet. Other obstacles to communication could be physical obstructions (you can't see each other well), distance, or language barriers. If you're trying to communicate with someone who doesn't speak your first language, that can create real challenges with communication. Industry terms (i.e., "gobbledygook") can also pose a communication barrier. It's amazing how many people will blame others for using the wrong nonsense words! Help improve this through using our recommendation in step six.

4. It's **received** by the person being communicated to.

    A. *Tip:* Even if you think you're being clear, your recipient might still misinterpret or misunderstand your communication. Remember the childhood game "Telephone?" A message is whispered from person to person and usually ends up being hilariously altered by the end. Make sure your message is received accurately through applying step six to avoid issues here.

5. The message is **translated** into meaning by your recipient, and they respond with action.

    A. *Tip:* A person's attitude, current state of mind, or prior experience can lead to miscommunications here too. Have you ever tried to compliment someone, and they took it as an insult instead? Their *translation* of your intended meaning went awry! Use step six to help solve problems here.

What is step six, you want to know? What is the silver-bullet solution to all your communication problems? It may not be a silver bullet, but step six comes darn close.

6. BONUS: Get a **feedback loop** going to see if what you meant to communicate is the same as what your recipient heard.
    A. *Tip:* Ask the person you're communicating with to restate or rephrase what they heard you say. If it's not quite right, adjust your communication by starting the feedback loop all over again. You can build your skill and speed in this feedback step with practice!

Effective communication occurs when everything goes well with the first five steps or is corrected during the feedback loop. *Miscommunications* occur when one or more of the first five steps breaks down and fails to be corrected. Imagine this dialogue which could occur between any number of bosses and any number of employees:

> Boss: "I told you what you were supposed to do, I told you what the deadline was. I told you that I wanted all the red things in box one, and all the blue things in box two. Why are you doing the reverse?"

> Employee: "I thought I was doing it the way you asked!"

Or what about this?

> Boss: "We talked about this on Monday. I told you I wanted this done, and that you should consider it urgent. Why hasn't it happened yet?"

> Employee: "I thought you were joking!"

There are all kinds of ways that communication can break down: your intention was one thing, but the message your employee received was another. In order to get your employees to perform the way your business requires, you must ensure that your communication is landing the way you intend it to land. In addition to implementing the feedback loop and other tips, we recommend *writing down* your employee's goals so that there's less room for misinterpretation. The SMART goals approach is a great way to provide needed clarity.

Also, we encourage you to genuinely value being a good communicator—and value your reputation as one. On days when you feel frustrated by miscommunications, this value for effective communication will help motivate you to care about continued improvement.

3. ACCOUNTABILITY

If you have SMART goals, and you have communicated them clearly, the next responsibility of a manager is to hold people accountable for meeting their goals. You need a system to ensure employees actually achieve the goals you've given them. By holding employees accountable to their goals, you'll increase your business's efficiency and level of trust.

> By holding employees accountable to their goals, you'll increase your business's efficiency and level of trust.

We can easily think of two types of manager behaviors that produce ineffective accountability: there's the no-accountability type and the random-accountability type. Both can lead to problems.

No Accountability

Let's talk about the no-accountability type first. Many leaders lean toward, "I'm busy. I don't have time to hold each employee accountable." This attitude is understandable; when you're juggling a million tasks to try to get your business to succeed, you might easily feel like your employees *should just do their jobs.* Maybe you even have a benevolent attitude in your lack of accountability: "I trust them! They'll get it done."

Unfortunately, that approach doesn't play out well. Let's say you give your employee an assignment, and they work hard on it. They feel proud of the end result. However, you never follow up with them. You never recognize the value of their contribution, and you give them zero feedback. Ultimately, that employee is going to feel like they wasted their time on that project. Your lack of accountability subversively communicates to them that their goal was not actually important.

Your employees' productivity will take a nosedive if they assume no one cares whether or not they do their jobs effectively. You might think that you're showing trust in your employees by giving them an assignment and never checking in to see how they got it done. Unfortunately, this does not lead to trust. This leads to demoralized, unmotivated employees.

Random Accountability

Now, let's talk random accountability. Other leaders may lack a consistent system to check their employees' work, so people get held accountable in random ways. Employees may end up getting held accountable for tasks they weren't asked to do or for a different goal than the one they'd been given. That's why effective accountability depends so much on effective communication! If a manager communicated a goal in a confusing way, she might get unreasonably angry with her employee for failing to achieve a goal she never successfully communicated: "I thought you knew! Can't you think for yourself? Can't you just *see* that this needs to happen?"

That's a poor system of accountability. It's not going to lead to happy, empowered employees, and it's not going to help your bottom line. Ultimately, you leave your employees guessing about what's really important: "I was working toward *this* goal, which I'd thought was the important thing, but I got in trouble for not doing *this* task, so apparently *that* was the important thing." Your workplace operations can get messy fast if your employees conclude that their stated goals are not actually important, and they should start guessing as to what *is* important.

Holding employees accountable can mean having difficult conversations, which many managers—understandably—would rather avoid. Maybe it feels nicer to just ignore an employee's mistakes. However, if you don't have any system of accountability, you end up creating an environment that leads to confusion, frustration, and demoralized employees. Accountability may require difficult conversations at times, but it's also crucial for establishing an environment of trust, where employees know where they stand and how they're doing.

Here's how you do accountability well. Start with clear goals and communicate them effectively. When you ensure that you and your employees are all on the same page about what needs to get done, get a system in place to hold them accountable. When goals are documented, measurable, and communicated clearly, there's less room for argument about whether or not an employee has achieved their targets. That makes those potentially difficult conversations less awkward and makes steps toward improvement clearer.

4. TRUST

When these first three key areas are in place—goals, communication, and accountability—something beautiful automatically starts to happen. You begin to foster an environment of trust.

In our Leadership chapter, we recommended the book *Speed of Trust,* by Stephen M. R. Covey.[37] Recall that Covey's research proves that a high-trust team works *faster* and *costs less.* They're more productive and profitable. Conversely, a low-trust team works slower, and they end up costing the company more money. There's more friction in the system, so each transition takes longer. Every additional minute added to operations ends up costing money to the company.

> "Trust is like the air we breathe. When it's present, nobody really notices. But when it's absent everyone notices." —Warren Buffett

Covey identifies **two areas of trust: competency and character.** If you can trust someone's *competency,* then you know that your teammate has the ability required to produce decent work in their position. You can give them a job and *trust* that if they do it to the best of their ability, the job will get done in the way that you need.

But what if they don't work at the best of their ability? That's where *character* comes in. You might have a skillful, competent

---

37   Stephen M. R. Covey with Rebecca R. Merrill, *The Speed of Trust: The One Thing That Changes Everything* (New York: Free Press, 2018).

employee, but if they're lazy, unmotivated, or unethical, you may not be able to trust their output.

Character, as Covey discusses it, involves someone's *intent* and someone's *integrity*. Intent refers to an employee's motivation. The employee who decides to give a project his all has *good* intent. You can trust someone with good intent. The employee who decides to complete a project as fast as they can, with as little effort as possible has *bad* intent. You can't trust someone with questionable intent—even if you know they're competent.

Integrity—the other part of character—refers to an employee's honesty and virtue. You might have a competent accountant who has the earnest intent to do everything possible to help your business succeed—but if that employee has questionable *integrity*, they'll still be untrustworthy. If they're willing to cheat or lie to get you the numbers you want, you can't trust the work from your accountant. In order to fully trust your team, you need to know that they will uphold your Core Values and maintain moral principles.

In discussing the different components that make up each area of trust, Covey ends up detailing an *anatomy* of trust. Managers can use his system to analyze how much trust is present in their team. Where is it broken? Where is it whole? Covey's system enables areas of broken trust to be identified and fixed, and employees are equipped to perform at their highest potential.

5. PUBLIC RECOGNITION

The four areas of management we've just discussed—clear goals, effective communication, consistent accountability, and trust— act as four cornerstones for a system of effective management.

After those are in place—and *only* after those are in place—it's time to implement systems of public recognition for your employees.

Here's an important point: public recognition won't work if one of the other cornerstones isn't solid. If the first four areas of management are not at a minimum level competency, public recognition is seen as insincere. It can even degrade trust or morale in the organization, because it can appear to be self-serving and manipulative by the leadership.

Imagine working in an environment where goals are unclear and there's no consistent accountability; then, your boss gives out celebratory bonuses to everyone who happened to do [this random accomplishment]. That celebration could end up feeling more frustrating than joyful, if it reinforces the fact that many employees never knew about the importance of [this random goal] in the first place. Employees will be reminded of the lack of clear communication from their supervisors. If the rewards were given out in a way that feels random, employees may even feel irritable with each other: "I work twice as hard as he does. Why would they give *him* a bonus, and not me?" It's easy to see how public recognition could actually erode trust and morale, when not supported by the first four cornerstones.

But let's say you *do* have those first four fundamentals of management in place. At that point, it's time to incorporate the turbo-power booster of public recognition.

Every human being—no matter how introverted or extroverted—desires to be recognized as competent by their leaders and peers. At our core, we want to know that the way we invest our time is worthy of respect. When there's no system of communicating respect in a workplace, people can easily assume they're actually viewed *disrespectfully*. They might believe they're the weakest link, dragging down the whole organization—even if they're actually doing good work. When employees assume they're disappointing their leaders and peers, they'll quickly become demoralized and unmotivated.

However, public recognition can have the opposite effect. The book *The Carrot Principle,* by Adrian Gostick and Chester Elton, unpacks the findings of a research study about public recognition.[38] The authors explain that, **when the first four fundamentals of effective management are at minimum competency, the addition of public recognition is a catalyst for exponential growth.** Public recognition helps a company's profitability and level of employee satisfaction rocket upwards, exponentially growing the overall effectiveness of the organization.

What does that public recognition look like? Gostick and Elton explain that managers need to be able to tell their employees *they did a good job*, and they need to do it in a way that best suits the personality of the individual. For instance, if an employee is hyper-introverted, you shouldn't call that person up in front of an entire company meeting to congratulate them for their good work. The discomfort experienced by that introverted employee at being the center of attention could be so intense, it might end up canceling out the message of appreciation. However, if you issue a message of appreciation in a way an introvert could appreciate— perhaps a sign of congratulations posted in the board room—that employee will experience gratifying public recognition.

Good managers need to learn their employees' "love languages"

---

38   Gostick, Adrian Robert., and Chester Elton. *The Carrot Principle: How the Best Managers Use Recognition to Engage Their People, Retain Talent, and Accelerate Performance.* London: Pocket, 2009.

(i.e., the method of communication through which an employee will best receive compliments and encouragement). Do they appreciate words of affirmation? Gifts? A day off? A public award? Do they like being the center of attention, or dread it? Getting to know your employees on a personal level will help you issue recognition in a way they'll appreciate.

It's also important that your recognition is *public* (i.e., made visible to the rest of your staff). This doesn't necessarily mean you call your introverted employee up in front of a room of a hundred people, but it does mean you need to publicize her accomplishments, and—even more importantly—*your appreciation.* **Your workplace community needs to be aware that you, as their leader, value them and recognize their good work.**

Public recognition will be more effective if it's *specific* rather than vague. Which of the following statements would you rather hear?

"Great job today!"

Or, "I was so impressed by how you spoke to that customer. You really showed that you cared about her questions, and I could tell that she left our meeting feeling great about our partnership. Thank you for your thoughtfulness and care for our people!"

If you hear a compliment from one of your clients about someone on your team, make a point to pass that on. These are great, spontaneous opportunities to affirm your employees with public recognition. Passing on affirmation doesn't have to be elaborate; the other day, when our employees Ben and Jeannie got a specific shout-out from a large client, we hollered out of our office door that we had an announcement. Then, as our team paused, we passed on the affirmation to Ben and Jeannie. The two of them appreciated it, and the rest of our team appreciated it too. When you take advantage of these moments, you'll help cultivate a culture where team members honor one another and recognize successes. That's a culture everyone likes to be in.

HIRING

Before we move on to discussing the "Things" side of running a business, there's one more crucial process on the "People" side that needs to be discussed—specifically, getting good people to work for you in the first place.

When it comes to people, you need to make sure you're finding the *right* person for the job—or at least, the right person for the job, at the moment. The people you have working for you will make or break your company. It's not technology or even a great product that will ultimately make your business succeed. No matter how great your technology is, you still won't get you very far without good customer service representatives to facilitate the customer's experience of the technology. Therefore, you'd better get the hiring part right.

There's a cost if you don't do this well, and the cost is turnover. Hiring well means you're stewarding the process of matching someone with a job that will suit their gifts, talents, and skills. When you hire the wrong person or set them up in a role that's a bad fit, it's not going to go well. Either the employee or the employer (or both) is going to be unhappy, and that's going to result in turnover.

Many people assume that turnover is primarily about bad management, but preventing turnover actually starts with hiring the right person and making sure you've got them in the right job.

We're guessing one of the most common reasons people leave companies is because the job they thought they were being hired for didn't turn out to be what they were asked to do; that's a sign that their job description wasn't effectively defined during the hiring process. You can't fight turnover if you ignore the first and most critical step in the process: hiring well.

"Turnover is an estimated $5 trillion annual drain on the US economy, making it the most significant cost to its economy and one of the most ignored economic factors in business history." —Adrian Robert Gostick and Chester Elton in *The Carrot Principle*[39]

Turnover is an epic problem, with epic implications. It is way less expensive to take the time to hire well and retain your employees, than it is to have to hire new people all the time.

Many companies struggle with the hiring process because they don't have a system. Maybe they don't have enough practice at hiring, or they don't know what qualities the employee really needs, or how to identify those qualities. However, hiring well can be learned. We've developed a process that has gotten us to a place where we've consistently been able to hire great people who are a great fit for our company.

If you're struggling with hiring great employees, you need to optimize your hiring process so that it is clear, complete, compelling, and can be replicated. Here's our system at a high level.

---

[39] Gostick, Adrian Robert., and Chester Elton. *The Carrot Principle: How the Best Managers Use Recognition to Engage Their People, Retain Talent, and Accelerate Performance.* New York, NY: Free Press, 2009.

KEEP CORE VALUES CENTRAL TO THE SEARCH

First: **hire, train, and fire to your Core Values.** If you haven't already completed the Vision creation activity outlined in chapter four, then make sure you do that exercise before you even think about hiring anyone new. Identifying your three to five Core Values is critical if you want to bring people into your company that will support your end goals. You're also more likely to attract great candidates. As we discussed in chapter four, it's far easier to attract people with Core Values than almost anything else, and you help ensure that your future employees will embrace your Core Values.

In an interview with a potential employee, discuss these Core Values. Ask if the candidate agrees with those values. Ask how they have lived them out in the last week or month. You can even ask the candidate how to define each Core Value; this will shed light on their thinking process and whether or not they'd align well with your company. Their answers will help clarify whether or not this person is going to be a good fit.

THE JOB DESCRIPTION

Secondly, write a clear **job description.** If you're going to hire someone for your company, you better know what you're hiring them for. Create a detailed written description before you ever put an ad anywhere for the job. You need to know the details for a compelling employment ad if you want to get great applicants. You also need to know what skills you need for the position.

Consider these questions as you're mapping out the job description:

- Is it an entry-level position?

- Does it require writing?
- Will there be any management of others?
- What's the basic job description?
- What skills are needed, and at what level?
- What tasks will they need to perform?
- What level of social interaction will they need to have?

After determining the answers to those questions and any others that might be relevant, write up a draft of the job description. Remember that any job has a certain level of competencies required, based on tasks the employee will have to perform. Every job will require some decision making, and relationships which will need to be built and maintained in a healthy way to be successful. So, what kind of person do you need?

Begin with the end in mind. Identify the specific job requirements, and then determine how you will assess the employee in the interview and on the job. If you know what the employee needs to do on the job and how you'll be assessing them, then you can determine in the interview whether or not they have the minimum competency required to do the tasks, or if they can be trained quickly.

THE JOB POSTING

Now, let's talk about the **job posting.** You want to attract great people to your company, so you're going to want to write a job listing like a commercial. We have a system we learned from Roy Williams at The Wizard Academy in Austin, Texas, that creates a long-format script which can go in an ad or on a video. Here are some recommended prompts of how to write up your job postings:

1. Write persuasively about the role that your new hire will play. Share why they will love the company and the culture. Help them envision their new potential job by describing a regular day at work.
2. Use second person in the description (speak directly to them, using the pronoun "you"): "Imagine yourself showing up on Monday morning, saying hello to your coworkers, grabbing a cup of coffee from the Keurig machine, and sitting down at your desk..." This second person voice feels immediate, relevant, and personal.
3. Describe how the job can help them achieve not only their salary goals, but also their dreams of significance and community.
4. Explain what a Passion & Provision job in a Passion & Provision company is all about. That's what you're building, right?

Then you put in *the secret sauce,* tucked in toward the end of the ad. It comes in two parts. First, tell candidates to write you a cover letter that they will submit with their resume through email. The cover letter should explain why they would want to work for your company and why they should get an interview. It's amazing how much you can learn about a candidate from this process.

Secondly, choose a secret code word and tell candidates to put it in the subject line of their email submission. The code word instruction isn't given until nearly the end of the long-format job ad. If you get an email submission without the code word, then you simply round file their application. If they don't care enough to read your entire job posting, you shouldn't have to read their application! You'd be amazed how many people won't read a long-form job description. That weeds people out very early on. For a sample of what this could look like, check out the resources link at the end of this chapter.

THE INTERVIEW PROCESS

When you receive submissions from candidates who have followed the directions successfully, you have cleared one big hurdle! Then, we recommend the following steps:

1. Do a phone interview first. If that goes well then;
2. Request writing samples. If their writing has the minimum competence required then;
3. Schedule your first "in-person" interview. If possible, do the interview with a small group of staff and a supervisor. If you have a small team, and they'll all likely be working with your new hire, it's important to ensure they're going to get along! If nobody can stand them, then the candidate doesn't make it to the next round. If they do make it, then;
4. Schedule final interview with the CEO or owner, and finally;
5. Choose the best candidate.

We have seen this process work over and over again. We didn't invent it; we learned it through mentors and then adapted and shaped it for our situation. Hiring well is one of the lynchpins for a Passion & Provision company. We have weeded out many applicants because they lacked either the competence or character to become the type of employee we needed to have in our Passion & Provision company. We've also successfully found candidates who help make our company awesome.

MANAGE LIKE A BOSS

Get your awesome people with your awesome hiring process. Then, manage those awesome people like a boss.

Provide clear goals. Communicate well. Develop a system for

accountability. Cultivate trust. And give public recognition to your team by telling them when they did a great job.

These five core pieces are at the heart of managing *everything*. Yes, they're strategies to manage people, but it's the people who are doing the tasks. As we move ahead into discussing operations, remember that all the operating systems that are often discussed in management operation books—resource allocation, supply chains, and so on—are done by your *people*. Care for them, and you'll have a massive head start on improving the smoothness, efficiency, and operations in the rest of your business.

OPERATIONS

In addition to Half a Bubble Out, the two of us also run a business called Rabbit Hole Hay (RHH), which sells high-quality hay to owners of small pet rodents. There's a long story behind how we fell into this—and no, it doesn't involve any personal ownership of small pet rodents—but that's not the story we want to tell right now. The story we want to tell right now is about stuffing hay into boxes.

In the early days of RHH, we struggled to turn a profit. Even though we were growing as a company, selling more products, and getting more customers, we were losing money on certain segments of our market. The biggest drain on our profitability seemed to be rooted in our labor costs, which made up 85 percent of the cost of goods for each sale. Simply put, the people putting the hay in the boxes were not putting the hay in the boxes fast enough. Somehow, we had to figure out a way to increase our efficiency.

At face value, packing hay in a box does not seem like something that would be a major time-suck. All that's required is to take an order, pull some hay off a bale, put it into one of six different-sized boxes based on the weight requested, and send it off. But guess what? It is possible to be laughably slow at packing hay—to the point that it would seriously compromise a company's profitability. Here's the good news, which we discovered after some experimentation: it is also possible to radically speed up the process of putting hay in a box.

When we got better at packing hay by addressing multiple steps in the packing process, we ended up *quadrupling* our efficiency in an hour. With a product that's so labor intensive, that changed our efficiency and our effectiveness at multiple levels. It also seriously increased our profitability!

Whatever you offer people as your product or service, you know that, "the devil is in the details." How you plan and manage the operational systems in your company will significantly determine how much Passion & Provision you have at the end of the month and year.

When you don't have good systems in place, both your people and your resources suffer. Imagine if we'd given a quota to our RHH employees to stuff one hundred boxes an hour, and they could only pack twenty. Their morale and motivation would plummet. However, good systems will empower your employees to succeed. In that way, management and operations are closely dependent on one another for success.

Whereas management involves the orchestration of people, you also need systems in place to orchestrate the assets and the resources which are required to create whatever product or service you have for the customer. Why do you need good orchestration of resources? So that customers can purchase your product and you can make a profit.

Here's a disclaimer: in order to really improve the operations of your business, you need to get specific about your very specific business. Are you dealing with a service or a product? Those two distinctions will require different operational approaches. Does your business operate in a hierarchal structure, divisional, flat, or matrix structure? Your operational improvements will need to be tailored to that particular structure. For example, there's no point in us giving you operations tips about dealing with international manufacturers in Asia if you're running a service-based company in the US.

For that reason, we're once again going to keep our discussion on Operations *high level*. We're going to provide you with two key areas of knowledge that will be universally relevant to business leaders: developing solid systems in Standard Operating Procedures and for troubleshooting. For further knowledge about operations tips that will work for your particular business, we recommend seeking out books that are tailored to your company's unique industry.

STANDARD OPERATING PROCEDURES

Operational systems can produce a beautiful form of autopilot. You develop a system, hone it, get it right, improve it—and then, let it chug, chug, chug along, revisiting the systems annually to ensure they're still running smoothly. Systems help you save time, save money, and avoid mistakes. They also make a company far more valuable when it comes time to sell it. These systems will help you be *efficient* in making your product and *effectively* delivering that product. Remember what efficiency and effectiveness add up to? *Elegance.* And who doesn't want to dress their company in an evening gown?

When you have elegant systems in place, you're able to spend less time down in the weeds and more time focusing on the high-horizon vision. That means you're more effective as a leader. You're able to make the right moves to grow. Likewise, your employees will be freed up to focus their energy on innovation, customer service, and doing their best work—rather than just getting their base-level tasks done.

If you want your employees to be consistent in the products or services your company offers, you need to create and document Standard Operating Procedures—what we fondly refer to as SOPs.

We use SOPs all over our lives, whether we realize it or not. For example, we are extremely particular about the quality of our morning coffee, so we taught our daughter, Jenna, to make coffee in a specific way:

1. Using the digital scale, weigh out 55 grams of whole bean Guatemalan coffee from delicious Cal Java coffee roastery down the street.
2. Grind in the burr grinder at a level eight grind.
3. Fill up the coffee pot with filtered water from the PUR water filter.
4. Fill the Mr. Coffee pot until the water is just below the over-flow holes.
5. Pour the freshly ground coffee in a brown, unbleached, flat-bottom coffee filter, and put it in the coffee pot.
6. Place the glass coffee pot on the coffee pot burner under the coffee-filter holder.
7. Close the lid over the grounds.

8. Turn on Mr. Coffee pot.
9. Wait until the coffee machine has finished brewing the entire pot and is no longer making any sounds.
10. Enjoy coffee.

That's how you build a system for making Guatemalan coffee in our home. It's the recipe that leads to a truly perfect cup of morning java. And in a sense, a recipe is exactly what you create with a well-crafted SOP.

When tasks in your business will be regularly repeated, develop your own SOP to maintain the ability to repeat tasks with similar quality and speed. SOPs also reduce the amount of time you need to train or micromanage the people in your organization. If you discover that your employees' quality doesn't match what is needed, then you can troubleshoot the process quickly. The SOP can streamline your problem-solving, enabling you to help people achieve their full potential in your organization.

In the early days of any company, systems are often created on the go and are usually transferred to other employees orally. If you think back to our coffee recipe metaphor, you can imagine that you're in the kitchen with Grandma while she shows you the family recipe for the perfect chocolate chip cookie. In a business, that usually looks like senior employees telling stories to newer employees about their best techniques, repeating the same instructions often. If someone forgets what comes next, they turn around and ask the expert. "Grandma, should I beat the eggs before adding them?" Or rather, "How soon should I follow up with the potential client?"

However, as time passes, those "family recipes" need to be written down. Why? Companies grow. Roles are passed from one person to another. People become busier, work farther apart, and often don't have any idea about how to do a task in a role different than their own. Grandma can't possibly instruct every single employee on every single next ingredient; systems need to be recorded so that people have the ability to independently reference what comes next.

Record your systems and make them easily accessible. In doing so, you'll ensure that everyone is doing the right things, in the right order, in the right amount of time.

TROUBLESHOOTING

When the two of us moved into our first home in Colorado, we attempted to take on some major home improvement projects. In chapter four, we already discussed the major issues that came up when we discovered two enormous cracks in our foundation—but that was only the beginning.

There were all kinds of projects we wanted to take on, and we gave ourselves a limited window to get them done; Kathryn was pregnant at the time, and we'd determined that everything needed to be finished by the time the baby arrived. That didn't entirely work out. In fact, Kathryn went into labor while she was trying to finish painting the kitchen.

In our minds, the projects seemed doable. We'd always set out with a clear idea of how we wanted the project to end up and how long they should take, but reality inevitably interfered. Problems showed up.

A lot of things got partially built, and then we'd realize that we would have to tear it apart because we'd built it completely wrong.

Sometimes we'd get to the end of the process, only to realize that the last part was supposed to go on first. The troubleshooting was maddening! We wasted time—and often resources. We both got used to Michael's repeated, "Uh-oh," said with the same quiet tone every time there was a new injury, a lost tool, or the realization that he'd built an entire wall four inches too tall and had to start over.

When you're leading a business, you might have a clear vision, great management, and good systems in place—but problems can still show up. Part of running your business with elegant efficiency means you're going to need a system to troubleshoot the inevitable problems that arise.

Many problems will be ironed out when you implement the operational systems and management techniques we've already discussed. However, even then, your company will likely run into issues that you could have never predicted. When that happens, what do you do?

You need to troubleshoot. And hopefully, you troubleshoot well.

Seven Questions to Troubleshoot Your Problem

We've experienced great success implementing a seven-question troubleshooting system that we learned from Robert F. Mager and Peter Pipe's excellent book, *Analyzing Performance Problems*.[40]

Let's say you need to troubleshoot a system in the office run by a few people who aren't hitting either the quantity or quality of results you had anticipated. Mager and Pipe recommend

---

40 Mager, Robert Frank, and Peter Pipe. *Analyzing Performance Problems: How to Figure Out Why People Aren't Doing What They Should Be, and What to Do about It*. Mumbai: Jaico Publishing House, 2004.

considering seven questions, which should be asked in a specific order. This system will help you uncover the rocks in your business's shoe that could be causing a problem with your people and daily operations:

1. **What's the problem?** The problem must be clearly identified and defined or you won't be able to ever solve it. Watch out that you don't misdiagnose the problem; in the medical world, that's called malpractice! In trying to correctly diagnose, consider these questions. One, whose performance is concerning you, and why? Two, what is the discrepancy between what you *want* to happen and what is *actually* happening? Once you can identify the problem adequately, then go to step two.

2. **Is it worth fixing?** Not all problems are worth solving. They will take too much time or energy, and they won't make any significant difference. If the problem truly *is* worth fixing, move on to step three.

3. **Can we apply a fast fix?** Not all problems are easily solved, but some are. If there is a fast fix, you can save your company a lot of wasted time and energy. Many people start solving a problem with a sophisticated overkill approach, or they'll use the only approach they have. If you need to dig a fence hole, you should use a shovel—you don't need to use dynamite and blow a giant hole in the ground. Look for fast fixes first, and if you can't find any, go to the next step. Consider these questions to determine whether or not a fast fix might work:
   A. Are expectations clear? If not, clarify them.
   B. Consider whether or not framing the situation in the SMART goals system could help resolve the issue. If so, SMART-ify the issue.
   C. Are the resources needed adequate for the job? If not, provide resources.
   D. Is it easy to recognize the performance quality you want?

Sometimes it's not easy to identify the quality level, so the people don't realize their work is below minimum quality levels. If this is the problem, provide feedback.

E. Is the problem sufficiently solved? If no, then go to the next step.

4. **Are the consequences appropriate?** If there are no fast fixes to the problem, then consider what might be happening with the consequences employees are experiencing. First, assess if you have consequences in place. If you do, are the consequences appropriate for the problem you're trying to solve? Are you unintentionally punishing good behavior or rewarding bad behavior? Here are a few ways consequences can go wrong, and create problems:

A. *The desired performance is punished.* Imagine that an employee does such a great job at a task, her manager piles on a bunch of other tasks as a "reward" and totally overwhelms her. The employee will be de-incentivized to perform well again, for fear of receiving even more work.

B. *Poor performance is rewarded.* Let's say a telemarketer has a hard quota of hitting thirty-dials-an-hour but isn't rewarded for sales. You might have a caller who closes 80 percent of his calls, but only makes ten calls an hour—he gets punished. Another employee might consistently make his thirty dials an hour quota, but only closes 2 percent of his calls—and he gets praised. You can see how that would create problems! Ineffective employees would get promoted beyond their competency, and the successful employees would change their habits to become less effective, just to ensure they kept their jobs.

C. *There are no consequences in place at all.* Sometimes things don't get done because it doesn't seem to make any difference one way or another. If the employee sees zero consequences whether they do the work or not, then this is something to solve. Bottom line, this step in solving the performance gap is about making the task matter. Clear expectations with clear consequences mean employees can take pride in a job well done, and that there is an undesirable consequence if the job doesn't get done.

5. **Does the person know how to do the job?** You need to determine if the people involved in the problem may simply lack the skills to do what you're asking of them. Find out first if the employee has the skill to do the job or not. Have they ever performed this skill in the past, at the quality you want? If so, was it a one-time thing, or could they consistently achieve that level? It's possible your employee simply needs a dose of good feedback on what's missing in their performance now, or they need some supervised practice to get up to speed. However, if there's a genuine skill deficiency, go to the next step.

6. **Are there more clues?** Check under all the big rocks to see if you missed any possible solutions, short of fully training your employee from the ground up. Consider: can the task be made simpler? Are there any obstacles you can remove? For example, in one manufacturing environment, the system was set up in a way that made the machine operator move the product off the machine, then go to another room to put the product in a box. Because of the distance, they had to slow the machine down. Everyone had missed that there was no good reason to keep the boxes in the other room, so when they moved the boxes next to the machine, production levels grew significantly. By looking for clues, a clear solution was found. If the issue is with an employee, consider: does the employee have the potential to change, or do they simply lack the personality/ability to improve in the way that's needed for this role? You may need to determine you simply need to replace this employee. However, if they can change, go to the last step.

7. **Apply training:** This step is listed as your last resort, because

it's the most expensive. If you're thinking about training, consider what type of training is going to get you the most bang for your buck. Calculate the cost of training against the return on investment. Select the best training solution(s), draft an action plan for the training, and then implement it. Once the training is complete, monitor your employee's progress and give encouragement or feedback as needed.

To some, this process can seem overwhelming. Others may view it as overly simple. Either of those positions can cause you to miss the power of this system to radically increase the profitability of your company. In our experience, this troubleshooting system has radically decreased the level of problems we've had. It's also helped us increase our productivity and avoid unnecessary challenges.

LET'S REVIEW

Here is a fact that just about every business leader can agree with: at the end of the day, *you've got to get stuff done*. After forming your high-level Vision, and dealing with your big picture Leadership, it's time to consider how you can most effectively get the tasks of your business done.

This chapter aimed to spell out ways to improve the efficiency and effectiveness of your company's management and day-to-day operations. We identified the five fundamental areas of management: clear goals, good communication, accountability, trust, and public recognition. We also provided a system to help you hire great people that will be a good fit for your company. We discussed the value of Standard Operating Procedures to improve the efficiency and efficacy of your business. We also recommended an effective system for troubleshooting unexpected problems.

When you combine Vision with strong Leadership, and then marry the combination to effective management and operations, your business will be more than halfway to providing you and all your staff with both Passion & Provision. Take a page from Bill Walsh's playbook: the change may not be instantaneous. It may not look pretty. There may be moments when you throw up your hands and say, "I don't know if this is going to work."

But if you can push through and hold fast to what you believe in— if you value community, dignity, competency, and the elegance of combined effectiveness and efficiency—if you're willing to do the work to transform your team—then the results are going to be a stadium's worth of fans, roaring their approval.

TIME TO UP YOUR GAME WITH PEOPLE AND TASKS

- Go to **fulfilledthebook.com** to download resources to assess and strengthen your management skills.
- How would you rate yourself on the five fundamental areas of management?
- How would your employees rate you and are you brave enough to ask them?
- What will you do to adjust your hiring process moving forward?
- What are two or three things in your business that can be organized and documented into repeatable systems?

CHAPTER SEVEN

||||||||||||||||||||

Marketing and Sales

"Marketing is not a function. It is the whole business, seen from the customer's point of view."

PETER DRUCKER

Not long ago, the two of us were driving down a freeway in Southern California when we suddenly spotted a humongous billboard. The billboard featured a Big Mac; in the corner was the instantly recognizable McDonald's logo. But the Big Mac wasn't what got us. What got us was the script printed underneath: "'Two all-beef patties...' You know the rest."

The line transported both of us back to childhood, when we first saw the McDonald's commercial on TV with the jingle that began "Two all-beef patties…" Decades later, we could recall the jingle instantly: *Two all-beef patties, special sauce, lettuce, cheese, pickles, onions on a sesame seed bun.* As it turned out, we *did* know the rest.

We looked at each other and started talking about the brilliance of that marketing technique. McDonald's had so successfully branded a jingle that they could put a fragment from the song on a billboard and immediately cause anyone who already knew the song to *identify* themselves with the brand. The two of us had felt an instant sense of pride for recalling the entire jingle, which means that McDonald's had triggered a proud, happy, nostalgic moment associated with their product. It cracked us up. It delighted our souls.

That's great marketing. So how do you do it?

WHY YOU NEED GOOD MARKETING AND SALES

In order to make a profitable company, you need people to buy your stuff. You want *new* people to buy your stuff, and you want *returning* customers to come back again and again, to buy more and more stuff. You want them to rave about your product or service to their friends, so that more people buy more of your stuff. Your main vehicle to accomplish all of that is successful marketing.

In order to successfully market your product, you need to do several key things. You need to get people to *notice* you, *like* you, *engage* with you, *spend their money* with you, and then decide they want to spend *more* money with you. Ultimately, you want to turn strangers into raving-fan customers who promote your brand, believing that your product or service solved their problems and made them the hero in their own story. Your marketing and sales experience should provide your customers with the narrative to take that journey. In this chapter, we're going to teach you how to construct that narrative.

The average person thinks that marketing is only about finding a stranger and getting them to purchase for the first time—but that's only the beginning. Marketing and sales involve managing the *relationship* between your company and the customer all the way through their buying-experience, including the windows before and after they buy your product or service. From a customer's perspective, every interaction they have with your company from the minute they discover you exist, through the sales process and on to their experience with your delivery of the product—that's all marketing. *Every* part of your company and your process impacts your overall marketing. We regularly have to remind our clients that every person on their team is in marketing.

Marketing and sales involve managing the *relationship* between your company and the customer all the way through their buying experience.

In that way, the initial *sale* is only one piece of a much longer marketing process—and ideally, by the time you get to that moment, there's no pushiness involved. Salespeople are notoriously viewed as untrustworthy characters who don't have the customer's best interests in mind—but in a Passion & Provision company, you *do* have the customer's best interests in mind.

Here is how we want you to think about sales. Your goal is to find people who need your product or service, find out if your product or service is a good fit for them, and— if it *is* a good fit—educate them in a way that helps them see the value of what you're offering. Then, you take the order!

If you have a service mindset and your goal is to connect people who need your product or service with what you offer, then you aren't pushing anything on them; you are helping them fulfill a need. Rather than come across as untrustworthy, you're actually establishing yourself as someone they *can* trust, someone who is genuinely trying to meet their needs.

You need a plan and structure that allows you to manage this relationship between customer and company in a healthy way, making sure that nothing falls between the cracks. If you *don't* have a process that effectively transforms strangers into raving-fan promoters, then you waste money and miss out on your best opportunity to thrive as a profitable business.

We have been doing Marketing for seventeen years, and when we sat down to write this chapter, we came up with enough material for an entire book on the subject. However, for the purposes of helping you as a leader build a Passion & Provision company, our goal in this one chapter is not to teach you how to do your marketing, but rather how to *think* about marketing.

We want to provide you with some fundamental principles to help you understand your customer and provide you with a framework for thinking about your marketing strategies. Some of our readers are probably doing their marketing internally; if that's you, then we'll give you some core ideas about ways you can be more effective in your marketing. Other readers might plan to hire a marketing person for their staff or hire an outside marketing firm like ours to work with. If that sounds more like you, then this chapter will make you a better marketing leader—and smarter client—which will make you a more sophisticated partner in the process. We'll also recommend further resources where you can go to learn more.

BASIC FEATURES OF THE MARKETING LANDSCAPE

Before we get into specific marketing structures, let's first get the lay of the land. Here are a few basic facts to keep in mind when approaching your marketing strategy.

THREE WAYS TO MAKE MONEY

There are three basic ways you can make more money as a company:

1. You get more new customers.
2. You get customers to purchase more in a single visit.
3. You get customers to come back and purchase multiple times.

Got it? Great, moving on.

RELATIONAL OR TRANSACTIONAL BUYERS

When people spend their money with you or any other vendor, they're going to purchase in one of two ways: transactional or relational.

Transactional buyers only care about the price. No matter what you do on behalf of your customer, a transactional buyer will switch to another company if someone can beat your price. If what you sell is a commodity (i.e., lots of companies sell what you're selling and there aren't many differences between your products), this will be a challenge for you. Price is a powerful buying motivator, but it's hard to beat competitors if you're relying on just price alone.

Relational buyers purchase from you because they like your product and they like you. Relational buyers are still looking to buy what they need, but they prefer to buy from someone they like. If you can provide something these buyers need, in a price range they can afford, and you make them like you, they'll choose your business every time. If they *really like* you, they'll even be willing to pay a little more and go out of their way to buy from you.

If you want a Passion & Provision company, it's far easier if you have a customer base made up of primarily relational customers. You want customers who buy from you because they're drawn to your brand and message. Knowing your Core Purpose and Values allows you to start creating messaging to attract these kinds of customers, people who align with your company and brand. Some marketers refer to these kinds of values-aligned customers as your *tribe*. Your message will draw them in.

Your message will flow out of your brand—but what is a brand?

BRAND VERSUS BRANDING

There is a lot of confusion around the concepts of brand and branding. Many people think your brand is simply your logo. That makes sense in some ways because the concept comes from the branding of cattle. Your brand on the hindquarters of a cow told everyone what ranch this cow belonged to.

We would argue, however, that while your logo may help people identify your brand, your **brand is actually your reputation.** The rancher with a specific cattle brand had a reputation, and that "brand" on the cow's behind went beyond identifying the owner when it was lost or stolen. Cattle thieves might think twice before stealing a steer from the cousin of Wild Bill Hickock, for instance. The brand triggered certain thoughts and emotions associated in a person's mind with that rancher, good or bad. That's how it works with modern-day marketing too. More than a logo, your brand is what your customers or potential customers think about who you are as a company. What do you stand for? How do you show up in the market space you are in?

If your brand is your reputation, then **branding equals *bonding*.** Branding is about getting people connected to you. That McDonald's billboard that instantly captivated the two of us with its jingle reference was brilliant branding. Although we hardly ever darken the doors of a McDonald's these days, the most powerful aspect of that marketing strategy was that it made us feel *reconnected* to the McDonald's brand, and remember how we used to enjoy eating there. Likewise, in your marketing approach, your goal should be to *bond* with your customer.

Your brand is your reputation. Branding equals bonding.

The more you bond with your customer, the more you build trust. The more shared trust between you and your customer, the more likely they are to choose to spend their money with you, in greater amounts and more frequently. That's a good thing!

THE MARKETING ARC

There's a journey that you will take on the road to market well, and we're going to call that the Marketing Arc. This arc helps you *think* about marketing well, helps you *know* your customer well, and helps you *communicate* to your customer well. Here's how it looks:

1. You first need to get a **framework** in place of how you're going to approach your creative marketing and messaging.
2. You need to **know your customer** by learning about their needs and figuring out how to speak their language.
3. Once you learn about your customer, you need to **be compelling with your message** so that it resonates.
4. Finally, you need to **get your message out** to your customer.

We're going to educate you about how to be effective at each stage in this process.

THE FRAMEWORK: HAVING THE RIGHT APPROACH

First, understand that your marketing efforts should aim to help customers bond with you. How do you do that? You *woo* them. We're going to explain how to get your customer to notice you, flirt with you, go on a first date, agree to wear your ring, and finally, toss their wedding bouquet in the air after smooching you at the altar—figuratively speaking, that is.

We credit Ryan Deiss of DigitalMarketer for coming up with this Eight-Stage Customer Value Journey.[41] DigitalMarketer is one of the world's largest and most respected educators for marketers

---

41 The Customer Value Journey is the copyright of DigitalMarketer. Used with permission.

today.[42] The Eight-Stage Customer Value Journey model walks business leaders through the process of taking a stranger from an initial introduction to your company, to converting them into a raving-fan promoter that tells other people about you.

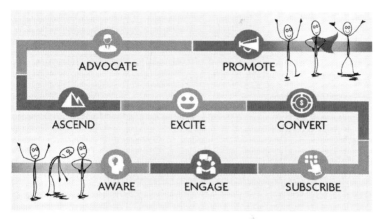

Deiss's model is built on the way healthy human relationships naturally develop, based on the work of Desmond Morris in his book, *Intimate Behavior*.[43] Morris was a zoologist who applied his studies to mapping out the progression of intimacy in "the human animal." What he came up with were twelve Steps to Intimacy which progress from an initial encounter, through various stages of physical contact, and—in the final steps—all the way to

---

42 DigitalMarketer's training material is used to train marketing departments like Uber and Harper Collins as well as smaller companies globally. As our company grew, we looked for the best places to learn from on the latest and best practices in an ever-changing world, so we could better serve our clients and train our staff. Ryan Deiss and DigitalMarketer was one of the best resources we found. Several years ago we joined their Partner program for agencies and we became one of their few Platinum partners as well as a certified trainer.

43 Morris, Desmond. *Intimate Behavior*. New York: Bantam Books, 1973.

"hubba hubba" in the bedroom.[44] Deiss's Eight-Stage Customer Value Journey mirrors the first eight Steps to Intimacy. Steps nine through twelve—where we start getting into the R-rated stuff—are, well...beyond the scope of this book.

As we talk through these steps, we're also going to build a romance between two fictional people—we'll name them Kevin and Jane. Kevin and Jane will represent the progressing closeness you want to model as a company while pursuing a customer. For the sake of clarity and all the rom-com feels, we'll say Kevin is the one pursuing Jane (i.e., he's the business and she's the potential customer).

Step One: Aware. The customer prospect becomes aware of you for the first time. Maybe they spot your ad or find you in a search. Maybe they hear your name through a friend's referral. In our fictional romance, maybe Kevin spots Jane across a cafe and catches her eye when she glances up. He holds her gaze for a second and smiles: now she's aware of him.

Step Two: Engage. You engage the customer somehow. You might get them to respond to a post on your company's social media page. Maybe they read your blog post or watch your video. You develop content that will interest them, appeal to them, and hopefully encourage them to engage with you. This is the point when Kevin walks up to Jane and says, "Hey! Did I spot a rock-climbing sticker on your laptop? Where do you like to climb?" Jane perks up and starts chatting back.

Step Three: Subscribe. The next step involves getting your

---

44 Giannotti, Paul. "Get More Customers: Zoologist Unlocks the Primeval Pathway to Intimacy (and Sales)." Content First. Accessed December 13, 2019. https://www.contentfirst.com.au/blog/get-more-customers-zoologist-unlocks-the-primeval-pathway-for-intimacy-sales.

potential customer's contact information and encouraging them to subscribe to your company's content. They choose to opt in to receive gated content, like a subscribers-only training or a special giveaway. This is the moment when Kevin asks, "Can I have your number?" and Jane willingly gives him her information. When he calls or texts later, she responds.

Step Four: Convert. Now, you get the opportunity to either sell your potential customer a low-priced product or service so they can test it out. In other words, you *convert* them from a bystander into a customer. In a service-based company, you might offer a free trial or consultation. In a product-based company, you might offer a demo or a product sample.

This is when Kevin takes Jane out to coffee. It's nothing big—just coffee—but it gives Jane a chance to think about whether or not she might want a longer date with him. Ideally, Kevin nails the coffee date with Jane and she goes home feeling giddy about how awesome this new guy is. If that's the case, then Kevin can move on to Step Five, the Excite stage. We'll explain more about that in a second.

But let's say Kevin's coffee date with Jane didn't go all that well. He asks her for a second date, and Jane gives him a line about wanting to "just be friends." In that case, Kevin is going to have to go back to Step Two: Engage—and the same is true for you as a business leader. If you can't successfully convert someone into a customer in Step Four, you need to go back to the Engage stage.

What does that look like for Kevin? He's got to keep Jane talking with him, in the hopes that she'll eventually change her mind and agree to a dinner date. He'll do his best to keep Jane engaging with him through his witty banter, fun social outings, and outgoing personality. What does that look like for you? You might continue to pursue that customer with clever marketing, engaging videos, and great social media outreach.

Once Jane decides she actually *does* want to have dinner with Kevin, and once your potential customer converts to an *actual* customer, then it's time to move ahead to Step Five.

Step Five: Excite. Now that your customer has purchased your product, you want to capitalize on that moment and make sure they're *excited* about the transaction. Maybe they made a small, tiny purchase: you offered them a sample size at 90 percent off, just to get them to try out your product. They took the deal in the Convert stage, tried your product—and loved it. They're sold. Now they want the full-size version.

The moment between Steps Four and Five is key. You want your customers to have a positive, exciting experience that makes them feel assured they got a good value for whatever time or money they gave you. That's how you're building trust. When you keep your word and give the customer what they were looking for, they're going to be willing to take the relationship a bit further: "I liked that. And I like you, so tell me about what your main product is."

Think of this in Costco terms. Imagine that you, a customer, are wandering those wide warehouse aisles, and at the end of every row are those delicious samples. Costco manages to convert thousands of customers every day using those samples; every time someone tastes a morsel on the end of a Costco aisle, they've successfully completed Step Four. They stop; they give a little bit of time and energy to consider the product; then they evaluate the core offer. Every time one of those samplers says, "Oh gosh, YES, where's the box?"—that's when they complete Step Five.

Step Five for our blossoming romance means that Jane concludes Kevin has a lot to offer and decides she *would* like to have that dinner date after all. The two of them are building a rapport of trust and she's willing to invest more of her time and energy into the relationship. Why? She's excited about him!

Step Six: Ascend. Step Six is when the relationship unfolds, develops, and deepens. Your customer purchases your core offer; perhaps they even agree to an upsell, adding on additional consulting services or featured products. Over time, they come back to you and purchase more; they agree to additional upsells. Each time they do business with you and feel satisfied with the value they get, the trust shared between company and consumer grows. Soon, the customer is seeking you out for other products and services, confident that they're going to have a good customer experience with whatever you offer.

On the human level, this is the stage in Kevin and Jane's relationship where they start getting serious about their commitment. They spend lots of time together and deepen their trust. Jane isn't just on the receiving end of Kevin's wooing anymore; she's ready to invest in their relationship—often, and in increasing measures. They discover new things about one another that they like, and find excuses to spend time together.

When your customer starts to buy more, and buy more often, they start naturally moving into Step Seven—which, for you, is a great thing.

Step Seven: Advocate. In Step Seven, your customer becomes an advocate. An advocate is a happy customer. They consistently have positive experiences in doing business with you. If you were to ask these customers to provide you with a testimonial or client survey, they would agree. If someone else asked them for their opinion about your business, they'd say great things. However, they're not quite at the point yet where they're taking the initiative to proactively go out and promote your business to other people.

In your own marketing efforts, this is the stage that we recommend aiming for. You want to try to do everything possible to ensure you're creating these happy customers. Perhaps you onboard the customer by offering personal help or attention to ensure their questions are answered. Do they know how the product works? Have they taken advantage of every part of the service? Are they fully acquainted with all the benefits? Hold their hand during the buying experience and make sure they feel important.

Other tools, like email marketing, communication loops, social media, and so on can help you not only stay in contact with your customers, but also make sure that their experience with you is consistently positive.

Back to Kevin and Jane. When Kevin says, "I love you," Jane happily says, "I love you too." When other guys pursue Jane, she tells them she's already committed to someone else—that's her, advocating for Kevin. The two of them start planning their future together, and Jane decides there's no better person out there for her.

The company that *doesn't* prioritize Step Seven sells their product or service without any further effort to communicate further with the customer. They don't bother trying to build a relationship with their customers; they simply thank them for their purchase and let them walk out the door. These customers might feel that they got what they paid for, but they're not going to feel any interest in coming back. Companies who neglect Step Seven are missing a huge opportunity to capitalize on their original investment. However, companies that *invest* in Step Seven are about to enjoy an exponential burst in marketing as their customers transition to Step Eight.

Step Eight: Promote. When customers reach Step Eight, they do your marketing for you as promoters. They are so excited about your product or service that they feel compelled to rave about you to anyone who will listen. They post about you on their social media accounts. They recommend you to their family and friends. They post online reviews, raving about your business.

In this stage, Jane gushes to anyone who will listen about the person who's made her fall head over heels. Cue the violins! (This is where the analogy breaks down. You obviously want more customers who will convince other potential customers to buy your product—but Jane does not want any other women to date or marry Kevin!)

These eight steps provide a process for nurturing the relationship with your customer, one step at a time. Here's an important tip: **don't skip steps.** You may be able to get away with skipping one step every so often, but if you skip two steps in that eight-step process, that's considered assault. If Kevin had asked Jane to marry him on that first coffee date, he'd probably send her running for the hills. Likewise, if you try to move the customer along without taking the time to build their trust, you're going to ruin their customer experience. They'll feel pushed and manipulated.

Now that's the framework so, don't blow it. Take the time to woo them. Stick to the plan and play the long game. In the end, your company will be more successful.

KNOW YOUR CUSTOMER

In order to collect your tribe of devoted followers, you're going to need to research your customers, learn the way they think, understand their pain points, and determine the problems they're trying to solve. Once you know all that, you can position yourself to help those customers be successful. You create the message that draws people in, and then build a tribe of customers by continuing to articulate who you are and what you do. So how do you get to know your customers? Use two valuable tools. First, you complete some effective Market Research. Then, you use all that information to build your customer avatar, so that you can genuinely get in the head of your target customer. Then, set up a cycle that lets you continue to understand your customer and update your customer avatar. Wash, Rinse, Repeat.

Market Research

When we started our second business, Rabbit Hole Hay, we began learning that there are a ton of city-dwelling people who own pet rabbits. Every one of them needed nutritionally rich food to keep their rabbits healthy, and the best kind of food happens to be hay. Even more, we learned that the best kind of hay for these bunnies was Timothy Hay, and really good, fresh, Timothy Hay was hard to come by, especially in the big city. Western Timothy Hay grows only in the part of the world we happen to live in—so what if we boxed it up and shipped it to their doorstep? It was a niche we'd never thought about. We'd learned about a specific group of people that had a specific need—and a business was born.

From there we learned everything we could about their problems. We learned about the customer, the rabbits, and the different needs associated with different breeds. We then found out how to get Timothy hay, box the hay, and ship the hay. (For the record, this sounds way easier than it was.) On a very basic level—that's market research: it's everything to do with the market surrounding your customer and product/service.

Market research is important for any business—but it can also feel like a great big pain. Market research reports can be hard to get, extremely expensive, and rarely is the data easy to translate into useful action.

Still—can anyone really afford to build a Marketing campaign with *no* market research?

For most of our careers, we've had to be scrappy to gather effective research for our clients which they could afford and which could be put to practical use. We searched high and low for the best technique that would get us actionable, practical, useful market research, which could translate into compelling messaging for ready-to-buy customers. We think we finally found that technique from our friend Ryan Levesque as he writes about in his brilliant book, *Ask*.[45]

Levesque's Ask Method® is the closest thing we've found to a "silver bullet" in gaining the kind of market research that can transform your approach with customers. The method aligns with our values and integrity, and we liked it so much, we became one of the few certified partner agencies in the world. We use this method all the time with our clients.

We recommend you get Levesque's book for yourself to fully

---

45   Levesque, Ryan. *Ask: the Counterintuitive Online Method to Discover Exactly What Your Customers Want to...Buy...Create a Mass of Raving Fans...and Take Any Business to the Next Level.* Place of publication not identified: Dunham Group, 2015. ASK Method® and Deep Dive Survey® are Registered Trademarks of Ryan Levesque and HB Media LLC.

learn the method. However, here is a simple "nutshell" version of what Levesque describes as the DDS or "Deep Dive Survey®," as part of the Ask Method®. This survey method will enable you to gather useful data and convert it into powerful messaging that cuts through the noise of distractions, capturing the attention of ready-to-buy customers. Here's how.

1. You **choose your customer group** you want to serve. Figure out the "who" even before you figure out the "what." In our experience, it's far easier to come up with a product if you can figure out the "who" you're going to serve first.
2. You decide what **specific product** or **service question** you want to ask them about.
3. Now, **you need to find out about their biggest problems** in relation to that product or service, so that you're equipped to frame the heroic narrative we discussed earlier.
4. You don't overload the customer group with questions; you **ask them *the single most important question*.** This "single question" component is key. Most people assume customer surveys should ask lots of questions, but that actually detracts from getting actionable results. If you do it our way, then you can probably go back at a later date and ask them more, but not yet. Start with asking the single most important question.
5. The question goes something like this: **"When it comes to [fill in the blank] what is your biggest challenge, frustration, or concern?"** Ask the customer to be as detailed as possible. Make the answer a free form, not a drop-down list of choices. You want to collect their actual words about their concerns. For example:
   A. In Rabbit Hole Hay we asked, "When it comes to buying hay for your pet rabbit, what is your biggest challenge, frustration, or concern?"
   B. For a property management company who helps Home-

owner Association Boards we asked: "When it comes to being a board member for your HOA, what is your single biggest challenge, frustration, or concern?"

6. **Use an online survey** and send the link out through emails, online ads, or maybe on a social media platform, like Facebook. You need 250 responses to be statistically valid, and you can use people on your email list if you have one. Get these responses however you can, as long as the people responding actually want or need your product or service. If you can't get 250, then you can do what we call a "Lean DDS" where you want to interview ten people and ask them the question. Record the answers and have them transcribed. You'll get better and more accurate data from a survey of 250, but a Lean DDS is still a solid start.

7. Once you have the completed surveys, **look for interesting quotes and themes.** Combine them into no more than three to five themes. Those themes become the different ways you can market or talk about your product. They become the angles you use to create various forms of content as you approach people.

8. **You're going to use the quotes from the answers as the exact language in your ad copy.** When someone says, "I hate icky moldy hay," we say in our ad copy, "Do you hate icky moldy hay? Then you'll love our hay: it's dry and mold-free." This technique is like a marketing version of "active listening," and its effect is golden. People get the impression that you've read their mind; they'll see that you understand their true needs and desires when it comes to buying your product. WARNING: Don't be fooled by how simple this is. So few people actually listen to their customers that this is almost as effective as a Jedi Mind Trick. We're going to talk more about effective copywriting in a minute.

Consultants like us get paid well to do this for our clients, but you can do this. Start the process, learn, and repeat. You'll steadily improve, and as you stick with it, you'll get solid, actionable market research that will help you grow your company and make more customers.

Before and After Grid: Customer Avatar

Now, you start *applying* the information you learned in your market research. In order to effectively talk to your customers, you need to think like your customers. You need to understand their pain points and recognize how your product or service meets their needs.

A key step in documenting how to speak to those true customer needs is called avatar development, also known as *persona development*. An avatar is a fictional representation of one of your customers that forces you to think through what they actually experience and how your product or service can solve a challenge they face.

The customer avatar is going to build on much of what you discovered when doing the DDS, helping you translate that information into a way that speaks to a person's needs, emotions, and context. The avatar works to remind you how your customer thinks and provides an easy way to communicate this information to your other copywriters. The customer avatar also allows you to ask some good questions from specific customer perspectives; many of the answers will come, once again, from the DDS.

To develop your customer avatar, we use a worksheet called the

"Before and After Grid," once again created by our friend Ryan Deiss, over at DigitalMarketer. When we started implementing this avatar development, we were blown away by the increase in sales we noticed from our new Marketing work. It's a simple tool but incredibly effective.

The Before and After Grid[46] has four main categories:

1. Before
2. After
3. Customer Segments
4. Products/Services

BEFORE & AFTER GRID

BEFORE	CUSTOMER SEGMENTS	AFTER
HAVE:		HAVE:
FEEL:		FEEL:
AVERAGE DAY:	PRODUCTS/SERVICES	AVERAGE DAY:
STATUS:		STATUS:
GOOD VS. EVIL:		GOOD VS. EVIL:

Let's start with the **Before** box. Imagine that Jane and Kevin are now engaged and Jane is looking for a wedding photographer. This box helps you to think about the situation that customers like

---

46 The Customer Value Journey and Before & After Grid is the copyright of DigitalMarketer. Used with permission.

Jane might be in *before* they have your product or service. Deiss's graphic prompts you to brainstorm five aspects of the customer's situation so that you effectively paint the whole picture. As you fill in each section of the Before and After boxes, write in first person (use "I," "me," "my" pronouns) so that you're pushing yourself to actively think like your customer avatar.

We're going to provide a couple of examples of how you might respond to each prompt; the first example (a) is what we've come up with for potential Half a Bubble Out customers, who are looking for marketing or business consulting help. The examples listed second (b) are our ideas of what Jane might come up with as she and Kevin look for a wedding photographer.

- **Have:** This is where you identify and talk about what the customer *doesn't* have but wants, or what they *have* and want to get rid of.
    - "I don't have enough customers and I want more but I don't have a big budget for marketing."
    - "I don't have a wedding photographer, and I need a photographer—one who will beautifully capture the happiest day of my life."
- **Feel:** This is where you identify how the customer feels. Emotions in the Before state often revolve around frustration, desire, or longing.
    - "I feel like I'm hitting a wall when it comes to lead generation and failure drives me crazy."
    - "I'm overwhelmed by the number of photographers out there and I've heard horror stories from friends who ended up with terrible wedding photos."
- **Average Day:** Your customer has an average day without what they want. If you can articulate to them what that typical day looks like, they'll feel understood and trust your

input. They'll also be more conscious of what they want and what is missing.

- ◦ "What we are doing isn't working as well as I'd hoped."
- ◦ "Every day that I don't have a photographer booked, I feel more and more stress that I'm not going to end up having a good one."

- **Status:** Respect and status are significant motivators of human behavior, but these desires are more subtle than some of the glaring facts in the other categories. In your Marketing, you're going to identify the customer's desire for status and then reflect it back.
  - ◦ "I am nervous that if I can't make this work, my company will fail. What will that say to my friends and peers?"
  - ◦ "My mom is obsessed with the idea that I need a top photographer and I'm sensing she doesn't trust that I can handle it."

- **Good vs. Evil:** Every problem has a cause. That cause can be personified as something evil, which stops the customer from getting what they need. If you can articulate the true battle, then you harness one of the oldest, most innate, and most compelling narratives we seek out as humans. Using this "good and evil" narrative will put you ahead of the competition, because most people don't even recognize the battle exists. When you describe this battle and get it right, it powerfully resonates with customers. For example:
  - ◦ The evil online ad companies are complicated and seem to favor big budgets, which keeps us from being seen by our prospective customers.
  - ◦ The photography industry is filled with amateurs who will charge an arm and a leg, but end up taking terrible pictures.

Once you've completed this brainstorming for your customer

avatar in the **Before** box, you move to the **After** box. Now, you're going to draft ideas about what your customer's situation is like *after* they have your product or service. How has their story changed? How has their status increased? How much better do they feel? Here's the easy answer: after your customer gets ahold of your product or service, they are ecstatic and victorious! Your solution was amazing and it's transformed your customer into the hero of their story.

In Jane's case, the **After** might look like this: she now **has** an amazing photographer. She **feels** confident and excited about her wedding day. Her new **average day** is less stressful, because she was able to check off a major part of her wedding plans. Her **status** has increased with her mom, because she's shown that she can book a great photographer and her friends are also super impressed. She's **conquered the evil industry** by cutting through all the marketing clutter and finding her amazing photographer!

And what are the other two boxes about? **Customer Segments** helps you note the different types of customers. For us at HaBO Village reaching out to business leaders, we would fill out at least three of these grids. One customer avatar grid would be filled out for entrepreneurs who want to start a company. We'd fill out a second grid for leaders of young companies, and a third for leaders of established companies. Each one of those Customer Segment groups has a different Before state, which means we need to tailor our marketing message approach differently for each. However, all of them want a similar "After" state: a successful Passion & Provision company.

The last part of the grid fills in what particular **product or service** we are selling to the target customer of the grid. Different types of customers may need different products; for instance, the entrepreneur we're looking to help might have very different needs than a leader of an established company. In this box, you identify which of your services or products is going to be the best fit for each Before customer.

When you identify all of these components and fully describe the Before state and After state, your language to the customer will be transformed. Rather than making guesses about what your customers want to hear, you can truly help them find their way to success—to being the hero in their own story. When you successfully do that, they will see you as their trusted guide and become your biggest fan.

BE COMPELLING

Let's do a quick recap. First, you're going to **approach your customer** like you would in a dating experience. Your goal is to help the customer to bond with you, trust you, and commit their loyalty and, yes, even their undying love to you. You want to inspire them to gush about how dreamy you are to all their friends. That's how we want you to *think* about marketing.

Then, you're going to get to **know your customer** so that you can set about this wooing process in a way that will appeal to them. You're going to do market research, create your customer avatar, and learn how to speak effectively to their needs.

Now, let's cover some helpful tools you can use to implement the romance. Casanova may have used roses and mood music; your tools are going to look more like powerful storytelling, strong market research, good copywriting, and frequency and reach.

Story and Messaging

Feel free to commit the next three lines to memory:

- Your customer is the hero.
- Their problems are the villains.
- You are their guide to help them defeat the villains.

Let's face it: you're not going to attract anyone to listen to your Marketing efforts if you don't have good messaging. If you bore people out of their skulls with your ad copy, you're not going to be successful at selling whatever it is you're trying to sell. On the other hand, if your messaging reveals something about who you are and what you value—that's going to be a message that resonates.

And who are you? You're someone who wants to serve the customer. You have a service or product that you created to solve real problems for real people.

Now, how do you communicate that message in a compelling, not-boring-people-out-of-their-skulls kind of way? As Donald Miller has reminded us so eloquently in his book, *Building a Storybrand*, you can boost the drama by harnessing one of the oldest, most effective forms of communication ever to exist: you tell a story.[47]

In this story, the customer is the protagonist. That means they're the hero. Your message is customer focused, spoken directly to them, acknowledging that they are the main character in this life story. The customer, as this story begins, is sad. They have a problem, and it's getting them down. Let's call your customer

---

47   Miller, Donald. *Building a Storybrand: Clarify Your Message so Customers Will Listen*. New York, NY: Thomas Nelson Pub, 2017.

Gerald. Gerald is grumpy and smelly. In fact, his whole family is grumpy and smelly. Gerald wants to feel like the hero in his story, but right now, he just feels like a shlump. Imagine Gerald with a big frowny face.

The customer's problem—whatever it is—is the villain in this story. In Gerald's case, he has a broken washing machine. No wonder everyone is so grumpy and smelly. Gerald wants to heroically solve his family's problems, but he doesn't know which new washing machine to buy.

Enter you—wizened, trustworthy, experienced Sherpa guide. Or, you can think of yourself as a Coach, simultaneously no-nonsense and nurturing. You need to communicate to the customer that you want to help them be successful. Everything you do or say should be about them. Present yourself as competent and trustworthy. You want to say, "Hey Gerald. I'm here for you. I want to help you turn that frown upside down. You need a new washing machine? What is the most important thing to you in getting a new washing machine?" After listening, then you point him in a direction: "I have this great washing machine that I'm really happy with. Based on what you told me, I bet it would make you really happy too."

Your marketing is not about you; it's about your customer.

Your marketing story continues: Gerald takes your wise guidance and gets that new washing machine. Now, he's made his family happy! The piles of dirty laundry are gone! His kids think he's awesome! His spouse thinks he's hot stuff! Remember, Gerald's initial problem wasn't so much the broken washing machine;

it was his grumpy family. The story ends with Gerald's *main* problem solved, by way of your product or service. Gerald is the hero of his family and life in general, and he now wears a great big smile.

Everything that you communicate to your customer needs to express the intention that you're there to serve them in their heroic endeavor. It's their journey from the sad Before state to the happy After state that will transform them from strangers into raving fans.

You will reiterate some form of this message and story at every stage in the eight-step Customer Value Journey, maintaining the narrative throughout. Your goal is to not only move them through the eight stages, but to reassure them at *each* stage of your honorable intentions. We're back in the vocabulary of romance, and this message about your intention is part of how you demonstrate yourself to be trustworthy. Your goal should genuinely be to help the customers overcome the challenges posed by the villains in their lives, to become the hero in their story.

When this message is authentic—when your desire to help your customer is genuine, connected to your Core Purpose, Core Values and Envisioned Future—then your messaging will be incredibly successful. Your Passion will emerge and customers will respond. That, in turn, is going to lead to more Provision, which will feed more Passion within your business. Once again, we can see how intricately connected all these pieces are.

Three-Step Copywriting Model

Now you've got your message figured out—but what words exactly will you use? When you produce any kind of marketing, you need to figure out what you're going to say. Those words are what we call copywriting. "Copy" describes the words said in your ads, in your trifold brochures, on your website, on your social media platform, and so on. "Copy" is anything that's written or spoken anywhere, on your forward-facing material. There are amazing books that are fully dedicated to copywriting. We thought we would give you a basic model to start with so you can apply what you have learned about your customer.

We've experienced great success using a simple three-step tool to make sure we provide our messaging in the right order; we learned this from Doug Hall's book, *Jump Start Your Business Brain*.[48] These three steps interlink with the idea that the customer should feel important and recognize the value you can offer them. In your copy, you want to make sure you communicate, in this order:

1. **The Overt Benefit**
2. **Reason to Believe**
3. **Significant Difference**

Let's go over each one in greater depth. Remember, with each of these steps, incorporate as much of your customer's *original language* as possible that you pulled from the surveys gathered in your market research.

The Overt Benefit

The *overt benefit* states, right up front, the biggest benefit your product or service will offer to the customer—*not* a laundry list of the features. It's a common rookie move to start telling people

---

48   Hall, Doug. *Jump Start Your Business Brain: Scientific Ideas and Advice That Will Immediately Double Your...Business Success Rate.* Cincinnati, OH: Clerisy Press, 2018.

about your product's various features before you tell them the overt benefit. This happens all the time and it's the fastest way to lose someone's attention. As an expert in your product, it's easy to assume people understand the benefit of your features, but they don't. Don't make this mistake! Only talk about the features *after* you've given them an overt benefit that is relevant to them. Then, the features serve their rightful purpose in your sales process.

"Overt" is another word for "obvious." You do not want to be subtle in stating the benefits of your product or service. Being too subtle with your messaging is another common mistake that nearly all businesses make; they believe that if they're too direct in their Marketing, they're somehow going to insult the customer. As professional copywriters who know the importance and value of direct communication, this assumption is bizarre to us—but it's common. If you assume it's better to be subtle than direct in your Marketing, know that you're not alone in that belief, and please allow us to correct you now.

People are busy and distracted. The average person receives over 5,000 marketing messages a day, not to mention the distractions that come from work stress, traffic, kid problems, and any number of other interruptions.[49] As a marketer, you do not have the luxury of your customer's undivided attention. If you actually believe that what you offer is valuable to your customers (and if you're building a Passion & Provision company, then it probably is), you've got to figure out how to break through all the noise to effectively communicate with them. The best way to do that is to **state the overt benefit that is most *relevant* to their life.**

---

49   Story, Louise. "Anywhere the Eye Can See, It's Likely to See an Ad." *The New York Times.* The New York Times, January 15, 2007. https://www.nytimes.com/2007/01/15/business/media/15everywhere.html.

Let's say you're in charge of a Honda dealership and you see a woman come in with three kids in tow. She wanders over to look at a minivan. Consider: what is this woman's *most pressing need* when she's shopping for a new vehicle?

Imagine that a salesperson approaches that woman—let's call her Beth—and says something like, "Ma'am, I see you're looking at this minivan. Well, let me tell you. It's got rack and pinion steering, and it's got power brakes. It's got..." The salesperson starts rattling off all of the features of this minivan. Unless Beth happens to be a very mechanically minded woman, then this salesperson hasn't cut through the noise—he's just added to it, and he will have lost her interest. Let's tell that salesperson to go on a break: you can take over.

So, you approach Beth and decide to learn more about her to figure out her core needs. (Remember, the Customer Value Journey is what you want to keep in the back of your mind.) Maybe you start with an introduction and a handshake. You might follow up with, "So what features are most important to you in a minivan?" Whatever Beth says in her response should clue you in to how to discuss the most *relevant overt benefits* of your product.

If Beth says convenience is big, discuss the overt benefits as they relate to convenience. Talk about the ease of loading kids in and out of the vehicle. Point out the headlights that turn off automatically, so that she doesn't have to worry about accidentally leaving them on. Show her the hands-free tailgate, which causes the trunk to open just by waving your foot under the rear bumper.

If she says she wants something safe, then speak to that: talk about how easy it is to steer and control the car, and how you'll be able to stop quickly when needed. If she says they're looking to shift into a more comfortable vehicle ahead of a big road trip, talk about the drop-down DVD player, the great sound system, the seat warmers, and Tri-Zone climate control.

Learn your customer's challenges so that you can cut through the noise with a message that feels immediately relevant to their needs. Be direct, be to the point, and state the overt benefit. Show them what's in it for them. "You guys are going to have such a great trip in this car. No more bickering in the back seat, no arguing over the temperature, and everyone stays safe."

We also recommend that you **write your ad copy in second person, speaking directly to the customer** in words like "you" and "your." That will make your copy feel more customer focused, personal, and relevant—once again, helping you cut through the noise.

Reason to Believe

You follow the overt benefit by giving your customer a *reason to believe* that the promise is true. **You need to prove to the customer that your product will deliver on the benefits you just described.** Think of photos that show a Before and After, or customer reviews attesting to the value of what you sell, or any kind of evidence that will convince the customer that they can trust in the benefits promised.

In your role as a Honda dealership owner, you're going to give Beth a *reason to believe* in the benefits by showing her the features that back up the benefit. You've told her it's a safe car, so now prove it. Demonstrate how the Honda suite of safety features works. Explain the Collision Mitigation braking system, and the Lane Keeping Assist System.

Remember, you're looking to establish a relationship of trust with your customer. Back up your promises with evidence and give the customer a reason to believe you.

The Significant Difference

Maybe Beth shrugs at this point and says she's heard good things about Chrysler's minivans. Now you need to show Beth the *significant difference* between you and your competitors. **Explain how and why you're different than the customer's other options.**

Because you are a savvy Honda dealership owner, you should be able to speak clearly about the difference between a Honda Odyssey versus a Chrysler Pacifica. Maybe you focus on the price or the reviews or the experience the customer will have at your dealership versus theirs. Part of the difference you discuss will relate to your product—but that shouldn't be the only difference the customer gets acquainted with.

Here's a great big tip: in today's competitive world, building a relationship with your customer has never been more important. Considering how many similar products are out there on the market, there may not be a significant difference in your product—so you have to create a significant difference through forming a relationship with your customer. As the old adage says, "People buy from people they like." A relationship can provide a majority of the significant difference that will lead your customer to go with you over a competing brand.

People buy from people they like.

Let's say Beth test drives a Honda Odyssey and a Chrysler Pacifica, but the Chrysler Pacifica dealership acted like her kids were a pain. At your dealership though, you engaged Beth's kids. You asked them about their sports and their favorite foods. When you and Beth started looking at paperwork, you gave the kids popcorn and a board game to play with. You made a point to talk with Beth about stuff other than cars. When she leaves your dealership, she feels like she made a friend.

If Beth likes both minivans she test drives, her deciding factor could very well come down to the fact that she liked the Honda dealership guy better than the Chrysler people. The customer is going to prefer to spend their money with someone that they *like*.

Establishing the significant difference is important. If Beth goes with your competitor, that's bad. You make no money. So, in your ad copy, make a point to clarify how you are *different* than your competitors, and work to build a relationship with your customer to strengthen that positive difference.

We've discussed these three messaging components as they would progress in an in-person interaction, but you can accomplish the same effect in your ad messaging. By stating *the overt benefit* clearly and directly, following up with a *reason to believe* in those benefits, and then clarifying *the significant difference* between you and your competitors, you're going to present a persuasive advertisement that is relevant to your customer and cuts through the noise. How do you know it's relevant? Because you already asked and listened with your market research and your DDS. Now let's tell the world.

GET YOUR MESSAGE OUT TO THE CUSTOMER

You're almost there! You've nailed the **approach,** you've gotten to **know your customer,** and you've written a **compelling message** in an effective way. So, now what? Do you book a TV commercial? Invest in digital advertising? Do a radio campaign? Here are some helpful tips to keep in mind when thinking about which specific advertising approach you want to pursue.

Be Repetitive: Frequency and Reach

You've collected data with your market research. You got inside your customer's head with the DDS and the customer avatar development. You've used their own words in the three-step copywriting model to come up with brilliant ad copy. Now you need to get that copy out to the world. So, what's the best approach? Who do you target and how often? Do you pay big bucks for the primetime spots or purchase cheaper ads that will play more frequently?

We hear this statement all the time from our clients: "I don't know where to spend my money and don't have any confidence that I'm going to actually benefit from it." Marketing is a confusing subject for most people. What they don't know is that there are rules of human behavior—psychological, neurological rules—that can tell us how human beings work. When we use those rules in our Marketing strategies, Marketing is *effective*.

Have you ever been to a party and introduced yourself to someone, only to have them inform you that you've already met? That first meeting with them obviously wasn't memorable—there wasn't enough of an impact for it to stick in your head. How do you make that imprint?

First, you need to make a neurological imprint on your customers, which means relevant, interesting messaging. If your message is boring, you're going to get tuned out, and nothing else that we're about to say will do you any good. Much of what we've already covered in this chapter will help you create a message that will cut through the barrage of ads that people get hit with every day. Use the Steps to Intimacy, show the customer that they're the hero, use their language, and keep your ad copy focused on *them*. That's step one: the message.

Step two requires *frequency*. **The brain needs to encounter a message at a frequency of three times a week for fifty-two weeks a year before information is successfully transferred to long-term memory.**[50] You need this kind of impact when you want people to have you at the top of their minds when they need your offering. This transfer happens in increments; there's a three-month, a six-month, and a twelve-month marker in which someone's knowledge of you goes from not even knowing you exist, to actually being part of their long-term memory. But essentially, if you want people to remember you when their need for your product or service arises—you need to get your message in front of them three times a week, fifty-two weeks a year.

When people are trying to make customers familiar with their product, but they don't adhere to this level of required frequency, marketing fails. Clients sometimes come to us and they say, "I bought an ad on the radio and it didn't work."

We'll say, "Okay, tell us more about that. How many times did you run the ad?"

---

50   "The Radio Success Formula." The Monday Morning Memo, June 18, 2018. https://www.mondaymorningmemo.com/newsletters/the-radio-success-formula/.

"Well, it was running twice a day, five days a week, for a month. I didn't get anything."

Their conclusion is that radio doesn't work. But that's not true. Think about all the marketing messages people encounter every day: billboards, radio ads, TV spots, internet pop-up ads, social media promos, everything in front of you that has a brand name on it— remember, the average person encounters over 5,000 of those, daily. A lot of advertising doesn't even register in our brains for the first three or four months. It's running along before we even notice it's there. In order to break through, you need a compelling message and then—this is crucial—you need sustained frequency.

If you want to reach somebody three times a week on radio, it takes about twenty-five spots. That's deploying twenty-five commercials per week for the average person listening to only hear it three times. Now, if you stop that ad campaign after a month, your potential customer is going to forget about you fast. They only heard your ad a total of twelve times, and they were distracted for most of them!

You need enough frequency to actually move the needle on somebody's memory. So, how do you pay for all that?

First of all, take advantage of social media platforms. If you join an online networking group, you can show up to the group every week, and then find two other opportunities each week to connect with people in that group. You're building frequency in a low-cost way, networking and building relationships. Social media, when done for business, is like networking in person. That's an effective and affordable way to slowly build your company.

Secondly, if money is tight and you're aiming for your potential customer to encounter you three times a week, fifty-two weeks a year, then you might need to invest in a cheap platform. Every town in America has at least a few radio stations. If your advertising budget is small and you have a product or service that is local or regional, then you pick the cheapest radio station, and advertise during the cheapest time of day, between midnight and 6 a.m.

Somebody might say, "Nobody's listening then!" Well, the radio station continues to operate between midnight and 6 a.m., so *someone* listens to it. You may only be getting your spot in front of thirty people, but you're better off advertising to those thirty people and getting a few regular customers out of it than paying for a single spot in the middle of the day. Sure, more people might hear it, but if you can't afford enough frequency to imprint, then your money is wasted. Your message will go in one ear, and out the other—forgotten.

People often want to focus on *reach* instead of frequency. They would rather try to reach 25,000 people in their target demographic *once* than reach fewer people, more often. This doesn't work. **Your reach is irrelevant if you can't afford enough frequency to make a neurological impression.**

As professional marketers, we know it's more effective to reach a hundred people with three-times-a-week frequency than a million people with not enough frequency. If you can afford a hundred people, go after a hundred people.

Use great messaging, get it out there as frequently as you need to be memorable, and you'll have even more success.

Tell Their Friends and Family Too

One final (kind of ironic) tip: don't just target your targeted customer when you publicize your ad copy. There are *two* customer groups to think about when you're developing your Marketing messaging, and you need to consider them both.

The most obvious group is the targeted customer (i.e., the people who actually purchase your product). The ability we have with modern technology to analyze customer data has given many companies the ability to target their ads to a demographic that is razor-sharp in its specificity. Many of our Marketing clients assume that targeting is the best thing in the world—the "nirvana" of all digital marketing. We hear something along these lines often: "If I can get my ad in front of women between the ages of thirty-five to forty-two who are white and French, I can get my product in front of my most-likely buyers without wasting a penny of my advertising money on anyone else!"

However, in our experience, targeting your Marketing isn't nearly as effective as people think. Why? Because of the weight of the *second* category of customers.

The second category of people you need to think about are the *influencers* around your targeted customers: their friends, their mentors, their significant others, and so on. These influential voices may sway your targeted customer to either buy or not buy your product. Here's an example.

Let's say our friend mentions that he likes taking his kids to McDonald's every so often for a Happy Meal. As we said earlier, the two of us haven't eaten at McDonald's in years—but their branding has worked on us. We're part of their tribe; we can sing their jingles and we "know the rest"! If our friend mentions that he plans to take his kids to McDonald's after he picks them up from school, one of us would likely say something like, "That's cool! I can remember getting Happy Meals as a kid at McDonald's, and I loved that." Even if we're no longer a McDonald's customer, we might influence someone else to spend money there—at least we wouldn't discourage them under normal circumstances.

However, we once had a friend who was never part of the McDonald's tribe—in fact, she hated McDonald's. Whenever someone mentioned McDonald's or suggested grabbing a bite there, she would immediately start tearing the brand down. She'd talk about how unhealthy fast food is and imply that anyone who took their kids to eat there was irresponsible. She's an influencer and we can guarantee she's causing McDonald's to *lose* sales.

As you approach Marketing, remember the importance of winning over both customer groups with your branding. It's not enough to simply acquaint people with your brand. You also need them to *bond* with you—to develop a positive opinion associated with your company. It's not just getting your ad in front of your targeted audience; it's shifting the culture to recognize and value your business.

BEHIND THE MARKETING

Let's circle back to the main point. In a Passion & Provision company, your goal is to solve the *real* needs of *real* people. We believe you're in business to serve others. You're looking to make an impact in the world—both inside the office and outside of it. Your Marketing is how you tell that story. Because of this, Marketing touches every part of your business.

It flows out of your Vision. It's shaped by your Leadership. As customers roll in as a result of your Marketing, your systems of Management and Operations receive the order and process it. It impacts your finances. It can even help shape your Culture.

Maybe because of how important and integral Marketing is, people often misdiagnose their company's needs in this area. Years ago, we had a company come to us, requesting a new website. This company has multiple offices throughout the state, with roughly a thousand employees. They felt confident that a new website was what they needed most to market their company.

We sat down with them to discuss this website. It only took about fifteen minutes before we realized that they didn't need a website—at least, not yet. We wouldn't have been able to build them a website anyway, because there wouldn't have been anything clear to put on it. The company didn't know how to talk about itself. They needed to do some serious soul-searching about who they were as a company and how they would talk about it clearly to outsiders before they tried to construct something as identity focused as a company website.

This happens often—companies self-diagnose their Marketing needs and come to us with requests for an ad words campaign or to run their social media or to do something with Google ads. They think they've discovered the missing piece. In these cases, we sometimes have to tell them that their Marketing is only a single piece of a much larger picture.

Imagine that we do a successful Google ads campaign for a company that has terrible customer service. When customers place their orders and interact with their customer service reps, they have a miserable, frustrating, experience. Those customers aren't going to come back. That company is dumping money into a leaky bucket.

"Failure awaits any writer who attempts to create an exciting ad campaign for a company that is not committed to delivering all that was promised in the ads." —Roy H. Williams[51]

Your Marketing messaging has to tie back to your Core Purpose, Core Values and what you're trying to achieve. If you *don't* have those in place, you won't convey any authenticity in your Marketing—and that means, you can't possibly build trust with your customer. When it's done correctly, messaging identifies who you are, what you offer, what you care about, and why your customers should want to do business with you. Get those pieces in place.

Then, go wooing.

51 Williams, Roy H. Wizard Academy. Accessed December 31, 2019. http://Wizardacademy.org/ stuff-roy-said.

TIME TO GET TO KNOW AND WOO YOUR CUSTOMERS

- Go to **fulfilledthebook.com** to download resources to further develop your marketing and sales tools and map out your Customer Value Journey.
- On a scale of 1–10, how well do you think people know who you are as a company?
- On a scale of 1–10, how good is your reputation?
- As you review the Customer Value Journey, can you identify areas where you are skipping steps and losing trust?
- How well do you know your customers?
- Have you taken time to identify who your ideal customer is and researched their needs and pain points?
- What are two main benefits of your product or service that can be seen from the customer's point of view?
- What promise are you making to your customers that is about solving a problem they know they have?

CHAPTER EIGHT

||||||||||||||||||||

Money

"We all long for noble purpose, and we also need to pay the mortgage."

ROBERT J. ANDERSON AND WILLIAM A. ADAMS

One of the most memorable stories we've ever encountered about a business going sideways was described in the book *E-Myth Mastery*, by Michael E. Gerber.[52] Gerber's earlier book, *The E-Myth*, is one of the classic books on business management—but Gerber acknowledges in his follow-up book, *E-Myth Mastery,* that there were a number of key points they missed in their original model.

---

52   Gerber, Michael E. *E-Myth Mastery: the Seven Essential Disciplines for Building a World Class Company*. New York: HarperCollins e-books, 2009.

Some of those blind spots, he confesses, affected him personally...
And ruthlessly.

In *E-Myth Mastery,* Gerber shares the story of how he almost
lost his company. At their height in 1985, his consulting firm
was worth multiple millions, boasted 850 franchises, and Gerber
himself was a nationally successful author. He recalls having
a particular meeting with his partner who handled all of their
accounting and finances. His partner assured him that everything
was going well—never better.

Michael Gerber confesses in his book that he had been negligent
in allowing his partner sole oversight over their finances. Gerber
had always preferred to focus on the company's big ideas and
vision; he hadn't kept track of the company's finances, prefer-
ring to delegate that responsibility. That, he acknowledges, was
a major mistake.

If Gerber had involved himself more in the finances, he might
have been able to avert the crisis that came. Instead, the gut-
wrenching announcement from his partner arrived as a shock.
On December 10, 1985, Gerber walked into his partner's office to
find him hunched over his desk, fingers pulling at his hair. Gerber
describes the scene in his book: "He looked up at me briefly with
a look that spelled disaster and said in a voice I could hardly hear,
'We blew it. We let it get away from us. I don't know what we were
thinking about.'"[53]

Initially, Gerber assumed his partner had found an error—a mistake. In reality, his partner was telling him that it was over. The
company was in trouble, beyond repair. They were $2 million in

---

53   Ibid.

debt. They were four months behind in their leases, five months behind with the phone company, three months behind with their payroll taxes, several hundred thousand dollars in debt in payables. Every bill was seriously overdue, and creditors were hounding them for payment. They couldn't get a line of credit for any new purchases. Gerber's partner had been trying to solve the issues for months, never sharing the troubles with anyone.

Although it would be tempting to pin all of the blame for what happened on his partner, Gerber accepts some of the responsibility. He admits that he would give someone a responsibility and then never follow up. He would simply say, "I'm going to trust you with it." He didn't keep his staff or colleagues accountable—in large part, because when it came to finances, Gerber himself was insecure. He didn't understand how to effectively evaluate the financial picture of his company, so he had no way of checking up on it. He also didn't know how to correctly manage the person who *did* have responsibility over the finances.

The company almost went completely under. Gerber's partner walked out, and Gerber's wife had to step in and help him save the company. They did manage to save it, which was barely short of a miracle. However, the stress and upheaval that went along with the recovery was almost unbearable.

AVOIDING FINANCIAL FAILURE

Whether you're a small company or a large company—whether it's obvious that you're struggling or whether it looks like you're a grand success—you could put yourself in the exact same position as Michael Gerber if you don't pay attention to the financial pieces of your business. Gerber's story represents countless other stories of struggling businesses who took a similar trajectory—many of which ended in outright failure.

The money part is stressful. It can be confusing. One of the big reasons the business failure rate is so high is because many business leaders get exhausted from treading water financially and decide they just need to close their doors. Most business leaders were not trained in finance. The language of finance is unfamiliar and intimidating. If we're old enough, maybe we were taught how to cash a check and balance a checkbook—but that doesn't translate to minimum competency in running the finances of a business. Not even close.

However—you *do* need minimum competency in this area. So take a deep breath, and let's dive in.

MONEY MATTERS

Money in a Passion & Provision company is a big deal; it's literally half the equation. Lack of provision will extinguish passion and destroy your dreams for the future faster than almost anything else.

"Money is better than poverty, if only for financial reasons." —Woody Allen[54]

Having basic competence when it comes to your accounting is critical if you are going to run and grow your company. Whether you do the accounting yourself early on or you pay someone to

---

54 "Forbes Quotes: Thoughts on the Business of Life." Forbes. Forbes Magazine. Accessed December 31, 2019. https://www.forbes.com/quotes/10385/.

take care of it for you, the difference between success and failure can boil down to a few financial basics: knowing how things work, what reports you should read monthly, and how to ask key questions.

When it comes to money in a business, there are two types of people: people who like numbers, spreadsheets, and all things accounting, and those who do not.

If you are one that loves numbers, great! Hopefully, this will be a good refresher for you.

If you fall into the second category, then you are in the majority of entrepreneurs who start and run businesses. Entrepreneurs often prefer to think big picture; they don't like the numbers. They don't feel confident wading into spreadsheets and account statements. In our consulting work with leaders running businesses ranging from startups to large successful companies, the biggest challenges usually involve insecurity about the money stuff. We have heard many a struggling entrepreneur say that they never really look at the books until tax time.

There's a common myth that people are either born with a financial acuity gene, or they're not—but that's not true. Take it from two people who would have placed themselves in the second category seventeen years ago: this stuff can be learned, and *you* can learn this.

As with our other chapters, we're going to keep things big picture, providing you with the nuts-and-bolts basics about key financial concepts you need to understand to achieve *minimum competency*, so that you can build a Passion & Provision company. This chapter is not meant to be an exhaustive guide to running your company's finances. It's meant to provide you with a strong foundation to build on and ensure you are equipped to have intelligent and regular conversations with your finance team.

So, what are the "big rocks" you need in place when you're dealing with the money flowing through your company? You need to be able to see and track things like your available cash, what people owe your company, what your company owes people, and how fast you can make more cash available. You also track things like how profitable the company is. Is it moving in the right direction? Do you know its value?

When done correctly, your accounting and reporting can reveal hidden opportunities to create more Passion & Provision in your company. It can also reveal dangers lurking in the shadows. Perhaps most significantly, you'll be able to answer the questions that keep many business leaders up at night:

- Can I pay the bills this month? What about next month?
- Are we profitable? What is my company worth?
- Can I afford to hire someone new, or do I need to make do with our current staff?
- Can I afford to keep everyone I have?
- Can I afford a bigger building?
- Am I on track for retirement?

When you don't have a basic plan for monitoring the money in your company, then you don't have the information needed to make good financial decisions—not for today, and not in the future. However, when you learn the basics of money and manage it well, you optimize your ability to achieve Passion & Provision. You'll also start sleeping better!

DEFINING "PROFITABLE"

We regularly encounter people with businesses that bring in thousands, hundreds of thousands, even millions of dollars a year—but when we dig a little deeper, we discover a disturbing story. These business leaders often assure us that they're "profitable," but what does "profitable" really mean? Often when we hear this, the business leader means they can cover all their expenses. They're able to "break even" or end with a little extra in the bank at the end of the month.

Hold up. There's a bit more to what profitable means.

From the startup home business, to retail shops, to restaurants on Main Street USA, we have been amazed at the response to this simple question: Are you paying yourself?

"Well, not yet."

"Well, no."

"Well, sometimes."

Hear this: you can't describe your company as profitable if you're not paying yourself. Working for free doesn't fit the definition of "profitable." It's one thing to float on no personal income for a year or two in a startup, but if you're still not paying yourself after three to five years—that's not a recipe for Passion & Provision. That's a recipe for destroyed dreams.

We do not say this without empathy or understanding—we get it. There have been a number of times over our many years in business when we could pay our staff but not cash our own paychecks.

There are seasons where cash flow is simply a beast. Still, to claim profitability and not be paying yourself is to claim a falsehood.

So what *does* it mean to be profitable? Let's review the Provision target we discussed in chapter two. Recall that "breaking even" means that you can afford to pay all your expenses, *and* you can pay yourself a consistent livable wage. From there, you become *profitable* when you're making a profit beyond breakeven. We recommend a target of 10 percent as that's going to give you "enough" for survival *and* progress toward your goals. Keep that in mind as we discuss ways to understand your finances.

YOUR EMOTIONAL RELATIONSHIP TO MONEY: KATHRYN NARRATES

We're about to give you some very practical information about dollars and cents. However, before we do, we have to get into some territory that many people would consider "impractical," or at least, intangible. We're talking about your emotional relationship to money.

Your emotions as they relate to money can have a profound impact on how you lead your business. In fact, the reason why Michael Gerber's partner mishandled the company's finances and hid the problems was because of his emotional issues surrounding money.

> Your emotional relationship to money can profoundly impact how you lead your business.

Money is an emotional topic. We all grew up in families that had different perspectives on handling their finances. One of our dearest friends would say that, in her family, money seemed to grow on trees, and so she never worries about having enough. Her husband, on the other hand, grew up in a family where his parents went bankrupt. Money always felt threatening and scary, and he usually thinks about money from an emotional position of scarcity.

Michael and I have waded through some deep waters when it comes to navigating our emotions around money. Neither of us were taught to manage money well by our parents so we each had our own ways of dealing with finances. Mine was to be hyper-responsible and never owe anything to anyone. In fact, when we brought in an outside consultant a few years ago, his biggest reprimand of me was that I paid bills too fast so I didn't manage our cash flow as well as I could have.

Another challenge for me was that I struggled when it came to investing in our own education, or in partnerships that would leverage our business. Michael could see the potential and the need, and all I could see was the dollars leaving our bank account. Michael lived in optimism and welcomed taking risks, and I lived in pessimism and dreaded almost every risk. It has made for some lively conversations over the course of our seventeen years of business, as well as our twenty-seven years of marriage.

All of us come into the world of running a business with different emotional perspectives regarding money. In order to gain financial objectivity as a business leader, you need to confront some major philosophical questions which will tie to your past experiences and emotions—questions like:

- What is money? Is it a tool? Is it the definition of your worth? Or is it something else?

- How does your upbringing inform your view of money?
- What does money mean to you? Is it a means to an end? Is it tied to your definition of success?
- Is money something you feel comfortable risking, or does it feel uncomfortable to risk money?
- Do you think of money usually in terms of its limits or its abundance?

As business leaders, it's also easy to get emotionally confused by our cultural narrative. As Americans, we live in a culture that says that you can have everything you want, and you can have it now—you just have to finance it. But that's a false narrative. It was that myth that eventually led our country into the Great Recession, as people found themselves with debt they couldn't maintain—even the country's biggest companies and banks. The "conventional wisdom" guiding financial systems inspired, encouraged, and made popular the idea that you can have it all and experience no consequences.

With that kind of landscape then, think about the standard emotional baggage that most business leaders bring to the accounting table: they're dealing with their personal family financial history; the attitudes of excess leading up to the financial crisis in 2008; the attitudes of regret and the pain of recession following 2008; any additional notions they might have about money related to their own self-worth. They bring all that to the table when they're starting a company.

It's a nice idea that entrepreneurs are intelligent enough adults that they can separate all of their emotions and perceptions about money from the way they operate their businesses—but it's not realistic. As business leaders, we take all that baggage with us into our leadership. As the stress of running a business puts pressure on us and squeezes, all those issues about money can come bubbling up to the surface and bite us in the beehive.

Because of all those different potential hang-ups, we risk the financial health of our businesses if we're not actively growing in the area of money management. We need to learn about our own perceptions, correcting the wrong ones and mitigating the areas where we're overconfident. We may need to overcome rampant fears about handling money and seek to understand the rules that govern how money works.

The goal? To get to a balanced, objective position where you can view money as a tool and understand how to use it most effectively to prosper your business.

STRATEGIES TO MANAGE THE BAGGAGE

So how do you achieve that goal? Here are some suggestions.

One: Recognize that your perspective on money is probably not universal, and surround yourself with people who think about money differently than you. We read a story in Patrick Lencioni's book, *The Advantage*, about a CEO who was comfortable taking financial risks so long as he was in control. However, once his company was big enough that other people started governing the finances, he started giving his leaders a hard time about every penny they spent.[55] Morale tanked, and when the leadership finally came together to have an open conversation about everyone's frustrations, it came out that the CEO grew up poor and he'd vowed that he would never be poor again. His ruthless driving of his staff, his scrutiny of expense reports—it

---

55   Lencioni, Patrick. *The Advantage: Why Organizational Health Trumps Everything Else in Business.* San Francisco, CA: Jossey-Bass, 2012.

all was informed by the pain of poverty he experienced as a kid. Rather than thinking about growth, he was thinking, "I managed to build this company. How do I protect it from falling apart, so I don't go back to being poor?" He could only play defense, and he frustrated anyone's attempt to go on offense. It was only when he came to grips with his own emotional relationship to money that he gained the clarity to listen to other people who could present different rationales about the best way forward.

Own the fact that you have emotions, preferences, and assumptions about money which may not all be accurate. Seek out knowledge in this area and let that free you from some of the current attitudes which may be controlling your decision making.

Two: Recognize that the people who handle your finances also have an emotional relationship with money—your accountant, your CFO, and so on. We heard another story from a friend who said that their CFO was always pooh-poohing every idea. He was always saying things like, "No, we can't do that. No, we can't afford that. No, there's no way that'll ever happen." Later, it came out that the CFO had grown up with parents who had been shaped by the Great Depression and felt constant stress and fear about money. For this CFO, every new venture seemed like a risk too big to take—but that negatively impacted his company's ability to take some of the risks that are necessary to grow. Like Michael Gerber's partner, whose emotional relationship to money dictated his mismanagement, your staff needs accountability.

As you hire or promote people into leadership, make sure that you're asking them about these issues of how they see and handle money. If you have somebody on your leadership team who doesn't have a healthy perspective about money, that will take some of the steam out of your company and slow it down. Consider asking them some of the following questions to get an idea of what their emotional relationship to money might look like:

- How do you feel about money?
- What's your attitude toward money?
- How do you feel about debt and how did your parents handle money?
- What's your earliest memory about money and finance? (People will say things like, "Well we didn't have enough," or, "Mom always gave me a quarter to go buy gum. It was easy. It was great." Their response will give you an idea about their default assumptions related to money.)

Your staff needs *you*, as the leader, to have minimum competency in this area so that you can oversee what they're doing and have a conversation with them if it seems like they're making emotional decisions which aren't in the company's best interest.

Three: Invest in your financial education and educate yourself. Read good books on the subject, like *Financial Intelligence: A Manager's Guide to Knowing What the Numbers Really Mean,* by Karen Berman and Joe Knight.[56] Learn the facts about money, and then learn about the attitudes about money that financially successful people have. It's important to educate yourself on both. Seek out additional books, videos, courses, and other trainings to constantly pursue continuing education. Do this, so that you can *grow* your business and *protect* your business—along with everyone connected to it.

Four: Surround yourself with good mentors. Seek out people

---

56 Berman, Karen, and Joe Knight. *Financial Intelligence: A Manager's Guide to Knowing What the Numbers Really Mean.* Boston, MA: Business Literary Institute, Inc., 2013.

who don't just have *opinions* about money and running a business, but actually have *experience* in successfully running a business. You want counsel that's wise and informed from people who have demonstrated they can manage money and their companies in a healthy way. When you're starting out as an entrepreneur, you'll need to find these mentors through your network. A common scenario is a volunteer advisory board made up of two to four successful people who believe in you and are willing to meet with you once a month. In larger companies, these advisors will likely be among your paid staff.

PRACTICAL STUFF: FOUR FINANCIAL SKILLS

Now, let's talk numbers. The concepts we're going to discuss throughout the remainder of this chapter were all informed by the excellent material we learned from Berman and Knight in *Financial Intelligence.*

The numbers tell a story. One of the mistakes we made early in our careers was failing to recognize that story. We knew there were different reports that our software could kick out, but we didn't know how to use the information in each report to inform the others so that we had the whole picture. We learned later that these reports are like chapters in a book. You won't know the entire story until you view them together and read the whole book.

That means, of course, that you need to become literate in comprehending these reports. Without a clear understanding of financial terminology and basic accounting, it's easy to misunderstand the truth of the financial picture of your company. If you've been in that position before, cut yourself some slack. Reading these reports is almost like learning a foreign language.

So, here's where you start: when you're reading this language that is the financial reports, focus on translating two things:

1. The text—what the numbers literally mean
2. The subtext—what the numbers *imply*

In the sections that follow, we're going to try to build your literacy so that you can effectively read and understand both.

UNDERSTAND THE FOUNDATIONAL BASICS OF MEASUREMENT

Financially intelligent leaders know what the basics of measurement are. They know how to read an income statement and how to balance a balance sheet. They understand cash flow and the difference between profit and cash. Most of all, a person with a strong financial foundation isn't scared or confused by the numbers.

There are five main reports that, when taken together, will tell you the first part of the story of your numbers. These reports provide the measurements that will guide your next steps forward. There are three main reports: the income statement, the balance sheet, and the cash flow statement. Small business owners will also need to pay attention to accounts receivable and accounts payable. We've provided samples of each report in a link listed at the end of the chapter, in our resources section.

We're about to talk more about each one to help you get to a place where the numbers don't scare or confuse you. If you already feel pretty savvy with reading these reports, you may want to skim over this next section. If you know you could strengthen your foundation with these foundational reports though, then we recommend finding a comfortable seat as you build your familiarity with these documents.

Income Statement

The income statement shows you what money you're bringing in, what money is going out, and whether or not your "bottom line" is a net profit or a net loss. The income statement is made up of three basic parts:

1. Your revenue
2. Your cost of goods sold (COGs)
3. Your expenses

The revenue shows all the different ways you take in money. Income comes from multiple departments, products, and services. For example, in our Rabbit Hole Hay company, we don't just sell hay—we sell multiple types of hay, in multiple sizes. In Half a Bubble Out, we sell marketing services like website design and production services, and we also provide business consulting. Similarly, your company likely brings in income from multiple areas of revenue.

The income statement will list all of those sources of income on a spreadsheet on different lines. Usually, each of those sources of income is assigned its own code in the general ledger, and they may be divided according to department or product. When added up together, those lines noting income tell you your top line or *gross revenue*. This is a fun column to look at. It's nice to see all the ways you've made money.

The **cost of goods (COG)** is what it costs you to create the thing you're selling. If you're a product-based business, like Rabbit Hole Hay, you're factoring in the cost of materials and labor. For us, that means the cost of boxes, hay, plastic bags, and our labor associates who put it all together. In a service business like HaBO, the cost of goods relates to what you're paying to carry out the service, like website design or video production. You might add in fees that are associated with the development or software, and so on.

These costs will also be listed on the spreadsheet in their own column and will also probably be divided up according to categories, like department or product type. If we were looking at the revenue and cost of goods columns together for HaBO, we could see how much *revenue* we brought in from website design and compare that with how much it *cost* us to make that website. The difference between those two numbers is our *gross profit*.

The third column is **expenses,** which describe your overhead costs like your rent, office supplies, salaries, and so on. It's anything it takes to run the business that isn't directly related to producing the product or service. At a basic level, all labor and salaries generally go in expenses.

But what about contract or hourly labor? Would that be something that counts more as cost of goods? As you get more comfortable with these reports, you'll be able to make them more sophisticated and complex. You can move percentages of your labor into cost of goods, and leave other percentages in your expenses category. However, if you're not confident reading these reports and/or you don't have an accountant that understands the various complexities, start simple. Keep labor and salaries in the expenses column.

Your revenue, minus the cost of goods, equals your *gross* profit. Your gross profit, minus your expenses, equals your *net* profit. Got it?

As you review your income statement month after month, you'll start to see your trends: what you typically bill out, what it costs you, and what your expenses are. If numbers are suddenly wildly variant, this is the first place to catch errors. First make sure the information you entered is correct. Do you have all the bills in? Are the numbers entered correctly? Does something look way off? For example, if you typically spend $1,500 in office supplies, and suddenly your office supplies line item says you spent $10,000, then you have some digging to do. What are the implications of this? Is there an expense that was super high? Or did someone key in $8,437.00 instead of $84.37? It happens! That's when you have a minor issue in your reporting. No big deal—go back and check the numbers. Easy fix.

Now you know the story told in the first chapter, the income statement.

Balance Sheet

The purpose of a balance sheet is to give any interested parties an idea of the company's financial position, in addition to showing what the company owns and owes. The balance sheet provides a snapshot at a single point in time of your company's accounts—including its assets, liabilities, and shareholders' equity. If you are ever looking to procure a loan, the balance sheet is one of the key reports your banker will care about. Having this set up correctly from the beginning can save you a lot of heartache in the future. Monitoring it month to month is a key part of your role as a leader in your finances.

A long time ago, we decided to start working with a fractional CFO to help us manage our finances with Half a Bubble Out. (A fractional CFO is a part-time, outsourced chief financial officer.) We sat down with him and began looking over our reports.

When we got to the balance sheet, there was a pause. Our financial expert looked at us and said as straightforwardly as possible, "It's a balance sheet. It's supposed to balance." Apparently, our balance sheet failed to balance. This was news to us.

We sat there as he smirked, and we sheepishly laughed. "Oh, right," we said. "Of course. The balance sheet...balances." He told us what we needed to do to fix it. The two of us learned our lesson, fixed it, and have never looked at a balance sheet the same way since. So, let's discuss what the numbers on a balance sheet represent and why it's so important that they balance.

First, at the top of a balance sheet, there will be a specific date—usually, the end of the month, quarter, or fiscal year. Although there are a couple different ways to write up a balance sheet, the traditional model shows *assets* on the top half of the page. On the bottom half of the page are listed the *liabilities* and *owner's equity*. When you use accounting software to run this report at any given time, **the balance sheet will show you what the company owns, what it owes, and how much it's worth.**

Your business's *assets* describe what you own, and the *liabilities* describe what you owe. Your petty cash? That's an asset. The money in your bank account? That's an asset. Your accounts receivable, or the funds owed to your business? Once again, that's an asset. What about a physical asset, like a vehicle, that you still owe money on? Let's say you bought a truck for $10,000 and still owe most of the money. You list the truck in the assets column, and the loan would be listed in the liability column. The value of the truck is weighted against the debt in the liabilities column.

The balance sheet also tells you about the *owner's equity*—in other words, what the owner has. That number is determined by the accumulated profit or loss that the company has experienced since it began. If the company has gained in profitability and value, the owner's equity is going to be a positive number. If it's taken on a ton of debt since it started and hasn't climbed out of that yet, the owner's equity is going to be a negative number. This number is added to the liabilities number, and their sum is listed at the bottom of the page.

So, on the top half of the balance sheet, you have all your assets, and the value of your assets is listed at the bottom of that grouping. On the bottom half, you have all your liabilities, added to the number representing the owner's equity; *that* number is listed on the bottom of that grouping.

Here's the most important thing to know about a balance sheet: **if everything on a balance sheet is entered correctly, the assets should equal your liabilities and owner's equity (i.e., they should be *balanced*).** That's why it's called a balance sheet, as our sassy, smirking fractional CFO explained to us so long ago. If the two sides of a balance sheet don't balance, something has gone terribly askew.

Frankly, understanding the balance sheet can be a bit challenging for those of us who are not accountants, and most of us will need to keep learning—*we're still learning*. We're not geniuses at this, but we have learned to understand enough to manage our finances effectively and get the right people in place, so we have the right information to make the right solution. The main thing you need to understand about a balance sheet is that it's supposed to balance; if it doesn't, then you might want to call in your CPA. We've learned the hard way that our CPA can fix something in thirty seconds that we would waste hours researching and probably still not solve!

Remember that we told you earlier, you need to take the "chapters" of these foundational documents *together*, in order to understand the whole story of your company's financial position. The balance sheet will show you things that don't show up on the income statement. For example, if you have long-term debt like a bank loan, that would show up on your balance sheet but not your income statement. Also, if you own multiple franchises, your balance sheet will reflect the financial position of your entire organization, not just the individual franchises, which would each have their own income statements. You need the balance sheet for a more well-rounded picture of your financial health.

Taken individually, either the income statement or balance sheet will only tell you part of the story, which can lead you to false assumptions. But wait—the plot thickens. We still need a few more chapters before we have the whole story in hand.

Cash Flow

Remember back in chapter two when we explained cash flow in the context of selling coasters? Let's revisit those coaster-selling days and see how they can shed light on our cash flow report.

If you recall in chapter two, you bought $10,000 worth of coasters and then turned around and found a buyer who wanted to buy all the coasters for $20,000. You've just made a fantastic profit of $10,000—but that profit doesn't hit your bank account immediately. Your $10,000 payment left your bank account when you bought the coasters from the wholesaler. Then, there was a delay while they were shipped to you. Then, there was another delay after you issued your buyer their invoice. Then, they had thirty days to pay you, but didn't manage to submit the payment until ninety days after receiving the invoice. Remember all that painful waiting? It was brutal.

So, your *income statement* reflects the sale of $20,000 worth of coasters, weighed against the $10,000 it took to buy them. You note the sale and the purchase according to the date they each were made. However, the money on the income statement doesn't translate directly to how much cash you have in the bank. Maybe you purchased the coasters from the wholesaler on March 1, and your payment was processed a month later, on April 1. You made the sale, let's say, on March 2, but the cash didn't arrive for another five months, not until mid-August.

How do you know how much money you've got to spend on other stuff? Clearly, there needs to be another document that reflects the reality in your bank account. This is where the cash flow report makes its grand entrance.

Whereas the income statement is designed to keep track of what you sold and what you bought, **the cash flow report actually reflects *when* the cash comes in and when it goes out.** One of the biggest questions business owners ask is, "Why don't I have any cash if I made a profit?" You may have made a profit— but if you purchased equipment or paid down a loan, these cash transactions don't hit your income statement. So, you can have a $10,000 profit, but if you purchased $20,000 in equipment, your cash had a net decrease by $10,000. Cash flow can also simply be impacted by timing. Remember our analogy of packing enough rations on your ship for your journey to the Caribbean? Your cash flow is significantly impacted by when you send and receive payment.

A traditional cash flow statement looks like a spreadsheet, except instead of capturing what you marked as a sale, expense, or a cost of goods, it would actually track when you *sent* money and when you *received* money.

So how does it work? Let's say that you sold a widget on June 1 for $1,000, which will come in over three payments. On your *income statement*, you would note the sale of $1,000 on June 1. On your *cash flow report*, you would jump ahead to whenever you would expect to receive those payments. If the customer has thirty days before their first payment is due, then you go to July 1 and write in the expected payment: $333.33. On August 1 and September 1, you note the same expected payment. The further out you go, the less accurate your cash flow projections will be—because life is unpredictable. Sometimes people pay early, and sometimes they pay late.

Every month, you reconcile your cash flow report. You'll note whether or not your projected payments came. You'll also note when *your* payments went out. The cash flow report helps you project what you'll have in the bank over the next month, two months, three months, and so on.

Every business leader needs to be able to take into account the expenses that are going to hit next week, next month, and so on. If you can't predict those expenses, you can't confidently know you're going to be able to pay your staff or keep your business open—even if it looks like, for the moment, that you have a positive cash balance. Similarly, if you can't predict when your profits will finally hit your bank accounts, you don't know when you're going to be able to time new purchases and investments. If you have a tendency to run by whatever is in your bank account, your financial picture is going to get troublesome quickly.

However, by paying attention to the cash flow report, you're going to be able to make sure you've got sufficient provisions to get you to the next port. You'll be able to safeguard against lags in payments, and time your big purchases wisely. Ultimately, you've got a much better chance at keeping your business afloat.

Accounts Receivable and Accounts Payable

In a large company, the leader may not need to review accounts receivable and accounts payable reports. However, in a smaller company, those will be the last two reports that will warrant your regular attention.

Accounts receivable is literally a list of all the people who owe you money, along with how much money they owe you and where they're at in their timing. Did they pay you within those first thirty days, or are they within sixty, ninety, or 120 days? Accounts receivable helps you stay on top of clients who are behind in their payments so that you can regularly remind them, "Hey! I'm still here! Still waiting for payment!"

Accounts payable shows what *you* owe to vendors, and where you're at in *your* timing. This is going to help you stay on top of your payments, so that ideally, no one calls you saying, "Hey! I'm still here! Still waiting for payment!" Who wants a call like that?

(And a Pep Talk)

Did you follow all that? If so, then you now have basic literacy to read the first few chapters of your business's financial story! Those five reports provide the basics of measurement to evaluate where you're at financially.

It's easy to be imprecise in business when you're discussing money. We say things like, "I made money, but I didn't get money," or, "We're profitable, but we're behind in our bills." It's also easy to avoid dealing with your financial reports altogether. Tell us if this sounds familiar: when your accountant hands you the reports, you push them to the back of your desk and decide you're going to work on something else that you like dealing with more. Then, you never get to the reports at all.

However, when you're in a position to comprehend these five reports, you're able to be more precise so you know exactly what's going on with your business's finances. Even more importantly, you won't be afraid to read them! That's going to make you a much stronger business leader and better equip you to lead a Passion & Provision company. You're going to know what's coming in, and what's going out, and how much you get to keep at the end of the month.

Remember in a Passion & Provision company, half of the equation is Provision. You need to have enough in your bank account to provide for all the bills of today, and the dreams and expenses of tomorrow. If you want to do that, you need to operate with a clear, precise view of where you stand financially. When you learn the language of these reports, that becomes possible in a way it's not when they feel scary and confusing.

UNDERSTAND THE ART

Now you know the essentials about the foundational basics of measurement. You know how you can use those reports to view the story of your business. But before you get too mesmerized by staring at all those figures on your financial reports, there are a few other financial skills that are important to learn—such as, the importance of understanding the *art* of accounting.

One of the most confusing things we learned as we sought to deepen our financial understanding was that accounting is *not* the exact science we thought it was. We always assumed accounting was a detailed, exact, mathematical process, chronicling each dollar and cent. But it's not.

Accounting is not an absolute science. It *is* a science, and there *is* specificity, but it's also an art. Think about it this way: information can fall into various categories. There are rules. There are estimates. And there are assumptions.

There are rules. There are estimates. And there are assumptions.

Through every step in accounting, you have to make estimates and assumptions on what happened. Why? You can never truly stop the world and count every last penny. The world of commerce just doesn't afford us the time to work that minutely.

People can easily get anxious if there's a difference between what their books said, and what their accountants report back for their end-of-the-year tax information. How could the accountants do that? Are they cooking the books? In most cases, no—that difference doesn't mean someone's cooking the books.

There are different ways to process your financial numbers—which, by the way, are fully legal and within the confines of Generally Accepted Accounting Principles (GAAP)—and the end rule for those different processes is that your figures have to be *close*.[57] There is a reasonable margin in which accountants

---

57 Generally accepted accounting principles (GAAP) refer to a common set of accounting principles, standards, and procedures issued by the Financial Accounting Standards Board (FASB).

estimate, because they can't know everything about every last cent you're spending and receiving. When the financial books get created, there are certain assumptions that are made along the way. If and when those assumptions change, the books can alter too.

You may have to make an assumption on where you put a certain expense or where you put a certain cost. For instance, our full-time employees are working to deliver our products and services to our customers. In theory, some percentage of their time should be put in expenses, and the customer-focused work they do should be categorized in cost of goods (COGs). So how do we figure out what number goes in each column?

Our employees can't devote 100 percent of their time to client-focused activities. Sometimes they're in staff meetings. They take their lunch. They go to the bathroom. Maybe one month, they're spending 52 percent of their time on customers; maybe another month, it's 68 percent. So, we make an estimate in our accounting that approximately 60 percent of what they do is client focused, and therefore categorized as COGs. It's not worth the effort for us to track down every single employee hour and put each hour in its respective category, but it still helps us get a better idea on what our COGs are than if we didn't enter that number at all. Good accounting means making assumptions and estimates.

Making these estimates can also help you tighten up your efficiency, if and when needed. Let's say you assume that your employees are devoting 60 percent of their work toward paid work for clients, and you note that in the books. At the end of the quarter or year, the business's leaders (i.e., you) will look over the books and determine you need to make more money to stay viable. Perhaps you're not making enough profit, or maybe you're even losing money. So, where do you make that up?

You may determine that the staff needs to be more efficient, so you decide to shorten your meetings during the week so that your employees can devote more time to client work. You might push for 70 percent of your employees' time to be devoted to client work, instead of 60. From there, you determine how that's going to work in operations, from a management perspective. You make a plan and implement it for the next quarter. Then you test your new procedures, hone your new processes, and get a sense of what amount of time your employees are now devoting to the client work. If it's looking like 70 percent, then you go back to the books, alter your numbers, and move 70 percent into your COGs.

Art in Action

Here's an illustration of how this played out for us. We shared in our chapter on Management and Operations that we were trying to tighten up the time it took for our Rabbit Hole Hay employees to pack hay into boxes. It was taking most of our warehouse employees about an hour to pack twenty boxes of hay. Our business partner would sometimes go out to the warehouse to work alongside the other employees and get a sense of the process. He works incredibly fast and incredibly hard; he could do thirty-five in an hour. Most of our employees weren't going to be able to work at his level, but we decided they might be able to do thirty an hour if they really applied themselves. That would make quite a difference in our cost of goods, as we're about to describe.

Let's assume our employees were building twenty boxes and we were paying them $15 an hour; in simple terms, that would mean that each finished box was costing us seventy-five cents in labor.

When they improved to thirty boxes per hour, then each finished box was costing us fifty cents in labor. Great improvement in our cost of goods!

We set a goal as managers and gave that goal to our staff in the warehouse. To their credit, the crew in the warehouse seriously stepped up their game and started managing thirty an hour. With that new metric, we changed our assumptions moving forward for the labor piece of our cost of goods.

However, neither of us are at the warehouse every day. As staff workers changed out and we stopped putting the pressure on, our warehouse staff started slowing down. The next time we took a good look at our numbers, we realized that our accounting assumption had gotten way off. Our assumption about their time meant we should have been getting thirty boxes an hour, but our production was way low. We had made estimates and reported it in our annual accounting, but the reality didn't work according to our assumptions, so we had to adjust.

As a business leader, it's important for you to be able to make assumptions and estimates to the best of your ability—and it's also important to make sure you're aware of the assumptions *other* people are making when they give you a set of books. If you don't know someone else is making an assumption, you'll misunderstand what's going on. Learning to estimate, adjust, readjust, and re-estimate is all part of learning the *art* of the accounting science. As with any art, you get better with practice!

UNDERSTAND THE ANALYSIS

Once you understand the fundamental basics of your reports, and you understand the art of how the numbers were put together, then it's time to *analyze* it all and start making decisions.

Let's imagine you have a basic report in front of you, and you want to look at your gross profit margin.[58] Your income statement says that you have $25,000—but what does that mean? Is that a 22.5 percent gross profit margin? Should you round up to 23 percent? As you become more comfortable looking over your numbers, you'll realize that **percentages provide more clarity than just dollar amounts, especially in your use of *ratios*.**

The Usefulness of Ratios

Ratios are used as a shorthand way to evaluate where you stand, financially. Essentially, a ratio helps you compare two numbers. Let's say you're trying to figure out if you have enough money, and for you, "enough" means you have twice as much money in the bank as what you owe people in liabilities, in case of an emergency. You want to compare your assets with your liabilities. So, if it costs you $100,000 to run the company, you may want to have an extra $100,000 in the bank. That means a.) you have the $100,000 you need to run the company to pay your liabilities, and b.) you have $100,000 in the bank as an asset. If you have $200,000 and the liabilities of the company are $100,000; that works out to a 2:1 ratio. If the ratio is more than one, you have more money than what you owe. CFOs and business leaders generally determine what their ideal ratios are and operate according to those goals.

---

58 When we say margin, we're basically talking about the "extra." For instance, for every dollar that a restaurant spends, it may cost them ninety-seven cents just for the cost of goods, which means they have three cents to pay for any overhead or expenses; that's a 3 percent gross margin. In contrast, a consultant may have 90 percent gross profit because their Costs of Goods is so small. Because they get to keep so much of the profit, there's more "extra," and the margin ends up being a much larger percentage.

Although there are some general rules of thumb, which we'll discuss in a moment, it's not uncommon for these "ideal" margins to differ from company to company. Everyone has an opinion about what's "safe." Some people are risk averse and want conservative ratios; others are comfortable with risk and feel fine operating with slimmer margins.

In sum, ratios provide a quick summary of how you're doing, financially. They enable you to look at your numbers quickly without having to do the math all the time. For instance, the "2:1 liabilities versus assets" is a ratio that tells you quickly if you're negative or positive. A CFO can come in, look at those calculations, do those ratios, and then have a conversation with you about where you stand. They don't talk about "$1,300,332 versus $1,040,266." They go, "You have a 1.25 ratio. That means you have more money than you're spending. You're good."

"You're good"—that's the kind of phrase that makes ratios so helpful. Ratios are going to help you understand whether the numbers in front of you are good, bad, or mediocre. For instance, let's say you want to look at the ratio of the gross profit versus the net profit. As a reminder, the gross profit is your revenue, minus your cost of goods. The net profit is your gross profit, minus your expenses. That comparison—that ratio—will tell you about your return on investment (ROI), which is key information about your profitability.

For instance, if your *gross* profit is 50 percent, you might think you're looking pretty good—but if your expenses are high, and your *net* profit only works out to 5 percent, that might be a sign you need to make some changes that work out to a larger number on the bottom line. Once you determine your target for your net income margin, you'll be able to see if your numbers are where you want them.

Another informative ratio might be the total amount of money you're spending on employees, versus your gross profit. Generally, you should have an idea of what percentage of your gross revenue should be allocated to pay your employees and try to align your budget with that. Keep your industry in mind when you're arriving at the appropriate percentage amount. Some industries, like the restaurant industry, operate with incredibly thin margins—they're often making only 2 to 5 percent beyond what they spend. Other industries, like consulting, have quite high gross profit margins, somewhere around 80 to 90 percent. They're not operating with a storefront, there are almost no cost of goods expenses, and they can operate with only a few employees. Every industry has a general rule of thumb for the appropriate percentage allocated to employee salaries.

However, in most industries, a good rule of thumb for employee salaries and benefits is that they should fall somewhere around 30 percent of your gross revenue. Without looking at that ratio, it might be hard to know whether or not you're spending too much or too little on your employees, just by looking at your income statement. But if you know that your total amount spent on employees should equal roughly 30 percent of your gross revenue—then, you have some useful information to make potentially necessary changes.

Depending on your Vision for your company, you may then create some additional goals for how you'd like to pay your employees. For instance, although the general rule for our marketing industry is to pay employees 30 percent of its gross revenue, the two of us have at times decided to shift that percentage down or up, depending on our circumstances. In one season, we decided we wanted to run a leaner operation so that we'd have more profits to invest for growth. We determined that we could do everything for our clients, do it well, and keep our labor costs at 25 percent; that way, we could take more of the profits and funnel it into growth.

More often, we're increasing the percentage that we pay to our employees. We value our people—they're good people—and we'd rather pay them more and keep them on than bring on new employees and risk a dip in quality with our clients. In recent years, we've decided to pay our employees 35 percent of our gross revenue, instead of 30.

This is the point: when you start analyzing the numbers according to these ratios, you're better equipped to use them to fulfill your Vision for your company. You can improve your Provision by spotting where you need to tighten things up, or where you have extra bandwidth to invest in a new tool. You also can enhance the Passion of your company by discovering ways to increase salaries and make work less stressful. These strategic, analytical moves are what we call *pressing levers*.

Pressing Levers

When soccer players are just starting out, they learn that they're supposed to kick the ball with their foot, and they're not allowed to pick it up. Intermediate soccer players learn concepts of offense and defense. Advanced soccer players can juggle the ball with all parts of their body, have skillful plays developed with their teammates, and can kick goals into the net that could only be accomplished with amazing athleticism.

Learning to read your financial reports is like learning some of the fundamental *rules* that define the game you're playing. Learning the art is like learning *concepts* about the game, like offense. Understanding the *analysis* is like recognizing key moves that could create a significant change in your game score. We call those rules levers. You become adept at pressing these levers with every bit of increased education and effort you invest toward your finances. Just like practice and working out increases the athleticism of a soccer player, experience in analyzing your numbers will make you freer and wiser about using those levers to make great financial moves.

What are some of those levers? Here are a few:

- **Increase your topline revenue:** On your income statement you can separate out your revenue streams by category, and then review the profitability of each main area: that's a lever. In our business, one of the largest revenue streams has been working as an ad agency and purchasing media on behalf of our clients. It can be a huge top-line revenue number, but the COGs on a media buy is 85 percent, leaving us 15 percent gross margin. That means, for every dollar in revenue, we're only making fifteen cents profit on media buys. By contrast, we charge much more for consulting services, because of the value of our time. Even though we're giving up valuable time when we consult, there are no COGs—so, the profit ends up being *much* higher. If we want to push a lever, it makes sense to increase our higher-end consulting, because more profit makes it through to the bottom line. That doesn't mean we say no to the 15 percent margin opportunities; it's still great to spend $1 and make $1.15. Still—if we can spend $1 and make $1.50, then it might be wise to focus our energy in that direction!
- **Predict the profits from price changes.** The reports can also allow you to see what would happen if you increased your prices. For example, our pricing on Rabbit Hole Hay was low and we weren't making nearly enough money for the company

to grow like it needed to. In working with our CFO, we set a target of having a 25 percent gross margin in our industry, but we were only at 18 percent. We did everything we could to get to 25 percent for our gross profit. We started by analyzing our cash flow projections and realized that we needed to increase our prices on all of our products. We also worked to improve our efficiency, as we discussed earlier. When we were able to bring our gross margin up to 25 percent, we knew the changes were effective and we were back on track.

- **Reduce COGs or expenses.** Seeing clearly what your expenses are on reports like the income statement can also help you make decisions that significantly impact the profitability of your company. For example, you may be outsourcing an area of your business because that made sense at one point. But if you're paying an hourly rate to an outsource person and they're working close to full time; you're probably paying more than if you brought that service in-house. You might be able to bring down your COGs by changing a vendor and getting a better price. If you're in a product business, you might be able to move up to the next price break in your quantities, which can shift things significantly. Seeing the reality of what your COGs are for particular items can motivate you to make changes, if you're able.

- **Understand your story.** Sometimes, these reports simply make key pieces of your story more obvious, which can help clarify your next steps as a business. For example, we were doing some vision and messaging work with a local nonprofit with a budget around $8 million. They came to us, insisting that we focus our messaging energy on one particular offering of their overall organization. As we dug into their background, their offerings, and their finances, we made an interesting discovery. While they were asking us to focus time, energy, and their cash resources on one area, that particular area was producing less than 10 percent of their overall revenue, and wasn't in a position to grow much beyond that. Meanwhile, the area that was producing 70 percent or more of their revenue on any given year was being completely ignored. We used a simple pie chart to diagram their revenue and expenses in each area. They knew the data. They gave us the information to draw the picture. But the picture told them a story they didn't see clearly before, enabling us to adjust the focus of the messaging to a more robust picture of what they were actually offering the community. That, too, is pressing a lever.

UNDERSTAND THE BIG PICTURE

There's the foundation: the rules and reports.

There's the art: the assumptions, estimates, and predictions.

There's the analysis: using the numbers to make decisions.

Then, there's the fourth piece: factoring the numbers into the big picture.

Here's a myth: the numbers tell you everything, and you should be able to understand everything about your business's finances with just the numbers. That notion is not actually true—maybe you got a hint of that truth with the last "lever" we just described.

Your reports don't tell the *whole* financial story, and the *whole* financial story is what we've been after all along. You've also got to consider the big picture: changes in the economy, changes in your customers, new strategies from your competitors, a shift in expectations, and so on.

We'll share another story from Rabbit Hole Hay as an example. A few years ago, Northern California (where the hay is grown) experienced a drought, which significantly impacted the amount of hay that was available. Three things happened: one, we got less hay. Two, the hay wasn't as good as what we'd sold before. Three, customers were frustrated.

Here's a tip about considering the big picture when you're looking at your numbers: they're always backwards. They tell the story in reverse. For instance, we could *predict* that our numbers were going to suffer as we watched the effects of the drought and started getting complaints from our customers. But as those complaints were rolling in, our numbers for the past month were still good. If we were to just look at the numbers, we would have said we should be able to forge ahead without any changes and continue in profitability.

But we *couldn't* just make decisions based on the numbers. We had customers leaving and buying hay from our competitors. Our competitors were struggling with the drought just as much as we were. We knew that once customers realized that similarity in quality, we could get them to come back to us—but that required some incentivizing. To woo customers back, we needed to lower our prices and offer discounts. We also determined we needed to offer a guarantee to give customers their money back if the hay was bad. We had to revisit our goal of 25 percent profitability and consider whether that goal needed adjusting, given the big-picture factor of the environment.

When the drought finally eased up and the rain came, good hay started growing again. We knew we'd be able to start raising prices soon and that customers would be pleased with our quality, but even as conditions were improving, that's when our numbers looked the worst; that's what we mean when we say your reports tell the story of the big picture in reverse.

That's an environmental factor, but there are economic factors outside of your control too, like a government's initiation of tariffs to another country if you're exporting. When tariffs go up, your expenses go up. For example, we sell Rabbit Hole Hay products both domestically and internationally. Recently, a distributor in the Philippines reached out to us and asked to buy our hay. We got almost all the way through the process before a new governmental law went into effect, which required any agricultural products coming into the Philippines to be fumigated. Nobody in our industry fumigates. It's too expensive, and we weren't about to start. What we thought was going to be a sale and a growth into a whole new country abruptly stopped because of a governmental requirement.

We had determined with our CFO that we needed to achieve a 25 percent margin for Rabbit Hole Hay, after subtracting our cost of goods. Then, we came up with ways to accomplish that margin. But when the big-picture factors come into play, your strategy may have to change. Those factors are necessary to consider when you're looking to make the wisest financial decisions for your company.

BUILD A TEAM

Of all the areas of business we discuss in this book, we can't implore you strongly enough to make sure you build a team in the area of finance. From the very beginning of our business, this was one piece we did right. We set our books up in a software that would allow us to grow, and we did so under the guidance of our CPA. Over the years we have come to learn that if mistakes are made in your books, having someone from the outside to help can save you not only time but money.

> We can't stress this enough: make sure you build a team in the area of finance.

Kathryn once spent three hours on the phone with the accounting software help desk after doing about an hour of research to try to figure out why something was out of whack in our accounting system. They couldn't figure it out, and so that was four hours of her life, gone. She relented and asked our CPA to come in and he literally found the issue and fixed it in under four minutes. Four hours versus four minutes. As one of the owners of the company Kathryn's time is worth a lot, so what an incredible waste! She swore she would call him first the next time.

So, build your team. For sure you need a solid CPA both for your year-end taxes, but also for assistance along the way. When you are able, bringing in a fractional CFO can help you really evaluate your levers and provide input into significant strategies for growth.

We know the objection: "I can't afford it." All we can say is that in the area of finance, you can't afford not to.

THE VALUE OF UNDERSTANDING YOUR FINANCES

Michael Gerber, the author of *E-Myth* and *E-Myth Mastery,* did amazing work in saving his company. He's brought incredible benefits to the business market and has educated many of us through sharing the lessons that he learned. He's introduced us to sound principles, which we use to run our own small businesses, and he has been candid about his own mistakes in his pursuit to help other people learn.

In spite of all that he's contributed, it's hard not to view his story as a tragedy.

Gerber's book wasn't just a how-to book about running a small business—it was also a confession. Gerber describes how he ran his company as a warning to other people. In the end, not only did the business go through tumultuous, stressful times on its way back to viability, it also required that Michael Gerber step down as the CEO. He moved to the board and was no longer involved in the day-to-day actions of his business. Most tragically of all, he and his wife got divorced—even though she had been integral in turning the company around and paying off its debts. The company survived, but the process of keeping it alive was so brutal, she finally told him that they were done.

The concepts and figures in this chapter may seem dry—we get that. But you *need* them. We feel so strongly that every leader of a Passion & Provision company needs to get this stuff. To fail to learn it could lead to the undoing of everything you're working for and care about. When you realize that you've let the money get away from you, you've got to make the horrible conclusion that you haven't managed your company well. As Gerber can attest, that's a miserable conclusion.

But *when* you come to understand and grasp this—and you will— you're able to get a Passion & Provision company in place. Not only will you avoid the stress of debt, lawsuits, bankruptcy, and pain and suffering, but you're also working to keep what matters most to you: your sanity, your closest relationships, and your health.

When you choose to stay on top of the four skills needed to accurately track and monitor your company's finances, then you're not only gaining Provision, you're also gaining fulfillment and meaning—not to mention, a good night's sleep.

TIME TO GROW YOUR MONEY SMARTS AND ATTITUDE

- Go to **fulfilledthebook.com** to download sample financial reports and additional resources to put together your business's financial road map.
- Take some time to reflect on your emotional relationship with money and how you view finances.
- Are there any life experiences that have an impact on how you view and deal with money?
- Are you running and reviewing your key monthly reports?
- Print out a current income statement for your business. Take a look at your revenue streams. Do you have your different products or types of services separated out and clearly labeled? Or are they lumped all together?
- Look at your cost of goods. Do you have them labeled and separated out to mirror your revenue accounts?
- If your revenue accounts and cost of goods accounts are not separated out, now is a great time to do that! Base your accounts on different revenue streams (types of products or services) so that you can start to track performance of those streams.
- Look at your cost of goods and consider which revenue streams are making you the most gross profit. These may be key areas to dive into a bit more as you lead your business.

CHAPTER NINE

‖‖‖‖‖‖‖‖‖‖‖‖‖

Culture

"Culture is not an initiative. Culture is the enabler of all initiatives."

LARRY SENN

Every spring in Northern California, the blossoms come. Thousands of acres of almond trees put forward their whitish-pink flowers. If you were to see Northern California from an aerial view, you would guess there had been a snowfall. You can't drive anywhere without seeing the blossoming almond trees. They're beautiful.

And every spring, the farmers hold their breath. They wonder, will the weather be right? Will there be enough water? Are we going to have a freeze? We rarely get freezes here, but they sometimes come. If a freeze comes too early, it can damage the blossoms, which ends up ruining the crop.

Most often though, the blossoms transition into robust green leaves. Then, the nuts come, and the graceful white dancers of the spring turn into stout, hardy trees, heavy with almonds. When harvest time arrives between August and September, the orchards are alive with workers, twenty-four hours a day. You'll drive past fields at night and see lights on, tractors humming.

We live in the almond capital of the world. Ninety-five percent of the world's almonds come from central and Northern California. We have over a million acres of almond trees—which locals actually call "a'monds" because when you knocked them out of the tree, in the olden days before mechanical shakers, you "knocked the L out of them." Plenty of us grew up making money by helping out at harvest time, and some of the old-timers actually remember whacking the "L" out of a'mond trees, using an ax handle covered with an old tire.

The United States Department of Agriculture maps out thirteen different growing zones across the country. Every growing zone has particular weather conditions, temperature ranges, soil types, and average precipitation. Citrus trees love zone ten, down in Southern California and Florida. Apples love zone six, like in Washington state or Massachusetts. Corn loves zone five, in Illinois and Iowa.

Our area is classified as zone nine, which apparently almond trees love. We have warm summers with hardly any rain, and we don't get extreme temperatures. There's rarely a freeze and almost never snow. The almond orchards also thrive because of the dirt of the Sacramento Valley. There are nutrients in the ground, stirred up by the snow paths of the Sierra Nevadas that melt off and drain into our creeks and rivers. In spite of all that agricultural goodness, plenty of produce doesn't like our growing zone. We have individual citrus trees here and there, but you won't see an orange grove. But almonds? The a'monds love it.

GROWING PEOPLE

People are not so different from almond trees—or any other growing thing, for that matter. Whether you're talking about plants or human beings, growing things need to be nurtured and cared for in a way that helps them grow. In the work environment, you determine your growing zone by cultivating your *culture*.

If you create a workplace culture that's equivalent to a cold and hostile growing zone, you can plant all kinds of good seeds, but you won't see good growth. Not even close. Your employees will perform poorly and won't grow or produce at the level you want. How could they? On the other hand, if you create an environmental structure that is hospitable to trust, creativity, community, communication, and so on—and if you maintain and nurture that culture—you are optimizing your growing zone so that your employees can flourish.

In every business there is a culture, just like there's a growing zone. As the leader, you have control over how you shape that culture to optimize the climate for what you want to grow. Think of it like having a greenhouse. You can set the temperature and the humidity and everything else inside your business, from the physical environment to the emotional environment. Here's the thing: the culture inside of a business is reflected in your people and it will grow no matter what. There *is* a culture that exists already in your workplace, and it's either helping or impeding your staff. Creating a good culture requires you to decide what the best conditions are going to be, create them, maintain them, and nurture the growth that begins so that you get the produce that you want.

An almond tree will thrive in Northern California, producing nuts to its fullest potential. Why? Because it was planted in the right environment. Similarly, if you can create the right environment for the human being—your team, your people, your company—they will be empowered to reach their full potential. They will produce a tremendous amount of fruit, which is efficiency, innovation, ideas, and teamwork. Similar to what we've talked about in so many of these Passion & Provision areas, when you transition from mindless default mode to intentionally cultivating something good—whether that's Leadership or Marketing or another core competency—you get a multiplication effect. The growth becomes exponential.

When cultivated well, your culture will help your team produce and profit. But it will also help the fruit produced to be *good,* sweet fruit. You'll be able to cultivate the values you want and help so many of the other Passion & Provision areas come together. Because of that, culture comes to be the anchor in a Passion & Provision company. It helps reinforce all the other areas, provided you're intentional in how you create it.

Everything thrives or dies in relationship to its culture. How you shape and shepherd your culture will determine if your people perform like rock stars for you—or just show up to punch a clock and get their paycheck for one more week.

WHAT CULTURE IS AND ISN'T

Culture comes from the Latin word "cultus" which means *care*. Cultural trends pop onto the scene often, but that's not what you want in your workplace. You want to care for and *cultivate* something more substantial, something that will inform the experience of every employee and client interacting with your business.

Having a fun company culture is a popular idea—tech companies, for instance, are famous for having ping-pong tables or napping rooms or areas to play video games. Companies want to propagate the cool-company culture so that they're featured on the six o'clock news and can attract good employees. But if the company's values don't support its attempt at creating culture, the environmental changes aren't going to help your employees much.

We used to partner with a company that had a nap room, and no one used it. When we asked why, one of the twenty-somethings said, "No young person who wants to move ahead in the company is going to be seen napping at work." That company clearly wanted to create a "cool culture," but only superficially; employees got the message that their productivity was more important than that post-lunch siesta. The nap room is now a conference room.

In the past, organizations assumed they could create a place where people needed to work. Now, however, they're realizing they need to create a place where people want to work. —Jacob Morgan in *Forbes*[59]

---

59   Morgan, Jacob. "Why The Future Of Work Is All About The Employee Experience." Forbes. Forbes Magazine, June 15, 2015. https://www.forbes.com/sites/jacobmorgan/2015/05/27/why-the-future-of-work-is-all-about-the-employee-experience/#7ddc40156f0a.

For many business leaders and HR managers, the obvious solution to attracting and keeping good employees is to offer more perks: catered meals, on-site dry cleaning, beautiful office spaces, modern technology, flexible work programs, and any number of others.

For the average small business owner, this might seem intimidating. Most small business owners can't afford to offer perks like these. Plenty of others might wonder why they should want to create a health spa for their employees to begin with. Aren't their employees already getting a paycheck?!

Here's what we think. When large companies seek to create an attractive culture using perks, they're essentially *bribing* people with external things like money, and polish, and fancy *stuff*.

In an effort to attract and retain great employees, employers can get desperate—but so often, they focus on the wrong things. We can remember reading a story about a man who demanded that he be able to work naked, so his employer created a night-shift position for him where he'd be the only one in the office, and he could work in the buff. But if employers keep capitulating to employees' demands for more perks, they're creating an environment that's based on greed—not one that's touching their employees' core needs.

Perks are nice on the surface—but after a point they only meet surface needs. Creating a positive work culture goes deeper than surface-level perks. If you want to create a genuinely healthy, positive workplace culture, it needs to be rooted in authentic values.

Don't get us wrong. We love benefits and perks and think that those are nice additions to a work environment. In the following pages you'll hear about one or two of our perks that our team loves and we wouldn't give them up for anything.

Perks and benefits aren't inherently bad, but they become empty and hollow when they are used as substitutes for real culture. Perks are not the things that help sustain motivation or even happiness. Perks are just that—nice extras after the fundamentals are taken care of.

Similarly, culture also isn't about just paying more money. Employees should be paid a competitive rate and we believe in the old saying, "The ox is worthy of its wage," which means the pay should be commensurate to the work they are doing. It needs to be fair and we might even say generous. However, there's a common misconception that if employees are paid more money, they'll want to work more—but that backfires. Why?

Imagine someone says, "I care for you, so here's $20." If that's the standard of care, then what happens when you *don't* give your employee an additional $20? Do they suddenly stop feeling cared for? Or what happens when someone offers your employee $25? If employees only feel as "cared" for as much as the amount of their paycheck, there's no reason to stick around if someone "cares" about them more, with more money. Healthy, positive culture, on the other hand, communicates to employees that they're worth more than just their dollar value.

So, here's what company culture is *not:* **company culture is not based on trends or perks.** It's not a matter of having a ping-pong table or on-site dry cleaning. It's not about whether or not you get to work in the nude. Everyone knows that their experience at work is defined by more than that—because that's not what culture is actually about.

WHAT CULTURE *IS*, ACTUALLY

From an employee's standpoint, culture is defined by the leader's management style, and the camaraderie (or lack thereof) on their team. It's defined by whether or not their creativity is invited, encouraged, and stirred up. It's defined by their manager's concern or apathy about their life outside of work. It's defined by their sense of purpose, and by their feeling of connectedness to something bigger. It's defined by their physical space. It's defined by their stress level. It's defined by the company's *values*.

Here's what culture *is*, first and foremost: **culture is informed by the company's Core Values.** In order to cultivate a lasting, thriving culture, you need to connect the culture to your authentic Core Values. Those values are going to be the roots that help your culture deepen and thrive—not just die out after one good season. Without the connection to your Core Values, superficial changes—even "cool" ones—are going to be rootless, and ultimately unproductive. A Passion & Provision culture, on the other hand, one that's based on Core Values, genuinely impacts the experience of its employees for the good. It communicates that they're valued as human beings, respected, and cared for. That's the kind of culture that cultivates the soil, creating that optimal growing zone.

Culture is also informed by how people are treated at work. We touched on this in our Leadership chapter: if your employees feel micromanaged, belittled, or undervalued at work—they're not going to perform well. If there's a culture of backstabbing or gossip or intimidation, they're not going to feel safe in putting forward their best ideas and they won't enjoy being around their coworkers. On the other hand, if you treat your employees with dignity, and work to create a relational culture of trust, they'll thrive. People have a desire to be known—to be connected to a bigger purpose, to feel their work matters, to be seen and appreciated. If you can cultivate that kind of culture, you're moving your workplace toward its ideal growing zone.

Culture is informed by its physical environment. It's not *only* about the physical environment, as we've discussed, but the physical space people work in does have a huge impact on their daily experience. Conan O'Brien, the comedian, famously mocked the microchip manufacturing company Intel on his *Late Night* show.[60] While his camera crew filmed, Conan went on a guided tour and made various remarks about Intel's now famously bad physical space.

He pointed out the gray walls: "I love what you've done with the color here. The gray works very nicely with the gray, which works well with the, uh, grayish-blue."

He riffed on the long rows of cubicles: "It's good. It makes people feel they're all basically the same. There is no individuality. There is no hope."

When he saw that the pillars in the giant cubicle room had alphabetical and numerical signs, he quipped, "H10. Is that what you'd see in a parking garage?" Conan pointed out that every aspect of the workplace culture at Intel was dehumanizing and depressing.

Here's something to know about creating a good physical environment: it costs you money up front. Paint, furniture, plants—all of the elements of creating a pleasant space to work in can be expensive. However, you can get creative about how you outfit your working space in affordable ways. Putting time and money

---

60   93, Conan. "Conan Visits Intel - Late Night w/ Conan O'Brien." YouTube. YouTube, January 10, 2016. https://www.youtube.com/watch?v=5aNPMEAejeo.

into nurturing your people is a worthwhile investment; that's how you're going to cultivate a culture that will bring forward the best work possible from them—and from you. And even if you can't afford just yet to splurge on new glass front doors for your offices, it doesn't cost you anything to start building your relational culture. It doesn't cost a cent to work on being kind.

So, in summary: what's the kind of culture you want to aim for? Here's what we recommend: **A Passion & Provision culture is a healthy environment that allows for everyone to win, people to be valued, and cultivates people's strengths so they reach their potential within the natural constraints in business. It should be nurturing, both relationally and in its physical environment.**

But wait—is culture really that important? Couldn't culture be considered a cosmetic feature? Nice to have, but not totally necessary? Or at least—it's probably less critical to have in place than something like management and operations, right? Wrong.

"The single, greatest advantage any company can achieve is organizational health." —Patrick Lencioni

According to Patrick Lencioni, in his book *The Advantage: Why Organizational Health Trumps Everything Else in Business*, Lencioni makes an overwhelming case that organizational health will surpass all other disciplines in business as the greatest opportunity for improvement and competitive advantage. Think about that. It's not knowledge. It's not efficiency. It's organizational health—and along with the other key areas of Passion & Provision, part of organizational health is what we are calling "culture."

CULTURE CAN DO SOME OF THE WORK FOR YOU

So how does that work? How could culture end up being a strategic advantage?

Let us explain.

The people within your company are going to work at their best and be engaged if they're in a positive culture. They're going to work more creatively. They're going to work more efficiently. You're going to get the best work possible out of them, which ultimately means your customers are going to be happier. So, positive culture, equals more Passion.

As a result of the great work your employees are doing, for all of the reasons just described, you're going to get a better reputation, which leads to people spending more money. You're going to get referred to other people as you become known for your amazing work and genuine care for your clients. You'll also retain more employees and save money when you would have otherwise had to rehire new staff, and retrain. That all leads to more Provision. The wheel rolls on and on and on. A healthy, positive culture correlates with excellent work, and excellent work helps lead to a strong bottom line.

When you walk into companies that have a phenomenal reputation for quality and service, who have happy employees and good retention, who enjoy longevity as a company—almost to a tee, you can recognize a fantastic culture that is being intentionally cared for.

We've worked hard to create an inviting culture at Half a Bubble Out, and we see people engaging with our space and culture in a way that attests to the fact that our *culture* is actually doing some of the work for us. It's helping us attract and retain good employees. It's helping us make sales with clients. It's helping to keep our employees happy and motivated. It helps us look forward to coming to work. Here are a few examples of what we mean.

We have heard clients say many, many times, "I love coming to your office. It just feels good." Other people comment, "It feels so peaceful here," or "It's comfortable. *I* want to work from here." If we can make clients actually *look forward* to coming to our office— you can bet that gives us an edge over our competitors and helps us establish lasting client relationships. Part of why people feel so comfortable in our work space is also due to the peaceful relational quality we've worked hard to cultivate. Our employees' attitudes, emotions, and perspectives are all informed by the supportive and kind atmosphere we've tried to create—and people sense that peaceful quality when they visit us.

Let's stop a minute and address one potential objection. Some of you might be saying, this seems way too calm. How can you stay competitive? How do you handle problems? How do you handle conflict? These are great questions and when we describe our environment we don't want to miss this.

Our team is competitive, works really hard, and gets a lot of stuff done for our clients. When we say kind and peaceful, we don't mean apathetic and milquetoast. Imagine a sports team that is tuned up, working together, and killing it. What you don't see on most high-performing teams is dysfunction, backbiting, or lone rangers. Everyone has their place and the GREAT teams have a strong team identity with mutual respect for their teammates. Take the 1980 Olympic Gold Hockey Team depicted in the 2004 Disney movie *Miracle*. Their story of success had its roots on learning how to play as one team playing for America rather than a bunch of superstars from competing colleges with giant egos. That's peace. That's harmony and that's kindness. It focuses raw energy and creates victories that we dare say inspire people.

The reactions our staff and clients have also come as a result of the physical environment we've worked hard to cultivate. For instance, we have a large wooden dining table in our conference room that seats eight people. We used to have an office manager who wanted us to get rid of it because she believed it wasn't efficient. She complained, "I swear, these prospective customers that come in, they linger, and they *linger*." She said, "I'm absolutely convinced they linger because of this table and these chairs." She wanted to move our prospective clients through faster.

We told her, "We *want* them to linger!"

When people come to our office, we've consistently experienced an incredibly high closing rate for our sales. As they enter our office, and they're greeted politely, they're offered coffee or another beverage, they spot the office dog, and they're invited to sit down in a comfortable space—we see their interest escalating. It's remarkable.

If you don't think about culture—about the relational, emotional, intangible side of culture, along with the physical environment of culture—you're throwing away a great opportunity for your environment to do half the work for you. Even if you've done good work on all the other pieces of your business, if you haven't thought about culture, you're giving up a profound advantage in cultivating Passion & Provision in your workplace. This is true whether you work out of your garage, your home office, a building, or a high rise. It's crucial to be thoughtful of what people experience when they engage with your business.

Your workplace environment primes people, just as you might prime guests that come over. When you want your guests to stay and enjoy themselves, you make them comfortable, bring them food, bring them beverages, and make them feel welcome. If you don't want them to stay long, you may not offer them anything to eat or drink; you may not invite them to sit down. People pick up cues from the environment you create and either stay or leave.

> Your company's culture tells people whether they'll be cared for or neglected.

Culture informs both your clients and your employees if they're going to be cared for or neglected. If they get the message that they'll be neglected, you'll struggle to retain employees or make lasting client relationships. You'll risk building a reputation of carelessness. Trust will be compromised. Think about it: if you visited a gardener, and noticed that their garden was run rampant with weeds—would you trust that gardener with your own yard? On the other hand, you can use the culture of your workplace to communicate to both your employees and clients that this place is good and safe and produces quality things.

There are two main environments in which your company's culture can be created: the physical and the relational. Both environments need to be intentionally created. Both environments have the power to sabotage the other if they're bad; for instance, a beautiful work space can still be a hostile culture for growth if everyone is mean to each other. And finally, both need to be rooted in your Core Values. Let's talk more specifically how you can cultivate each environment.

PHYSICAL ASPECTS OF CULTURE

One of the most original thinkers and inventors of the twentieth century, R. Buckminster Fuller, aptly said, "You can't change people. But if you can change the environment that the people are in, they will change."[61]

Think about that: if you change the environment that people are in, *they will change.* You can make nice people nasty, and nasty people nice, by changing their environment.

The people behind all the Disney parks get this. In fact, Fuller's quote came from a book called *Be Our Guest* which describes some of the "secrets" Disney uses to help inspire the elation and giddiness that their parks—some of the "happiest places on earth"—are so known for.

In *Be Our Guest*, Ted Kinni notes some of the key components of physical setting that help create a physical environment which informs culture:[62]

- Architectural design
- Landscaping
- Lighting
- Signage
- Color
- Texture of floor surface
- Internal/external detail
- Music/ambient noise
- Smell
- Touch/tactile experiences
- Taste

---

61   Kinni, Ted. *Be Our Guest: Perfecting the Art of Customer Service.* Glendale, CA: Disney, 2011.

62   Ibid.

Anyone who's been to Disneyland or Disney World can start to think of all the ways these elements of physical culture are enhanced in the theme parks. The air is pumped full of the smell of popcorn and churros. There's cheerful music everywhere you go. The buildings are colorful. There are flowers and bushes and topiaries lining the streets. Every detail of the physical environment has been considered and tended to—and it works. People *love* being at Disneyland.

So, what does this mean in an office space? Let's roll up our sleeves for a second and talk interior design. Here are some of the ways we've tried to enhance our physical environment at Half a Bubble Out, which may get your own creative juices flowing.

- Entry: There's an old concept of interior design that recommends an interim space between the outdoors and the interior space. Supposedly, that interim space helps people adjust to a new type of environment. In our workplace, we have a front entryway that mostly conceals the rest of the office. The window is frosted with a dynamic logo, and through it, you can get glimpses of what's inside. You can spot our conference room and might see the office dog. In the front area you can see the drum set, and the piano, and a desk. These represent the rhythm, tempo, and tone of marketing and communication. You can see a table with an ancient typewriter, that looks cool and speaks to the beauty and magical quality of words, and a four-foot-long carpenter's level that looks over a century old. They're little touches and all of them are metaphors for what we do, but we think they communicate our personality and our attention to detail.

As you move through the office you'll also see:

- Color: The colors are warm. The doors on most of the offices are glass. We use these elements to try to convey—can you guess?—a sense of warmth and transparency.

- Signage: We have creative signs and illustrations on the wall. There are curves, which convey motion and talk about our work. One wall has a huge canvas print of Trafalgar Square in London. It features a bus going by the fountains and the lions. Why? The UK matters in our story, and looking at the print makes us happy.
- Furniture: On the other side of the office, near the actual offices and staff, there's a living room area. We've set up a couch, a love seat, two chairs, and a coffee table. Our employees sometimes like to hang out there to work with their laptops, flowing with productivity in the afternoon.
- Architectural design: We elected to rent an office space that has more square footage than we actually need because we wanted a sense of spaciousness. The conference room sits in the middle of the office, and a hallway circles it. We've found that this helps create motion and energy in the office. When you move around corners, you find new views, surprises, and interesting things. We think this keeps people's minds stimulated.
- Attention to detail: In our recording and film studio, we decided we wanted to create the feel of old England, because that's such a part of who we are. It was important to us that the studio look warm and feel authentic, so we built a real stone wall as a backdrop for filming videos in our studio. We often use our studio to record content for our clients and ourselves, and we know that people can tell when something is fake. Sensing inauthenticity can change people's level of trust, but the opposite effect happens when you've done the work to make something look appealing and genuine.

When we set up the physical space of our office, we thought about color, size, spatial relationships, and detail. We thought about creating warmth and energy. We used all the concepts we knew about graphic design, architectural design, and interior design. After we exhausted that knowledge, we tried to think of everything else we've learned about how human beings perceive the world and recognize beauty, comfort, and safety. We looked at those concepts and thought, how can we *interpret* those rules so that, as you move in our office from space to space and portal to portal, you're always looking at something different?

MAKE IT YOUR OWN

We encourage you to consider how these concepts could work for you. Your physical space will look different, based on your office size, layout, and industry. But hear this: these fundamental concepts about what appeals to people *do not change*. They are universal, because human beings are human beings. Even if you're running a mechanic's shop and you think your clientele would roll their eyes at a baby grand piano—they're still going to appreciate music. Even if you think they'd scoff at a love seat—they'll still appreciate a comfortable place to sit. Consciously or unconsciously, people value nice lighting, nice smells, an atmosphere that's inviting, and an environment that demonstrates competency, trustworthiness, and attention to detail. Most people don't even notice the way they're impacted by design—but they are, all the time.

Many leaders of small businesses know this intuitively, and have taken care to set up an inviting physical environment. If that sounds like you, well done! Consider the ways these ideas can help you codify your efforts at culture and take it to the next level as you further incorporate your values into the physical space.

Other business leaders don't think much about their physical space. They're focused on functionality. If their office looks messy, who cares, so long as the work gets done? The space is functional enough, and if the staff is able to maintain decent attitudes and values—that's good enough.

If you're in a "good enough" scenario though, consider what opportunities you might be missing out on. Clients may feel unimpressed and decide not to come back. Your staff may not work at their full potential if they recognize they're only expected to do "good enough." Right?

Consider this: how would you feel going to a doctor's office that had peeling paint on the walls and plastic folding chairs to sit in? You might assume that doctor wasn't maintaining a very successful practice. You might even start to worry about the quality of care you were going to receive or wonder if the doctor was even legitimate. On the other hand, if you went to a doctor's office with soothing colors, nice carpet, and rich furniture, you might feel assured that you were in a place that would give you quality care.

Your workplace's physical space is going to lead both your employees and your clients to make assumptions. You can either direct their assumptions in a good direction, assuring them that they can feel confident and good about what happens in your workplace—or, your physical space can lead people to assume you'll neglect to care for them.

We know that the physical environment impacts culture, but it's not the only thing that impacts culture. Let's go back to Disneyland for a second. It's not just the smell of popcorn and flower baskets that makes Disneyland such a happy place. It's also the relational environment.

Managers at Disneyland ensure that every visitor's interaction with a Disney "cast member" is positive. Cast members greet visitors with a smile and are eager to be helpful. This tips us off to the other major component of shaping culture: our experience relating to others. The *relational* environment is huge in shaping the way people experience your culture. Let's talk about that next.

RELATIONAL ASPECTS OF CULTURE

Imagine that you're going to work in an amazing physical space, but you work with catty coworkers. You know they're talking about you behind your back and evaluating your outfit. You suspect they're also sending nasty emails back and forth to each other about the work that you do. That relational culture is not going to be conducive to you producing your best work—right?

Cultivating healthy work relationships is every bit as important as how lovely your building is. In fact, we would say that's what every other part of this book is about. Throughout our other chapters, we've talked about the importance of building trust, reinforcing your Core Values, and so on—those are all important elements of building a healthy relational culture, and that's one reason why we waited to discuss culture until all of the other pieces were explained first.

But there's something more to be said here. In his book *The Culture Code,* author and journalist Daniel Coyle researched what common traits could be found in organizations with great culture. He discovered that the organizations which people described as having amazing culture consistently had three core skills. They were all able to:

1. Build safety

2. Share vulnerability
3. Establish purpose

In our experience, we've found Coyle's three skills to be dead-on accurate, in terms of what leads to positive relational culture. In a healthy relational culture, there's strong community, mutual trust, mutual risk, openness, honesty, and a strong sense of purpose. You can help cultivate all those qualities by targeting Coyle's three skills.

> In a healthy relational culture, there's strong community, mutual trust, mutual risk, openness, honesty, and a strong sense of purpose.

BUILD SAFETY

Remember the Allegory of Good Government, and the thriving prosperity that took place when people were confident in their safety? When employees feel safe and protected, they're empowered. They feel confident that they can risk being vulnerable and honest, which builds a culture of trust. You can't trust without vulnerability and you can't have vulnerability without trust. Once you achieve a culture of trust, there's more creativity and more efficiency that follows.

So, what are some practical ways to cultivate that safety in the culture of your workplace?

First, **honor people's dignity.** If one of your employees says something asinine in a meeting, don't tell them that they're being an idiot in front of everybody else. You may have to address that issue in the meeting for the sake of moving forward productively but you don't need to tear them down. Instead, do what you can to take your feedback offline and pull them aside for a chat. You might need to do that immediately if their behavior warrants immediate attention—but don't embarrass them. Just say something like, "I disagree and that is probably something we should talk about after the meeting." If you can, wait a bit before giving them that feedback. They're going to be more open to hearing correction after they've had some time to calm down, and they'll appreciate that you didn't publicly embarrass them. Unless an employee is being so unruly that you have to publicly shut down their behavior, do your best to correct them privately, in a way that honors their dignity.

You don't ignore toxic behavior—doing that would produce its own set of weeds in the garden you're trying to cultivate. You prioritize communication, but you do so in a way that enables people to retain their dignity. You may need to bring in facilitators as necessary to help people build up life skills they may simply not have.

With that said, **hold people accountable.** If and when an employee or client violates your Core Values, make it clear their breach of those values was unacceptable. If you don't do that, you're failing to weed the garden and the weeds are going to end up taking over. Even if a leader is working hard to create a good culture, their efforts can fail if there's no accountability.

Sometimes, leaders simply aren't paying close enough attention, and they're not noticing that people are breaking the Core Values. Other times, they don't want to have the uncomfortable confrontational conversations, so they turn a blind eye. However, failing to hold people accountable to the Core Values ruins the atmosphere of trust and safety that you need.

Here's one way you can set up a system of accountability: if someone violates the Core Values, communicate firmly that their behavior was unacceptable, and give them a warning. If they do it a second time, make sure they understand how and why they violated the Core Values, and then form a plan to change their behavior. Communicate clearly that they need to either adhere to the plan, or they're out. If they violate the Core Values a third time, they're fired. Some business leaders may not want a "three strikes approach"—they'd rather fire someone the first time there's a major violation of Core Values, so that the bad behavior doesn't contaminate the rest of the environment.

It's also important to manage conflict in a healthy way. We often hear complaints from older business leaders that their younger employees don't know how to handle conflict or being told no. A lot of people think—perhaps unfairly—that the generation of people under forty mostly grew up being told that they were great and they deserved an award for almost everything they do. We're also up against the social media culture, which is rampant with mean remarks. Our American culture doesn't do us many favors when it comes to teaching healthy ways to resolve conflict.

Many older people in the business world want to reject the idea that it's somehow their responsibility to teach their younger employees how to communicate and behave. In their minds, those are basic human skills. Their employees should learn them at home or from somewhere else! They need to come to work knowing how to do it!

Here's the deal though—on a practical level, that attitude doesn't work. If you're going to fire someone every time there's a badly handled conflict or poor communication or someone flies off the handle—you're going to end up firing a lot of people.

As leaders in business, we sometimes have to take on the responsibility to nurture our employees if we want them to be successful and stick around. There *are*, in fact, life skills that need to be taught. Some of those life skills, like effective communication, go directly toward maintaining a healthy relational environment. We've discussed ways that employees can be trained in some of these skills in many of our other chapters; for instance, our troubleshooting model could help a manager work with a difficult employee.

The five areas of management, the troubleshooting process, the reinforcing of our Core Values—those are all ways we nurture safety in our relational culture.

BUILD A TRIBAL EXPERIENCE AND LANGUAGE

Coyle's second skill is to share vulnerability. Modeling healthy vulnerability is critical in your leadership if you want your team to connect with each other. More than just a "touchy-feely" thing, vulnerability sparks cooperation and trust among coworkers. The simple ability among your team members to share a weakness, say they need help, and not be shamed for either remark can have a profound impact on your culture.

Dr. Jeff Polzer, a professor of organizational development, says it this way: "[Vulnerability is] about sending a really clear signal that you have weaknesses, that you could use help. And if that behavior becomes a model for others, then you can set the insecurities aside and get to work. If you never have that vulnerable moment, on the other hand, then people will try to cover up their weaknesses, and even a little micro task becomes a place where insecurities manifest themselves."[63]

---

63   Chatham, J., J. Polzer, S. Barsade, and M. Neale, "Being Different Yet Feeling Similar: The Influence of Demographic Composition and Organizational Culture on Work Processes and Outcomes," *Administrative Science Quarterly* 43 (1998).

Being vulnerable includes the courage to share places where you struggle or need help without fear of judgment. It is owning your mistakes but not wallowing in them. It is allowing your employees to be honest with you and with each other.

"I've yet to come across a company that has both a shaming, judgmental culture, and wonderful customer service." —Brené Brown, *Dare to Lead*[64]

We also believe that **healthy vulnerability can be increased through building up your sense of *tribe*.** If you like where we start going in this next point, check out *The Power of Moments,* by Chip and Dan Heath for more great ideas about using shared experiences to enhance your relational culture.[65]

The Power of Moments recommends that you create cultural moments to reinforce your values. At Half a Bubble Out, we have a high value for relationships, good rapport, and employees knowing each other on a personal level. When all those areas are good, we think people more often enjoy coming to work. So, about nine years ago, we developed a weekly "moment" to help reinforce all those values for our staff.

We started meeting every Friday at four o'clock to do what we call Wrap, which is our way of wrapping up the week. We provide snacks like cheese and crackers, along with beer and wine. Essentially, it's a one-hour wind-down at the end of the week where we sit together and chat. We chat about the week, we chat about our lives, we chat about what's coming up during the weekend. It's

---

64 Brown, Brené. *Dare to Lead: Brave Work, Tough Conversations, Whole Hearts.* Place of publication not identified: Random House Publishing, 2019.

65 Heath, Dan, and Chip Heath. *The Power of Moments.* Random House UK, 2019.

become our time to celebrate events in different people's lives, like birthdays or work anniversaries or becoming an aunt for the very first time. For one hour at the end of the week, we pay our tribe to eat, drink, and be merry.

Wrap has become a workplace tradition that our new interns or hires are invited into; it's part of our culture, and it's *reserved* for our tribe. No one comes who's not an employee except in rare moments. For our team, it's become almost sacred—they're protective of it. Wrap has developed its own traditions and rituals, almost like a family develops for certain holidays. It's a way we're able to communicate to our staff that we care about them as human beings. We want to know them. We want everyone to genuinely enjoy each other's company, because when coworkers like each other, that creates a major impact on the environment.

In our third year of doing Wrap, we began to feel concerned that it had run its course. We felt like maybe people didn't care about participating very much anymore. During one Wrap, Michael said to the crew, "We're thinking about maybe not doing Wrap anymore. What do you think of that?"

We expected our people to say something along the lines of, "We don't care either way. It's nice, but we have other things we could do..." Instead, our employee Natasha balked. She said, "That's like saying you're going to cancel Christmas!" Everyone on the staff began nodding and agreeing with Natasha—"Yeah, what she said!" We looked at each other and shrugged. Neither of us wanted to be the Grinch who canceled Christmas. Plus, we liked it too. That was seven years ago and Wrap lives on.

By creating these moments—these traditions and rituals—you're inviting your team to be part of something bigger than each individual. It's human nature to want to be known, and these tribal experiences help reinforce a sense of belonging to something powerful and strong. Is that going to help your employees stick around and stay motivated? You bet it will. It's also going to help infuse your workplace with the Passion that we all want.

You can also build this tribal identity through language—insider vocabulary, shared jokes, references to shared memories and shared stories. You can see this "insider" vocabulary among members of the military or in medicine. Those snippets of conversation prove that you belong to something bigger, which touches a core need in people.

Especially in a day and age where there's more superficial connection happening over social media than real connection in person, people are searching for something real—for something to belong to. Many recent studies show that people have never before felt so alone.[66] They want a *tribe*.

We didn't invent this idea—many people have written books about the characteristic elements that define a tribe. Most of them agree on the same thing: being part of a tribe calls forth greater involvement and commitment, because the more people feel like they belong to something, the more they are willing to commit and invest. For the sake of the tribe, they'll give above and beyond themselves—and then they'll give a little bit more beyond even that.

The price of that commitment is your dedication, as a leader, to create a culture that signals belonging. In fostering real belonging

---

66 Brandt, Andrea. "Why Do We Feel So Alone?" Psychology Today. Sussex Publishers. Accessed December 13, 2019. https://www.psychologytoday.com/us/blog/mindful-anger/201911/why-do-we-feel-so-alone.

and real community—you also foster real commitment and real engagement.

ESTABLISH AND COMMUNICATE PURPOSE

People want to know that the work they're doing matters. All of the concepts that we've discussed related to Vision and a larger mission—those concepts play a major part in creating a healthy culture. They signal belonging and meaning and purpose to your staff—which matters a great deal.

Remember the Big, Hairy, Audacious Goal? The BHAG is massive; it's profound, it's enormous. To achieve it will require persistence, perseverance, and commitment. Your team may experience failures in the pursuit of its achievements and will have to work together to make it through those failures and come out the other side. The BHAG requires deep commitment—and that means that you're going to have to connect with people at a deep level.

There's a reason why Vision is pictured at the center of the wheel of all our core competencies: Vision touches on *all* the pieces of core identity. It's a major factor of what enables leaders to cultivate a sense of tribe. When your team is inspired by your company's Vision and BHAG, they're going to be willing to strain under the weight of effort so that they can achieve that goal. We've seen this firsthand: people are willing to make sacrifices to achieve a larger purpose. But *without* a compelling Vision to motivate that commitment and sacrifice, your employees will pull the ejection lever when things get hard.

We recently made a promotional video for Half a Bubble Out, titled "We Believe." The video features short clips of the two of us, along with members of our staff, stating simply what values we believe in. Some of the statements are earnest, like "We believe in kindness." Some of them are half-serious and half-joking: "We believe if the office dog doesn't like you, we probably won't like you either." It was an amazing exercise for us—to say and preserve out loud what some of our Core Values are—and it's also been incredibly effective as a marketing tool.

When people see this video, they figure out quickly whether we're their kind of people—or whether we're *not* their kind of people. We know that some viewers might hear the line about the office dog and immediately conclude, "Not my people." But we're okay with that, because we want to work with people who share our sense of humor. As we present our values to the customer base, we're drawing people to us that we'll enjoy working with and likely be able to create lasting relationships with. In essence, we're saying, "This is who we are. Want to come over and play?"

It's also been a phenomenal HR tool, because it taps into people's universal desire to *belong*. When given a chance, they want to belong to a tribe that likes them and *is* like them; for many people who watch our "We Believe" video, that's exactly what they feel. The video has helped us recruit new potential staff, because even when people didn't have a reason to buy our product or service, they started telling us, "Can we figure out a way to work together? I just like you guys."

The other day, we met the PR representative for a client we're working with. She was warm and friendly, and explained that she'd graduated from college within the last four years. When we introduced ourselves, she said, "Funny story, I actually applied to your company when I was still in college."

Both of us froze. We had no memory of her whatsoever.

She went on to explain that she'd sent us a resume without a cover letter. If you remember our hiring tips from the Management chapter, you know that the lack of a cover letter meant we didn't give her resume a second glance. Apparently, when we'd returned her resume, we said, "Thank you for your interest, but we need a cover letter with your application. Just as a tip for future job applications—always submit your resume with a letter of interest."

After getting our response, she felt embarrassed, but she also told us she appreciated the fact that we'd responded and given her the tip about always submitting a cover letter. She never made the mistake again, and it paid off.

She also described when she saw Michael guest lecture at her university. Out of fear that he might recognize her, she sat in the back and slouched down. But in spite of her embarrassment, she mentioned that those moments had all made her want to be part of the company. She saw our business as interesting and appealing—she felt like our culture would fit her. Years later, she's landed on her feet with a job she loves, and we're happy to hear it. Still, we felt the weight of her compliment: she noticed our culture, our values, and our people—and she wanted to be part of the tribe.

THE LEADER'S ROLE IN SHAPING CULTURE

Let's get direct now about your role, as the leader of your company, in helping to shape your workplace culture. At the end of the day, your job as CCO—chief culture officer—is about more than just buying comfortable couches and posting your Core Values in a visible way. As we discussed in our Leadership chapter, everything trickles down from the leader. If you want a culture where your employees are bringing their best to work—then *you* need to bring your best to work. If you want employees that are bought in and fully engaged, *you* need to model the standard of engagement.

In no area is this more important than the area of building safety. Leaders, are you practicing vulnerability? Are you willing to be honest? Are you engaging people on a personal level and showing them that you care about them as human beings? Are you rewarding your staff when they take a risk, even if it doesn't work out, or do you punish that behavior? Do you honor their dignity when they're honest about a mistake, or do you humiliate them? Your leadership makes a profound difference in whether or not you're creating a culture of safety or of fear.

People have to feel safe to bring their best selves to the table. If your staff feels afraid that they're going to get laughed at or slammed every time they offer input, they're going to stop offering input. As the leader, you're in charge of protecting employees from ridicule. If one staff member scoffs at another person's idea—what are you going to do about that, to make sure that doesn't happen again?

Being vulnerable is not always easy for leaders, but if you want to create a culture of safety and trust, vulnerability has to start with you. How will you model what it looks like to own your mistakes? Can you admit in front of a group that you dropped the ball, and recognize that you need to correct it now? When you model that willingness to be vulnerable as a leader, then it's safe for an employee to admit when *they* dropped the ball. And when they do, and when you respond with grace, honoring their dignity—what happens? Your staff learns that this is a safe place to bring their best, to experiment, to risk mistakes in pushing forward.

No matter how big the company is, water runs downhill. If there's a jerk at the helm who doesn't honor the company's stated Core Values, it says to everyone else in the company that there's a lower standard by which they can and should operate. Remember what happens to a company being managed by a reactive leader, who's controlling and self-protecting? Everything contracts, slows, and worsens. Creativity is squashed, stress is high, and communication is terrible. Now, remember what happens when there's a creative leader at the helm, who's supportive and others focused? People thrive and prosper.

Keep your values central and live them out. Hire, train, and fire according to your values. Keep your employees accountable to maintaining them. Reinforce your values in meetings, in emails, and in your decisions. By taking the Core Values seriously and working to maintain them, you're helping impact your company's culture for good.

Many of America's most cherished documents speak to the values that help create a positive culture—documents like Martin Luther King Junior's "I Have a Dream" speech, or our Constitution. These speeches emphasize key truths about humanity—that all of us are created equal, and we all have a right to the pursuit of happiness. Going even deeper into history, we find that the most ancient writings all point to the fact that human beings *matter*. Are you living out those values? Do you embrace those values in a way your staff can see?

And are you *balanced* in your priorities? In business, it can be easy to elevate one priority at the expense of other equally important priorities; for instance, either money is viewed as the only important goal, or employees' experiences at work are valued so much that you ignore good business practices. If you focus too much on money, you create a terrible culture with unhappy employees. If you focus on people at the expense of the business's health, then the business fails and everyone loses their jobs. In either case, people lose Passion & Provision.

As leaders, we have a responsibility to make sure that we're leading people toward dignity, toward prosperity, and toward happiness—and not away from them. We need to bring our people toward unity and health, not toward destruction.

How do you do that? You start with you.

One of your foremost jobs as a leader is to grow internally as a human so that you can create a culture that is full of Passion & Provision. Grow in your competency. Grow in your skills. And most of all, grow as a human being. As the leader, you win all around.

A NOTE ABOUT HOURS

We can't finish a chapter on culture without touching on the amount of hours you expect to work—and expect your staff to work. When people say they just worked an eighty-hour work week, they're usually not gushing about how much they love their job. More often, working long hours is something people mention when they're talking about how much they *hate* their job. Likewise, we can think of any number of entrepreneurs who burned out mainly because they worked too many hours and it was destroying their lives.

Still—if the business demands it—then what other option do you have?

It's a good question, and one we've had to wrestle with personally.

We're going to try to define a rough idea of what it means to work a "healthy" number of hours, as a leader who's trying to build a Passion & Provision company.

A long time ago we heard a speech from a successful business owner. We can't recall his name, but his message stuck. He talked about how he had built his business and gained great success, but like many others, he'd realized he was missing out on massive chunks of his life. He was absent during key time with his kids and their activities, missing time with his bride, time with his friends, and so on. He wasn't able to exercise or do other activities he enjoyed. After making that realization, he instituted a new rule for himself, and that rule is what we have adopted.

The "rule" has three key parts:

1. Always take one day off a week.
2. Don't work more than ten hours a day, preferably no more than five days a week.
3. As often as possible, get a full night's sleep.

The first part of the rule means you're taking a *full* day of rest. You've got to discipline yourself to not work—to take a break, to be restored. We don't believe human beings were designed to work seven days a week over a long period of time, and when they do, their quality of work begins to diminish. You've been there, right? There's so much to do that it feels like you can't stop, but the longer you go, your capacity to think well, problem solve, create, and even accomplish basic tasks is compromised. You *have* to stop. You have to take a break. One full day a week is ideal. This will be good for your soul, and—believe it or not—good for your business.

The second part of the rule specifies a "healthy" number of working hours: ten hours a day, preferably five days a week. There will be times when you really do need a sixth day, or at least part of it, but overall, you're aiming to work no more than fifty to sixty hours a week; that's the "rule." Having said that, there will be exceptions. We've probably all experienced seasons with massive deadlines or huge projects that require a full-court press. We think occasional exceptions are fine, but not for a sustained season. If it happens three or four times a year, sure. However, if you're working more than sixty hours a week, six to eight months at a time, you will risk burnout. Even worse, you will definitely miss out on the rest of your life.

Finally, don't underestimate the value of a good night's sleep. Some CEOs and entrepreneurs have bought into the idea that it is heroic to sleep only a couple of hours a night, but we disagree and so does the research. If you want to build a Passion & Provision company, you need to sleep. Much like the "day off" concept, your brain needs sleep to be able to do its best work. Creativity, problem-solving, and optimism are at their best when we are not sleep deprived. If you need to pull an occasional all-nighter to meet a deadline, sure—but on a sustained basis, sleep is your friend.

DANGERS OF NEGLECTING CULTURE

On Michael's desk is a little quote block, which says, "How do you expect me to think outside of the box if I work in a cube?"

We're guessing the leaders at Intel haven't seen that quote.

Almond trees won't grow in a desert, and employees will struggle to produce if they're in a barren environment. On the other hand, flourishing happens when you make the investment to cultivate a thriving workplace culture.

The idea of good culture leading to more money is a good reason for most business leaders to start dealing with culture—but don't *just* do this to make more money. As you work on your workplace culture, remember that *people* are just as important as *money*.

Here's a fact: it's possible for companies to become very lucrative when there's no attention given to physical space or a healthy workplace culture. During the industrial revolution, factory owners got rich by employing children and women who worked in horrible conditions. You can be very profitable by pushing humans to work like machines, in a machine-like environment. The only problem is, eventually your workers will rise up to say, "No!"—just like the labor unions did when they were created as a result of those terrible environmental conditions.

Those factories have mostly gone away in our country, but the factory owners' attitudes haven't. We can think of many business leaders who operate with the attitude that business is all about efficiency and making money. "I'm not here to make my employees happy," they'll say. "I'm here to make *me* more money."

In the factories of the industrial revolution, work was efficient, and work was productive—but it wasn't *honoring* people. That's a big deal, especially in a day and age where there's far greater competition for good employees.

If a competitor does the same thing that you do, pays the same wage, and can also boast an environment that is emotionally healthy and physically safe, then you are in danger of losing your employees to that competitor.

If, that is, you have neglected your workplace culture. That's the profound risk you take by neglecting culture: you lose employees. You lose clients. You lose Passion & Provision as negative culture spreads like rot throughout your organization, retarding growth, retarding fruitfulness, retarding productivity.

What else do you risk? The loss of creativity and experimentation. If you create an environment which punishes employees when things don't go perfectly every time, they won't feel safe taking risks or even offering their opinion. In order to grow, you *need* new ideas, new opinions, new efforts in new directions. All the risks you need your employees to take, they won't take, unless you've established a culture that affirms and invites their risk-taking.

Hear this: it's possible to run an efficient, productive business that still honors people. In fact, we'd argue that investing in a good culture actually leads to *more* efficiency and productivity, provided there's a balance achieved in caring for both your people and your business. For instance, being kind doesn't mean you never hold anybody accountable. The rest of this book provides strategies to help you set up the paradigms for effective and efficient work, which can occur in a nurturing and safe atmosphere.

We're not just saying all this—we've *lived* this. In our book's Introduction, we talked about the "boom" days of Half a Bubble Out, when clients and money started pouring in—but our culture was terrible. We both hated going to work. We didn't hire properly, we didn't hold people accountable to the Core Values (because we hadn't even articulated them yet), and we didn't let people go fast enough. We were both consumed with putting out fires and were so fed up with work, we were nearly ready to shut down the business.

Then, we fixed those problems. We addressed the aspects of the environment that we didn't like—not just superficially, but by starting with our Core Values and our own leadership. Our company got better—but what changed the most was our culture. All of the very tangible changes made, which we've talked about throughout the book, most noticeably affected our culture.

And guess what? Work started to become fun again. We felt more passion, and our employees were more motivated. There was a stabilized, reliable stream of provision because we smoothed out our operations. The machine wasn't constantly squeaking anymore, which meant we were able to take on "high horizon" projects to grow and enhance our business, not just put out fires.

GROWING GOOD FRUIT

There's an old proverb that says something along the lines of, "You will know a tree by its fruit." If a tree produces oranges, you know it's an orange tree. If the oranges are small and sickly, then you know something's wrong at the root—there's a virus in the tree, or it's planted in bad soil. If the tree produces oranges in abundance, and they're sweet and juicy, then you know it's a healthy and thriving tree.

Workplace culture produces evidence, and the evidence is the fruit. When an organization produces an abundance of good, healthy fruit in the way of quality products, good customer service, positive employee attitudes, customer and employee satisfaction, and so on—you can tell, that workplace has a healthy, thriving culture. They are working in an optimal growing zone. That fruit is good to taste, and it leaves people feeling nourished.

There are sophisticated tools and details and rules to help build a good culture, but at the end of the day, it's pretty simple: culture makes itself known by its fruit. If there's no good fruit, something's wrong at the root.

As a business leader, you must intentionally care for your workplace environment with the love and attention of a good farmer caring for his crops. If you neglect your culture, you invite weeds to grow instead which will threaten the growth of anything good. Pay attention to the fruit you're producing and do your best to cultivate a healthy environment for growth.

The result will be good to taste.

TIME TO SHAPE YOUR CULTURE ON PURPOSE

- Go to **fulfilledthebook.com** to download resources and questions to help you evaluate your current culture and look for ways to improve.
- Evaluate your culture. Does it feel safe or do you need to start changing things in your organization?
- Are you being intentional in how you shape your culture or are you just letting it happen?
- Does your office or workspace enhance your culture or detract from it?
- Are you modeling healthy vulnerability with people in your leadership?
- Would your employees describe your company as a "safe" place to work?
- What traditions do you have that help create a sense of "tribe" in your company?

Conclusion

"I am looking for someone to share in an adventure that I am arranging."

J.R.R. TOLKIEN

THE GIFT AND THE TRAGEDY: MICHAEL NARRATES

I still have a very vivid memory of the night that someone left groceries on our front porch.

Our daughter, Jenna, was still young. I'd been doing all of our shopping at the ultra-discount grocery outlet which sold groceries that the mainline stories hadn't been able to sell. We were just barely making it—literally struggling to put food on the table. That night, we'd had to scrounge dinner together from the very little that we'd had in our cupboards.

And then there was a knock. We opened the door to find two paper bags, stuffed full of produce, meat, eggs, bread, and all kinds of good food. We scanned the driveway and street, looking for the person who'd left it. No one was in sight.

It was an incredible gift, and it made us feel thankful to have friends who would love us in such a practical, needed way.

But that hungry night was also one of the lowest points of my life. This wasn't what I wanted our lives to be. That's not why we had a company.

Kathryn and I had started our own business to achieve our goals and dreams. We'd thought we were setting about to make our lives better. We expected that running a business would help us find more meaning, purpose, and happiness in our lives.

When I looked at those groceries left in the dark on our front step, I thought, "My God—what am I doing? Is this ever going to turn around? Am I ever going to get off the ground, or are we going to spiral into the dirt?"

Growing a business can sometimes feel like these hungry nights. That's what it was like for us after we started Half a Bubble Out. We had no idea how hard it was going to be.

Can you relate? Even if you think you've counted the cost, you don't actually *know* how hard it's going to be until you experience it. That was another lesson we learned early in our married life, long before we started Half a Bubble Out, when we were still in Colorado working on that old house of ours.

"KNOWING" VERSUS KNOWING: KATHRYN NARRATES

It was September of 1995. I was thirty-two weeks pregnant and on my way out the door to a baby shower—my baby shower. As I kissed Michael goodbye, he was dressed for construction work and focused on our kitchen. The goal was to transform our 1950s *Leave It to Beaver* kitchen, complete with pink linoleum counter-tops and metal cabinets, into a workable modern kitchen. I was all in.

I knew when I left that this was demolition day. I knew.

This was, however, long before the days of *Fixer Upper* and watching Chip and Joanna go after an old house. I had never seen demo day in real life. My parents rented homes. There was no remodeling in my history.

I will never forget coming home from the baby shower, a car full of really cool gadgets and cute clothes, getting out of my car and walking into my home.

Michael had recruited our whole youth group to help and an enthusiastic junior high boy with a sledgehammer raced past me and said, "Isn't this great?! We're smashing your kitchen!"

Everything from my kitchen cabinets was in my living room covered with plastic, which was covered with a fine layer of sheet rock dust. I walked into my kitchen, looked up, and saw my attic.

That's when it struck me. I *knew*, but I didn't **know**. I really had no concept of the implications of what I was signing up for. Zero. I didn't understand what "down to the studs" actually meant. I didn't realize I'd be able to see my attic. I was unprepared. I walked through the kitchen, out the back door to the far edge of the property, sat down on a pile of sheet rock and wept.

I have thought of that story many times during our years of owning a business. Many times I have looked at Michael and said, "I knew this would be hard, but I didn't *know*."

The learning curve. The blood, sweat, and tears. The risks. The fact that everything takes twice as long as you want it to. The challenge of walking through failures as well as triumphs. Of days when the future looks bright and days when you are convinced the end is imminent.

Why tell that story at the end of this book? Because even though I didn't understand everything we were getting into and it has been far more difficult than I thought, I wouldn't trade what we have learned and what we have built for anything.

It isn't just business for us. It is our life's work that we have stepped into as the story has unfolded. This quest is to have "work" be a place of purpose, profit, and legacy, not drudgery and toil. Our hope is that somehow the lessons we have learned along the way can help you lay a solid foundation much earlier on in your business so you can achieve your goals. This is why we keep moving forward.

I wanted that new kitchen, much like I wanted a successful business. The process was challenging, but we got there in the end. And fear not—Michael warns all newly married young men that remodeling during pregnancy is a no-fly zone. Lesson learned.

We think about these moments in contrast to where we are today— and all we can feel is profound gratitude. The work paid off. All the effort to turn our business around, to educate ourselves, to lean into best practices and uphold our Core Values—it's led us to a starkly different place than where we were so many years ago.

BUSINESS IS PERSONAL

These challenging times—the hungry nights or the moments when you realize you knew but you didn't *know*—can come to business leaders in a lot of different forms. For some of us, they come in the form of doubts. For others, tossing and turning in your bed as you think of the bottom line. For still others, when your family waits for you and dinner gets cold because you just couldn't resist hashing it out with that client. Those hungry nights, in all their shapes and forms, have taught both of us that business is personal.

Most of the time, we as human beings put on our armor in the morning. We go out and try to defend our soft spots so we don't get shot or stabbed by people's words or actions, or wounded by the events of the day. We try to bluff and bluster our way through, and we do it so often that it becomes a habit. We start to believe those people who say it's normal to work for the weekend. We start to accept that it's not personal; it's business.

But when it's 10 p.m., and all the noise is gone, and you're sitting there having a whiskey or beer, and you're starting to get honest with a friend—the truth comes out. We've had a lot of those middle-of-the-night moments with other business leaders. When they decide it's safe to get vulnerable and shed the armor, they get personal about what it means to them to run a business.

They talk about their core desires and, in some cases, their deep fears. They sometimes wonder whether or not their marriages are going to make it. Or they talk about feeling scared that they may not be able to provide for their family. They wonder if their kids hate them, and have to remind themselves that their kids love them. Some wonder what people will think of them if the business fails. And their train of thought never stops with, "I don't know if I'm going to have enough money." It always goes deeper than that.

Business is real life. It concerns your quality of life, for the majority of your waking hours. It has everything to do with the life you dream to live. It *is* personal.

Our Passion & Provision concept isn't just about boosting morale, or making a little more money. This is about living into the "more" of what life is supposed to be. When we talk about Passion & Provision, we're talking about fighting a battle against despair, against the status quo, against fear and failure and loss. In this battle, with three out of every four businesses not making it to five years, there have been too many casualties already. Too many people have lost as they've tried to start a business and do something good.

> Passion & Provision is about living into the "more" of what life is supposed to be.

But this battle isn't against an unbeatable foe. When there's hope and knowledge and help and a plan to move forward, every soldier is strengthened. The two of us have gotten bloodied in those trenches, but we've also experienced victory.

LESSONS ALONG THE WAY

The two of us love our lives, and that's no accident—we got here with intention and purpose. We put in our blood, sweat, and tears. We worked hard at growing personally and becoming better at business. We educated ourselves about the different skillsets we needed. We've struggled and we've learned. We're *still* on a journey of growing and learning.

It continues to be hard at times. But we remember the days when we didn't know if the company would succeed, when we didn't know if we would lose our home, when we didn't know how to pay for groceries. That's not the way we wanted to do it—that's not the way *anyone* wants to do it. Those memories make us incredibly thankful for the lessons that took us to the place we are now.

We learned first that *passion matters*. We learned that as kids, watching our parents. We learned that as adults, in dead-end jobs. We learned that when we had plenty of money and a miserable culture in the early years of Half a Bubble Out. We learned that our marriage, our mental and physical health, our relationship with our daughter, our values, our enjoyment at work—all of that matters too.

We learned next that *provision is equally important*. The stress of trying to keep our company afloat in those lean days was almost too much to bear. In order for our company, our employees, and our*selves* to thrive, we needed sufficient provision to meet our expenses and pursue our dreams.

Through trial and error, we realized *everything in business is holistically connected*. When we propped up one area, many areas improved as well. When one area suffered, it dragged down our whole enterprise. We realized that we had to achieve minimum competency in all areas of running a business so that we could get a healthy foundation underneath us.

Then we began to identify those key areas and sought out as much good training as we could to build our skills in each competency.

- We learned about *Vision*, and how to craft the Core Values, the Core Purpose, and the BHAG, and then how to translate all of that into a Strategic Plan.
- We learned about *Leadership*, and the ways we could pursue healthy creative leadership through growing our inner game and our outer game.
- We learned about effective *Management and Operations,* honing the five fundamentals of good management. We improved our Standard Operating Procedures and trouble-shooting process.
- We constantly sought to learn more in *Marketing and Sales,* so that we could improve our offerings to clients and grow our capabilities. We learned about the Eight-Stage Customer Value Journey, the power of storytelling, and best practices in terms of frequency, reach, and ad copywriting.
- We pushed past our limits in the area of *Money* and learned how to read our reports, dig into analysis, remember the art, and factor in the big picture.

- We learned about *Culture* and began to incorporate our values throughout the physical and relational environment of our workplace. As our culture thrived, we saw our people thrive as well, and we strengthened our identity as a tribe.

It was often hard to find the information that we needed to learn—we didn't have a lot of people teaching us. But the hunt and the journey was worth it. We have a passion for our business, and it's that much more rewarding because we know exactly just how hard it is to be on the other side. Now, we've tried to assemble the best of what we found into one place, for the benefit of all who read it.

OUR HOPE FOR YOU

We want to get this message out to all entrepreneurs: you can beat the business failure rate. It's possible to run your life and your business in a way that allows you to enjoy the fulfillment of both Passion & Provision. You can experience meaning, purpose, and joy along with financial success. You can actually look forward to going to work on Monday mornings and lead a staff who like coming to work too.

We've tried to drive that message home, and then provide you with the basic nuts and bolts of what it will take to get you there. We've put some of the best research we've come across in one place so that you have the information you need to continue building your competency in each of the six core areas.

We've shared our personal stories so that you have something concrete to envision about what a thriving company could look like, in a small business context. We wanted you to have a clear idea that a Passion & Provision company is achievable and be able to understand what next steps you could take to move forward.

We've tried to show you *a* way, so that you can find *your* way.

What steps will you need to take?

1. Know that this is possible! Have hope that you can experience more Passion & Provision in your company when you pursue growth in these areas.
2. As you start to strengthen your competency in each of the six core areas, don't hesitate to seek out help. Check out some of the additional resources we've listed and find mentors. Join the HaBO Village (habovillage.com) and enjoy the camaraderie and advice from other small business leaders who are looking to transform into Passion & Provision companies.
3. You'll need discipline to see this through, and you're going to have to persevere. But, like any good BHAG—it's worth the journey.

We hope this book has given you the vocabulary to identify potential problems, and strategies to codify your improvements. We hope we've shown you a way. Most of all, we hope you feel confident that you can discover *your* way to fulfill the dreams you set out to achieve.

BEGIN

"You don't have to be great to start, but you have to start to be great."
—Zig Ziglar

So, now it's your turn. Build a Passion & Provision company. Change your life and change the world around you.

Do this for your own sake—for your own physical and mental

health, for your own bottom line, for your own fulfillment. Do this so that you have more fun in your daily work and can sleep better at night.

And do this for your family. Your family needs you. The failure of a business can wreak havoc on your marriage and your kids. Do this, so that you can show up more often, and be more present with the people you love.

Then, once you've done this for yourself and your family, build a Passion & Provision company for others. Do this to make an impact in your community. Do this to change the lives of your employees. Become a leader who can cast a purposeful Vision for your employees—one that's compelling enough that it can help them find their own way, and experience their work as something more meaningful than *just* work.

Do this, so that your employees go home and tell their families about how much they love their jobs. Do this so they tell their brothers and sisters and parents and spouses, and children as they're growing up, that they feel fulfilled; that they feel passion for what they do; that they're working toward a greater purpose with people they enjoy. Build a Passion & Provision company so that an ever-widening circle of communities and generations understand what sort of life is *possible*, and go after it.

We want you to have hope in this dream—but not false hope that's based on wishes. We want to offer you *real* hope that you can actually take this journey. Real hope gives you a goal and shows you a path. After that, it gives you faith that if you endure and persevere, you can actually accomplish the dream which you've envisioned. With this book, we've tried to offer you the practical strategies which will enable you to transform your business into a Passion & Provision company. We want you to experience *real hope* that will lift you up and help take you forward.

If we've succeeded in doing that, then we've begun to fulfill our own Big, Hairy, Audacious Goal. We hope to spend the next twenty years of our lives helping business leaders experience the fulfillment and satisfaction that comes with transforming their businesses into Passion & Provision companies. We're not looking for a buyout; we're not going anywhere. *This* is the legacy we want to leave. We believe so strongly in the worth of this goal, that we want to pursue it as our contribution to creating a better world.

Will you join us?

If you found our book useful, we'd love to hear about it! Please leave us a review on Amazon, or shoot us an email at info@ halfabubbleout.com.

Appendix

WHAT IS THE HABO VILLAGE?

HaBOVillage.com is a membership site that gives leaders the encouragement and training to build Passion & Provision companies full of profit, purpose and legacy. HaBO stands for Half a Bubble Out, which is the name of our Marketing and Consulting company. The name comes from a carpenter's level, which was a description of Michael years ago by one of our mentors because he sees business and the world from a different perspective. That different perspective led us to launch HaBO Village and to write *Fulfilled*.

If you are "half a bubble out" too, and you dare to believe that your business can have both Passion & Provision, then we invite you to join us in HaBOVillage.com, the place where you will find your tribe. Come and check us out. We would love to meet you.

RECOMMENDED READING
VISION

"Building Your Company's Vision," by Jim Collins and Jerry

I. Porras. From the Sept./Oct. 1996 issue of the Harvard Business Review, found online at: https://hbr.org/1996/09/building-your-companys-vision

Built to Last: Successful Habits of Visionary Companies, by Jim Collins & Jerry I. Porras. Harper Collins, 1994.

Start with Why: How Great Leaders Inspire Everyone to Take Action, by Simon Sinek. The Penguin Group, 2009.

LEADERSHIP

Mastering Leadership: An Integrated Framework for Breakthrough Performance and Extraordinary Business Results, by Robert J. Anderson and W. A. Adams. Wiley, 2016.

The Partnership Charter: How to Start Out Right with Your New Business Partnership {or Fix the One You're In}, by David Gage. Basic Books, 2004.

Primal Leadership, with a New Preface by the Authors: Unleashing the Power of Emotional Intelligence, by Daniel Goleman, Richard Boyatzis, and Annie McKee. Harvard Business Review Press, 2013.

The Speed of Trust: The One Thing That Changes Everything, by Stephen M. R. Covey and Rebecca R. Merrill. Simon & Schuster, Inc., 2018.

Stuck!: Navigating Life and Leadership Transitions, Revised and Updated Edition, by Terry B. Walling. Leader Breakthru, 2015.

Wooden on Leadership: How to Create a Winning Organization, by John Wooden and Steve Jamison. McGraw-Hill, 2005.

MANAGEMENT AND OPERATIONS

Analyzing Performance Problems: How to Figure Out Why People Aren't Doing What They Should Be, and What to Do about It, by Robert F. Mager and Peter Pipe. Jaico Publishing House, 2004.

The Carrot Principle: How the Best Managers Use Recognition to Engage Their People, Retain Talent, and Accelerate Performance [Updated & Revised], by Adrian Gostick and Chester Elton. Simon & Schuster, 2009.

The Ideal Team Player: How to Recognize and Cultivate the Three Essential Virtues, by Patrick M. Lencioni. Jossey-Bass, 2016.

The New Mager Six-Pack, by Robert F. Mager. Center for Effective Performance, 1997.

The Truth About Employee Engagement: A Fable About Addressing the Three Root Causes of Job Misery, by Patrick M. Lencioni. Jossey-Bass, 2015.

MARKETING AND SALES

"Eight Stage Customer Value Journey," by Ryan Deiss of Digital Marketer. Can be found online at: https://www.digitalmarketer. com/digital-marketing/digital-marketing-strategy/

Ask: The Counterintuitive Online Formula to Discover Exactly What Your Customers Want to Buy... Create a Mass of Raving Fans... And Take Any Business to the Next Level, by Ryan Levesque. Dunham Books, 2015.

Building a Storybrand: Clarify Your Message So Customers will Listen, by Donald Miller. Harper Collins Leadership, 2017.

"The Radio Success Formula," by Roy Williams of Wizard Academy (discussing Frequency, Reach, and the Psychology of Buying). Can be found online at: https://www.mondaymorningmemo.com/newsletters/the-radio-success-formula/

The Wizard of Ads: Turning Words into Magic and Dreamers into Millionaires, by Roy H. Williams. Bard Press, 1998.

FINANCE

E-Myth Mastery: The Seven Essential Disciplines for Building a World-Class Company, by Michael E. Gerber. Harper Collins, 2005.

Financial Intelligence, Revised Edition: A Manager's Guide to Knowing What the Numbers Really Mean, by Karen Berman and Joe Knight. Business Literacy Institute, 2013.

CULTURE

Be Our Guest (Revised and Updated): Perfecting the Art of Customer Service, with Theodore Kinni. Disney Enterprises, 2001.

The Culture Code: The Secrets of Highly Successful Groups, by Daniel Coyle. Bantam Books, 2018.

Gung Ho! Turn on the People in Any Organization, by Ken Blanchard and Sheldon Bowles. Blanchard Family Partnership and Ode to Joy Limited, 1998.

The Power of Moments: Why Certain Experiences Have Extraordinary Impact, by Chip and Dan Heath. Simon & Schuster, 2017.

Acknowledgments

As first-time authors, the concept of writing a book was daunting, especially while juggling the rest of our lives. Indeed, it eluded us for several years. If it weren't for the encouragement of friends, family, colleagues, and clients, this book would not have been possible. While there are not enough pages to list everyone who has shaped our journey to this point, we would like to highlight a few by name.

First of all, without the love of Jesus in our lives we would be in a very different place. There is incredible peace that comes from knowing that we are loved unconditionally, and we have deep gratitude for the reservoir of grace that has sustained our lives.

Our heartfelt thanks to our team at Half a Bubble Out and the HaBO Village. You are an incredible crew that works with passion, integrity, and teamwork. You are in the trenches with us every day. You have encouraged us, kept us on track, and kept meeting our client deadlines while we were buried in a manuscript. You embody what we have tried to describe in these pages and we are deeply grateful for how you work with excellence and protect our

Passion & Provision culture while you are doing it. You make us want to come to work every day.

To our daughter, Jenna, who is part of our team at the Bubble, but has lived this book a bit more extensively over the past couple of years with her parents. Conversations at work, at home, in the car as we drive and talk, and sometimes even over dinners! Thank you for your consistent support and love. We adore you.

To our extended family who have watched our crazy journey, loved us through the good times and the hard times, and told us to keep moving forward even when you all had no idea what we were really up to. Thank you.

To our clients, who have trusted us to help them grow their businesses and have pushed us to always keep learning and growing so we can better serve them. We are privileged to call many of you friends, and we do not take that for granted.

To the amazing authors, thought leaders, mentors, and teachers we have drawn on for more than thirty years in both our personal lives and our business. Some are in the pages of this book and some are not, but all have mattered. As King Solomon once said, "there is nothing new under the sun," and everything we offer in *Fulfilled* is built on the work of others. Some know us well, and some have no clue who we are. Thank you for the legacy each of you has poured into our lives.

And finally, to Greta the Great and our publishing team. You know who you are. What a gift you have been in this journey. Thanks for believing in this book when we weren't sure it had value. Thanks for helping us bring it to life.

About the Authors

KATHRYN AND MICHAEL REDMAN are sweethearts, best friends, and the husband-and-wife team behind Half a Bubble Out (HaBO), a marketing and business consulting firm based in Chico, California. They're also founders of the HaBO Village, a membership site which helps leaders build Passion & Provision companies, full of profit and joy. For more than seventeen years, they have helped business leaders across the world grow their companies through marketing, business coaching, and leadership development. Their second company, Rabbit Hole Hay, is an international e-commerce company that has grown 300 percent every year since 2014. Michael and Kathryn have both taught at the university level and are frequent guest speakers. They currently reside in Chico, where they love going to work every day.